# Deference

# Deference

*The Legal Concept and the Legal Practice*

GARY LAWSON
GUY I. SEIDMAN

OXFORD
UNIVERSITY PRESS

# OXFORD
## UNIVERSITY PRESS

Oxford University Press is a department of the University of Oxford. It furthers the University's objective of excellence in research, scholarship, and education by publishing worldwide. Oxford is a registered trademark of Oxford University Press in the UK and certain other countries.

Published in the United States of America by Oxford University Press
198 Madison Avenue, New York, NY 10016, United States of America.

Library of Congress Cataloging-in-Publication Data
Names: Lawson, Gary, 1958– author. | Seidman, Guy, author.
Title: Deference : The Legal Concept and the Legal Practice / Gary Lawson, Guy I Seidman.
Description: New York : Oxford University Press, 2020. | Includes bibliographical references and index.
Identifiers: LCCN 2019024756 (print) | LCCN 2019024757 (ebook) | ISBN 9780190273408 (hardback) |
   ISBN 9780190273415 (pdf) | ISBN 9780190273422 (epub)
Subjects: LCSH: Deference (Law)—United States. | Law—United States.—Interpretation and construction. |
   Judicial review—United States.
Classification: LCC KF450.D44 L39 2019 (print) | LCC KF450.D44 (ebook) | DDC 347.73/7—dc23
LC record available at https://lccn.loc.gov/2019024756
LC ebook record available at https://lccn.loc.gov/2019024757

1 3 5 7 9 8 6 4 2

Printed by Integrated Books International, United States of America

**Note to Readers**
This publication is designed to provide accurate and authoritative information in regard to the subject matter covered. It is based upon sources believed to be accurate and reliable and is intended to be current as of the time it was written. It is sold with the understanding that the publisher is not engaged in rendering legal, accounting, or other professional services. If legal advice or other expert assistance is required, the services of a competent professional person should be sought. Also, to confirm that the information has not been affected or changed by recent developments, traditional legal research techniques should be used, including checking primary sources where appropriate.

*(Based on the Declaration of Principles jointly adopted by a Committee of the American Bar Association and a Committee of Publishers and Associations.)*

You may order this or any other Oxford University Press publication
by visiting the Oxford University Press website at www.oup.com.

*In loving memory of my mother* Lea Seidman *(né Carmi), 1934–1999*
*Prof. Guy Seidman*

*As with all things, to Patty, Nathaniel, and Noah*
*Prof. Gary Lawson*

# Contents

# Acknowledgments

Professor Lawson is grateful to Boston University School of Law and Philip S. Beck for generous support and to *Constitutional Commentary* for permission to reprint portions of Gary Lawson, *Interpretative Equality as a Structural Imperative (Or, Pucker Up and Settle THIS!)*, 20 CONST. COMMENTARY 379 (2003). Professor Seidman is grateful to the Max Planck Institute. We are both grateful to Oxford University Press and Jamie Berezin for believing in this book.

# 1

# Introduction

## The Puzzle of Deference

If you run a WESTLAW search for appearances of the term "deference" in American jurisprudence, using any one of the "All Federal Cases," "All State Cases," or "Law Reviews & Journals" databases, you will get the dreaded, search-engine-breaking "10,000" response, meaning that your search has yielded so many hits—more than 10,000, and perhaps many multiples of 10,000—that the program is hectoring you to come up with a different and more limited search. These numbers do not include decisions or scholarly commentary in which the *concept* of deference is invoked or applied without specific use of the term; that body of material seems to us likely to break the "10,000" barrier as well in all relevant databases if one could come up with the appropriate search terms. We are confident that similar results would be found in comparable searches, in any appropriate medium, involving virtually any developed legal system anywhere in the world. All of this is a good indication, if one is needed, that deference is among the most important and widely employed concepts in jurisprudence, whether one looks at the usages of judges, lawyers, or scholars. In the law, deference is omnipresent.

A moment's reflection reveals obvious reasons why deference, both as a concept and as a practice, is so prevalent in the law. Deference is a concept and practice fundamental to any real-world legal system.[1] Anytime one encounters multiple levels of decision-making, and/or a system of decisions that accumulate across time, one must always ask what weight, if any, subsequent decision-makers should give to the judgments of prior decision-makers (or, conceivably, to future decision-makers, though that introduces complexities that we will not pursue in this book). This is even true, and perhaps especially true, when a decision-maker is considering the weight due its own prior decisions. Even if the decision-maker never explicitly considers how the present decision should accommodate the efforts of other legal actors, including one's own temporally prior self, there will always be some value attached to prior decisions. If one does not openly ask or think about

*Deference.* Gary Lawson and Guy I. Seidman, Oxford University Press (2020). © Oxford University Press.
DOI: 10.1093/oso/9780190273408.001.0001

the appropriate weight to be given to prior decisions, one will necessarily re-solve that matter implicitly, even if the implicit resolution is to assign a weight of zero. Deference is omnipresent, and questions about deference in the law are inescapable.

In a great many contexts, the law[2] openly recognizes and addresses questions of deference. Doctrines proclaiming that one governmental actor will, should, or must defer to the views of others are legion, involving vir-tually all possible combinations of governmental (and non-governmental) bodies: courts deferring to agencies, agencies deferring to courts, legislatures or executives deferring to courts, courts deferring to legislatures or executives, executives deferring to legislatures and vice versa, courts defer-ring to other courts (both domestic and foreign), and government officials of any stripe deferring to public opinion or private expertise. Later in the book, we will discuss some of these different manifestations of deference in more detail. For now, it is enough to note that the concept of deference lies at the core of every system of precedent, appellate review, federalism, and separa-tion of powers. All of these systems center on how one actor should deal with decisions made by another actor (treating each decision-maker as a series of actors across time).

Deference is not merely prevalent in the law. Deference matters in the law. It often matters a great deal—or at least is thought to matter a great deal. In the United States, one single judicial decision from 1984 involving one distinct species of deference[3] has become, in the span of just a few decades, one of the most cited US Supreme Court decisions of all time.[4] Judicial deference, of varying degrees, to juries is a fundamental—and constitu-tionally entrenched—staple of American civil and criminal justice; the US Constitution declares that in civil cases "no fact tried by a jury, shall be oth-erwise reexamined in any Court of the United States, other than according to the rules of the common law,"[5] and in criminal cases jury acquittals are unre-viewable and thus receive the highest level of deference possible.[6] Deference to trial judges on the admissibility of evidence or other matters of trial ad-ministration probably determines the outcome in an uncountable number of appellate cases. The extent to which courts do and/or should defer to legislatures or executives is perhaps the central question of American con-stitutional theory. A quick trip across the Atlantic Ocean immediately yields, inter alia, *Wednesbury* deference from England, so named for the 1948 de-cision in *Associated Provincial Picture Houses, Ltd. v. Wednesbury Corp.*,[7] and the "margin of appreciation" doctrine from continental and European

Union law,[8] both of which we very briefly discuss in a subsequent chapter. An unadorned list of vital doctrines involving deference could go on for several pages. Collectively, those doctrines come very close to defining the key features of any legal system. All things considered, deference is quite possibly the single most important concept in all of legal thought.

Thus, there is nothing at all surprising about the widespread usage in legal decisions and legal scholarship of the term "deference" and of other terms, such as "margin of appreciation" or "comity," that express the same idea. What is surprising is the lack of sustained and systematic attention that the term, and the practice represented by the term, has received in the United States. To be sure, scholars and judges in other common-law countries, as we discuss later, have paid considerable attention to deference, and we draw on their work throughout this book, but that attention mysteriously seems to stop at the American border. The term "deference" is tossed about routinely in American law and scholarship, but it is very rare to see the term carefully defined or analyzed. Everyone is just supposed to know what it means. To some extent, perhaps everyone does know what it means. But with regard to something as basic to virtually everything that happens in the law as the concept of deference, "I know it when I see it" is a bit intellectually unsatisfying.

We are not alone in observing that "deference is an underexamined subject in American legal scholarship."[9] To be sure, there is prodigious writing, both scholarly and judicial, on specific applications of deference. As Professor Paul Horwitz has aptly observed:

> [D]eference has featured in countless discussions in the academic literature of constitutional law and its cousin, administrative law. The constitutional doctrine of separation of powers, for example, revolves around the extent to which one branch of the federal government must defer to another branch's interpretation of some constitutional question. Within administrative law, vast forests have been felled on the subject of deference to administrative agencies. And scholars have often discussed deference to other specific government institutions, such as the military, prisons, public schools, and universities.[10]

What is lacking, however, is a study of deference itself rather than deference as it appears or is applied in specific legal contexts. Even at this late point in the development of jurisprudential thought, "deference . . . has never been analyzed in depth as a fundamental issue."[11]

We are aware of no systematic treatment of the concept of deference in the law. The statement is remarkable enough to bear repetition: We are aware of no systematic treatment of the concept of deference in the law. Massive amounts of judicial and scholarly writing apply, describe, and criticize various applications of deference across all of the settings noted above, but there is strikingly little, in either the case law or the scholarly commentary, by way of systematic analysis of the concept. The term "deference" is generally employed—often with some adjective, such as "*Chevron*," "*Skidmore*," or "*Thayerian*," preceding it—as though the base concept is a primitive and careful analysis is therefore unnecessary.

Consider the treatment of "deference" over time in *Black's Law Dictionary*, which has long—though, as we will later see, not always—been the preeminent legal dictionary in the United States. For many editions, the volume did not contain a definition for the term "deference" at all. The fifth edition, acquired by one of us when he was in law school in 1980, has no entry for "deference." Its only account of "defer" is "Delay; put off; remand; postpone to a future time,"[12] which clearly is not the core meaning for the legal term "deference." The term did not merit an entry in *Black's Law Dictionary* until the seventh edition in 1999, which offered: "To show deference to (another); to yield to the opinion of."[13] Apart from defining a verb rather than a noun, this definition at least nods toward an attitude of giving way to another's view, which is surely within the orbit of whatever "deference" normally means in the law. The more recent tenth edition moves the previous definition of "deference" to "defer" (where it grammatically belongs); and "deference," in its first definition, becomes primarily a linguistic and conversational, rather than a distinctively legal, concept, describing nothing more than old-fashioned courteous social conduct: "1. Conduct showing respect for somebody or something; courteous or complaisant regard for another."[14] The second definition in the tenth edition finally links the term, albeit indirectly and non-exclusively, to legal analysis: "2. A polite and respectful attitude or approach, esp. toward an important person or venerable institution whose action, proposal, opinion, or judgment should be presumptively accepted."[15] That is all that is said. It is (or so we think) somewhat jarring to see a term as old, central, and vibrant as "deference" receive such limited treatment.

To be fair to *Black's Law Dictionary* (and its extraordinary editor, who we both revere), defining deference presents lexicographers with an impossible problem. Legal actors who employ the term generally do so without explicit definition, so there is no obvious canonical source to which one can turn with any confidence for a definition. Furthermore, as we will see in this book, the range of legal practices that are explicitly identified by actors as instances of deference is so wide and varied that drawing out a single dictionary definition from those usages would require a book in itself. Accordingly, we set out to write one. Indeed, the two of us on occasion, and only half-jokingly, have described this project to ourselves as providing the raw material for a definition of deference in a legal dictionary.

As it happens, an older law dictionary from the nineteenth century provides a much more elaborate, if ultimately unsatisfying, definition of "deference"; we will examine that dictionary entry in some detail in a subsequent chapter. Scholarship is also thin on attempts to define deference with any precision; we will discuss the major—and relatively few—scholarly attempts at definition (primarily from scholars in common law countries other than the United States) in a subsequent chapter as well. Our point for now is only that the gap between the importance of deference as an activity and concept in the law and the attention paid to the term by legal actors is strikingly wide. It is comparable to, for example, having human rights law take center stage as a legal-political idea for centuries with hardly anyone seriously analyzing the concept of rights of which it is an application. That would be startling. We think the lack of attention given to the concept of deference is equally startling.

We aim in this book to begin to fill in that gap. We place strong emphasis on the word "begin"; we have no pretension of actually filling in the gap or even coming close to filling in the gap. If the concept of deference is as important, variegated, and equivocal as we think it is, one book can only start a conversation. Fortunately for us, starting a conversation is our goal. We hope to bring the concept of deference to the forefront of legal discussion; to identify, catalogue, and analyze at least the chief among its many manifestations and applications; to set forth the many and varied rationales that can be and have been offered in support of (some species of) deference in different legal contexts; and thereby to provide a vocabulary and conceptual framework that can be employed in future discussions.

We *do not* intend to recommend, as a policy matter, any particular scheme of deference in any particular context. We *do not* plan to criticize the way that any legal system chooses to allocate authority among institutions or across time. We *do not* set out to construct an ideal system of deference for any specific set of problems or institutions. We are not legal reformers, policy analysts, or moral or political theorists. We are humble lawyers, with nary an advanced degree in anything other than law between us. Our project is descriptive, and when we are critical of others, whether courts or scholars, our criticism is directed at a perceived lack of clarity, definition, or identification, not at anyone's favored set of answers to any particular legal problem. In short, we believe that clear understanding should precede critical analysis, and our sole goal in this work is to facilitate clearer understanding of one of law's most crucial concepts. Those who hope to find in this book answers to questions such as "to what extent should courts defer to the legal interpretations of administrative agencies?" or "should courts engaged in review of government action that affects human rights use reasonableness review, proportionality review, or something stronger?" are going to be disappointed. We are not trying to answer those questions. We are trying to make it easier for those people who do want to try to answer those questions to do so with intellectual rigor and clarity. We think, and hope, that our discussion is potentially useful to anyone who approaches questions of legal doctrine or legal design, from whatever perspective and with whatever priors they possess.

Indeed, our original goal was to study deference globally—and we mean "globally" in both a conceptual and literal sense. Because deference is not a concept confined to any specific legal system, our initial ambition was to conduct a comparative study which would examine how different legal systems define and employ the idea of deference. We continue to believe that an adequate account of deference as either a concept or a practice requires that kind of comparative analysis, especially since our impression is that scholars outside the United States have taken deference as an object of study far more seriously than have their American counterparts. Frankly, the original proposal for this book that the publisher graciously accepted had a strong comparative focus. Unfortunately, in pursing that comparative project, we encountered the same difficulty that has apparently plagued others as well (and which may explain the absence to date of a thoroughgoing comparative study of deference): There simply is not enough English-language material on the subject from civil law countries to make such a study possible, at least not for authors limited in their language skills to English and Hebrew (and a smattering of German).[16] We hope in a future project to engage directly with scholars in other countries who can speak, with both scholarly and linguistic authority, to their countries' practices. In this book, we will make very modest mention of how deference is dealt with in some civil law countries, but for now we must primarily limit our focus to the common law world.

More precisely, we have elected to center our study on a relatively narrow band within that common law world: We concentrate primarily (though not quite exclusively) on the use of deference in the United States by federal courts and, to a lesser extent, other federal institutions and actors. This is partly due to the same considerations that we suspect have discouraged others from taking a broad look at deference rather than concentrating on specific applications. Even within the common law world, different countries have developed their systems of judicial review in different ways. There are some commonalities among those systems, and we will try to draw on some of those commonalities in this book, but a fair treatment of deference in common law countries would require separate treatment of, at a minimum, Australia, Canada, New Zealand, and the United Kingdom. That is the work of a separate book—or at least of a separate book-length doctoral thesis.[17] Moreover, the potential field of study for an exploration of deference encompasses literally all of law, so a project that looked at all possible applications of deference even within a single country would be a lifetime of volumes rather than a book. But our main reason for looking primarily at the use of deference by federal courts is a methodological move that we believe, or at least hope, can provide a window into the broader account of deference that is our ultimate object of inquiry.

In order to study deference, in any setting, one must know what one is studying. Even if one does not have a formal definition of deference to guide inquiry, one must have enough of an idea in mind to recognize instances of deference when one comes across them. There must be some criteria that identify the phenomena that count as deference. There are a number of ways to approach that problem of definition.

One approach would be to start with a conceptual account of deference, derived from first principles of jurisprudence, and then to test the practices of legal institutions against that account to see how well they conform to it. That is, one first thinks philosophically or jurisprudentially about the problems of layered decision-making and then derives from that consideration a set of norms for coordinating the various levels of the system. This would be the methodology of a critical, or prescriptive, project that aims to identify what kinds of legal arrangements are desirable or effective. In its application to real practices, the method is largely deductive: One knows what deference should look like, and the question is to what extent legal practice looks that way and how legal practice can be modified to be more in line with the ideal.

Another approach is inductive. Instead of starting with a theoretical conception of deference, one could try to derive the conception from practice. That is, one could observe the practices that legal actors describe as deference, induce from those practices some common or defining characteristics, formulate a definition from those data points, and then see whether that inductively derived definition has broader explanatory or analytical power in contexts beyond the observations from which it was derived.

Because our inclinations run far more toward descriptive than normative scholarship,[18] we have chosen the latter method. We draw our initial definition of deference from the practices of US federal courts. We observe what kinds of activities they describe as instances of deference and we construct our account from those descriptions. As it happens, those courts describe a wide range of practices as instances of deference, so the body of material from which we can draw is very substantial. We also draw from those courts the rationales that they advance in favor of deference in different circumstances to construct a framework and vocabulary for understanding the relevant practices.

We could, in principle, stop at that point, content with a descriptive account of the practices of deference of US federal courts. We want, however, to explore whether that account can be applied, either descriptively or analytically, in settings beyond the database from which that account was derived. We want to ask, in other words, whether an account of deference inductively derived from the practices of US federal courts can serve as a framework for a wider, even if not entirely universal, study of practices in other settings, performed by other institutions, perhaps in other legal systems. We wonder whether deference as a general concept is best understood from the ground up rather than the top down.

There is no a priori way to determine how successful such a project can be, so the proof is in the pudding, If, at the end of the day, there is no pudding, we will still have a descriptive account of deference as it is practiced by US federal courts (and other federal institutions) that is of some utility. We think, however, that we will wind up with a bit more than such a descriptive account. But that is ultimately something for the reader to decide.

Chapter 2 of the book lays the groundwork for the project by identifying a range of practices that US federal courts explicitly describe as instances of deference. We do not intend exhaustively to catalogue uses of the term or concept of deference. Instead, we focus on some widely applied instances of what the courts themselves describe as deference. Our goal is to examine enough practices to warrant inductive generalizations, not to account for all of the "10,000"s of uses of deference in the federal courts database. Even this limited focus turns out to generate a substantial body of material from which a definition and a framework can be induced. It is, of course, conceivable that there are important tails in the distribution of deference usages that we are missing, but we think we have hit the main instances of federal court legal practice.

Chapter 3 then tries to derive a definition of deference from those materials. Because the range of practices covered in Chapter 2 is so broad, any definition that captures all of them will surely be very broad as well, and the definition that we induce does not disappoint in this regard. To give away the ending, we eventually (after a false start in a slightly different direction) define deference in this book as: "the giving by a legal actor of some measure of consideration or weight to the decision of another actor in exercising the deferring actor's function." Any definition that is narrower will miss some important practices that legal actors consider to be instances of deference. Any definition that is broader is likely to be of little use.

Chapter 3 also surveys the reasons that courts have given for deference in various settings, and we induce from those reasons a framework for describing and analyzing deference. We think that deference can be either *mandatory* or *discretionary*, depending on whether it is commanded by positive law or is a choice made by the deferring authority (keeping in mind that following rather than flouting or ignoring positive law is a choice, so even mandatory deference is, in some ultimate sense, discretionary). Deference is justified by legal actors by invoking some combination of the relative legitimacy of decision-makers, the relative likelihood that different decision-makers will reach good answers, the costs of independent decision-making, the signals sent to other actors by independent rather than deferential decision-making, and the expected effects of non-deference on the legal and political status of the deciding institution. For lack of better labels, we call deference based on these various rationales, respectively, legitimation deference, epistemological deference, economic deference, signaling deference, and prudential (or strategic) deference. These categories seem to describe the principal rationales identified by deferring actors or readily seen as lying behind their actions. This framework is inductively rather than deductively constructed. That is, we did not sit down to try to ascertain the best possible categorization of kinds of deference or the most persuasive reasons for (or against) deference in various contexts. Instead, we think we are just describing what federal courts, and other legal actors, do and say.

Because our account of deference is induced from a limited context, that raises the obvious question how valuable such an account can be when applied in other settings.

Chapter 4 starts to answer that question by comparing our account of deference to other accounts advanced by legal scholars. In some sense, it is an odd comparison even to attempt, because the mission of most other scholars is normative rather than descriptive. It would be strange, one might think, to imagine that a purely descriptive account could have much to say to people who are trying to make normative assessments and vice versa. But that is precisely why we think the comparison is worth making. If it turns out that the various accounts of deference have far more commonalities than differences, that is an interesting result that suggests that there is enough of a common core to the notion of deference to make systematic study a worthwhile endeavor. Again to spoil the ending: We think that the accounts of other scholars turn out to have some very important insights to add to our own account (and we freely and unapologetically appropriate those insights), but those additions do not fundamentally change the definition and framework that we derive from the federal courts. There are differences across different accounts, but there is a great deal of convergence as well.

Chapter 5 then asks directly whether our framework, as modified by the insights of others, has any descriptive or analytical value with respect to practices that are not, or are not always, identified as instances of deference but which seem to share some of the features of those practices that are explicitly identified in that way. Such practices include precedent, including precedential practices among courts, among executive institutions, and between executive (and legislative) institutions and courts; intra-agency allocations of authority; and the use by courts of decisions of foreign tribunals. We think that the framework provides a useful way to think about a broad range of practices, though we will not be shocked if others disagree with our assessment. Indeed, we look forward to hearing about those disagreements. After all, the goal here is to start a conversation.

Deference is too important to the law to be left undefined or without an analytical framework that can be employed across contexts. There is, of course, always the possibility that no such definition or analytical framework is possible. Perhaps deference is too vague for any definition to capture and too varied for any framework to describe in anything other than purely local settings. Maybe there is no existing systematic study of deference because such a systematic study is impossible, and we are therefore two (old) fools on an errand. We hope not, but there is only one way to find out.

## Notes

1. *See* Yoav Dotan, *Deference and Disagreement in Administrative Law*, at 4 (manuscript on file with authors) ("Deference is a fundamental concept in legal discourse.").
2. As a default, when we speak of "the law" we normally mean the US legal system. Sometimes we use the term to mean the Anglo-American common law system. When we intend to include a broader international scope, as we sometimes do, we usually try to say so. Nonetheless, we believe that many of the observations that we make about "the law" in the narrow, United-States-centric sense have universal, or at least near-universal, application.
3. Chevron U.S.A. v. Natural Resources Defense Council, Inc., 467 U.S. 837 (1984).
4. *See* Chris Walker, *Most Cited Supreme Court Administrative Law Decisions*, Oct. 9, 2014, http://yalejreg.com/nc/most-cited-supreme-court-administrative-law-decisions-by-chris-walker/.
5. U.S. CONST. amend. VII.
6. *Id.*, amend. V ("nor shall any person be subject for the same offence to be twice put in jeopardy of life or limb").
7. 1 K.B. 223 (1948).
8. The margin of appreciation doctrine, adapted from French origins, first appeared in European Union law in 1958. *See The Cyprus Case (Greece v. the United Kingdom)*, 2 Y.B. OF EUR. CONVENTION ON HUM. RTS. 172 (1958–59).
9. Paul Horwitz, *Three Faces of Deference*, 83 NOTRE DAME L. REV. 1061, 1069 (2008).
10. *Id.* at 1069–70.
11. Daniel J. Solove, *The Darkest Domain: Deference, Judicial Review, and the Bill of Rights*, 84 IOWA L. REV. 941, 945 (1999). *See also* Dotan, *supra* note 1, at 4 ("deference—as a concept of its own—remains largely understudied and undertheorized by legal courts and scholars alike").
12. BLACK'S LAW DICTIONARY 379 (5th ed., 1979) The definition adds, somewhat un-helpfully: "The term does not have, however, the meaning of abolish."
13. BLACK'S LAW DICTIONARY 432 (7th ed., 1999).
14. BLACK'S LAW DICTIONARY 513 (10th ed., 2014).
15. *Id.* at 514.
16. *Cf.* PAUL DALY, A THEORY OF DEFERENCE IN ADMINISTRATIVE LAW: BASIS, APPLICATION AND SCOPE 13 (2012) ("I have confined my study entirely to common law systems. The decision is partly due to restrictions of time, expertise, language and resources.").
17. *See* ALAN FRECKELTON, THE CONCEPT OF DEFERENCE IN SUBSTANTIVE REVIEW OF ADMINISTRATIVE DECISIONS IN FOUR COMMON LAW COUNTRIES (2013), https://

open.library.ubc.ca/cIRcle/collections/ubctheses/24/items/1.0073508 (surveying the law of Canada, the United Kingdom, New Zealand, and Australia).

18. To be precise, Professor Lawson's inclinations run far more toward descriptive than normative scholarship, and he has effectively bludgeoned Professor Seidman into putting up with that position in their joint work. Professor Lawson's attitude toward normative scholarship is best summarized by an observation from his very first law review article in 1988: "It is conceivable that the ethical, epistemological, and metaphysical problems of the ages will be solved by an article in a twentieth-century, English-language law journal. But I rather doubt it." Gary Lawson, *The Ethics of Insider Trading*, 11 HARV. J.L. & PUB. POL'Y 727, 778 (1988). Professor Lawson does not have higher expectations in this regard for either English-language books or the twenty-first century, and he believes that the normative efforts of legal scholars in the three decades that have ensued since his first article validate his doubts.

# 2

# The Many Faces of Federal Court Deference

Recall from the previous chapter that *Black's Law Dictionary* offers a (secondary) definition of deference as "a polite and respectful attitude or approach, esp. toward an important person or venerable institution whose action, proposal, opinion, or judgment should be presumptively accepted." To what extent does this definition accurately represent, either wholly or partially, how the law applies the idea of deference?

Our initial ambition, as we have noted, was to take the term "the law" literally and attempt to survey how deference is understood and applied across different legal systems worldwide. For the reasons given in Chapter 1, we had to abandon that ambition at a relatively early stage of this project. Accordingly, we are really addressing here only "the law of the United States" rather than "the law" in general. But even with that limitation in hand, there is no reliable way universally to answer the question posed above. Most obviously, it is impossible to catalogue and survey comprehensively all, or even most, of the appearances of deference in judicial decisions and scholarly commentary on those decisions. There are simply too many of those appearances, including appearances that will escape word-based searches or search engines because they employ the concept of deference without using the word or any similar term, for any project to capture. Nor is there any reason to expect all of those uses to be fully consistent across time and context. There is no canonical legal source for the meaning of deference, so individual users of the term have no standard to which they must conform. It would take many volumes, and many lifetimes, exhaustively to canvas enough uses of the concept to generate empirically precise information about how US courts use deference. (It would also require researchers who are trained in empirical methods, which we are not.)

Perhaps less obviously, but perhaps more important, courts are not the only governmental institutions for which deference plays an important role. A full account of deference in the law must consider how it is employed by

*Deference.* Gary Lawson and Guy I. Seidman, Oxford University Press (2020). © Oxford University Press.
DOI: 10.1093/oso/9780190273408.001.0001

courts, legislatures, executives, and administrators, among other actors; and identifying systematically how deference is used and applied in those non-judicial contexts is likely to be impossible. The opacity of deference in non-judicial settings poses an intractable methodological problem, to which we have no answer other than to retreat to what is better known. Accordingly, although deference is a practice that can and does occur in all branches[1] of government (and in everyday life), and we do our best to take account of deference in executive and legislative institutions at various points in this book, we observe deference most clearly and accessibly in the judicial branch. For at least three reasons, therefore, our study is and must be primarily court-centric.[2]

First, executive and legislative branches of government are usually more complex and multilayered institutions than are courts, which effectively forecloses any generalizable descriptions of their activities at the granular level necessary to analyze a concept such as deference. Even unitary executives, who in theory personally possess all vested executive powers,[3] in practice carry out almost all functions through a Byzantine network of subordinates that is virtually impossible to monitor, much less to control. It is possible to imagine legislative bodies that operate with a large dose of internal centralization and discipline; casual inspection of US legislatures suggests that they do not much follow this model. Accordingly, even identifying within the executive branch or within a large multimember legislature effective exercises of legal authority in which deference might play a role is a task calculated to, as James Madison said in another setting, "puzzle the greatest adepts in political science."[4] Even more importantly, *failures* to exercise authority could involve deference as much or more than do positive actions, and those kinds of activities are elusive, and perhaps even undetectable in principle by anyone who is not directly embedded in the deferring institution. Even with courts, "negative choices remain in most cases undetected"[5]; trying to locate and analyze negative choices or non-action within complex legislative or executive institutions is much harder. This does not mean that one cannot identify instances, either positive or negative, in which legislative or executive agents defer to others. Such identifiable instances abound, and we address some of them as best we can later in this book. It does mean, however, that any database of legislative and executive decisions that one constructs is going to be purely anecdotal, and we know of no mechanism for assuring the representativeness of any sample within those databases.

Second, courts, and especially appellate courts in the common law tradition, often explain their decisions in written opinions. If one indulges the assumption that, most of the time, these explanations can be taken at face value as accurate representations of the judicial reasoning process, they provide material that one can examine to see how and whether deference is operating. Executive and legislative decisions do not leave as consistent or accessible a paper trail, especially within executive agencies that value deliberative secrecy. To be sure, one should not make too much of this putative difference in the rate and degree of explanation across branches. Many executive decisions, in the form of either rules or adjudicative orders, also come with explanations (and sometimes published dissents in the case of decisions by multimember administrative agencies). Indeed, in US administrative law, agencies that do *not* explain, in excruciatingly lengthy detail, the reasoning behind their major decisions will have their work product rejected by courts until the agencies can prove to the courts, via their publicly available explanations, that the agencies have taken a "hard look" at the relevant problems.[6] Legislators, for their part, are often prolific producers of "legislative history" in attempts to guide, or even control, outcomes involving statutory interpretation before agencies and courts. And, approaching matters from the other side, while appellate opinions in the common law tradition normally come with statements of reasons, that is less true of trial court proceedings, especially when cases are disposed of by summary order. Furthermore, even many "reasoned" appellate opinions are unpublished, which makes them relatively inaccessible. Nonetheless, all things considered, common law courts have a more thoroughly developed tradition of transparency than do common law executives or legislatures, which makes them an easier object of study than are the other branches.

Third, and perhaps most importantly, the judiciary in common law countries is a reactive branch. (This may not be true across all legal systems.) It does not initiate disputes or investigations but merely passes judgment in cases and controversies brought before it by others. The US Supreme Court chooses its own docket, but the lower courts do not have that luxury. Accordingly, a court's decision *not to intervene* in a matter, when the reason is grounded in what we will ultimately consider to be deference, is a relatively easily observable occurrence. One can track a case going into the court system and track its path outward. Executive and legislative decisions not to act, by contrast, may be wholly unobservable, and the reasons for nonaction (if indeed those reasons are anything other than inertia) are likely unknowable. This helps explain why failures of executives or legislatures to act, on grounds of deference or otherwise, are so hard to identify and analyze.

For all of these reasons, and probably more besides, we begin our study of deference by looking to the practices of courts. More specifically, we look to the practices of federal courts in the United States. A survey of fifty different state court systems (not to mention several hundred other national court systems) is beyond our capacity and probably beyond the patience of any reader. As it happens, the federal courts have employed the idea of deference in many different contexts, so even confining our attention to that limited universe yields a diverse body of doctrines that we think is sufficient to ground our study. Once we derive some tentative conclusions from the practices of federal courts, we can later consider whether different institutional actors employ the term differently and whether an analytical framework designed to describe the practices of federal courts is potentially useful in other contexts as well.

Our method is both inductive and conceptual. We start in this chapter simply by identifying certain practices that courts expressly label as acts of deference. In Chapter 3, we then try to draw out and analyze the core ideas represented by deference in those contexts and to explore reasons why an actor might defer to another. In Chapter 4, we examine other definitions of deference put forward by other sources and scholars to see whether their insights warrant refinement of our own conception. And finally, in Chapter 5, we apply that inductive-conceptual account of deference to practices that are not always identified or recognized by courts or other actors as deference but which substantively fall within its umbrella, and we ask whether that broader focus requires any kind of reconsideration or reformulation of our initial definition.

Our methodology is thus "ground-up" rather than "top-down." We do not start with an ideal conception of deference and then use that conception to criticize the practices of courts that do not conform to it. Rather, we start with the practices of courts as the raw material and work from there. Nor do we set out to assess critically from any particular interpretative perspective the various doctrines that embody deference. To be sure, we are already, both together and individually, on record regarding some of those doctrines (indeed, probably enough on record to fill another book), and we will occasionally—more randomly than systematically—offer passing commentary on some doctrines or practices, but our mission is not to instruct courts or other actors about the appropriate ways in which to take into account other decisions. That would require, at a minimum, a full specification of an appropriate model of judicial decision-making in all relevant settings, and that is a project that we happily leave to others. At least initially, we come neither to praise nor bury the way that US federal courts employ the concept of deference but simply to identify and describe it.

We have no ambition here of cataloguing every doctrine or practice that US federal courts label as an act of deference. That would be some combination of tedious and impossible. Our goal in this chapter, rather, is to identify a hopefully representative, or at least useful and accessible, sample of especially visible doctrines and practices from which we can induce some generalizations about deference in the law. In identifying those practices, we do not mean to provide a comprehensive account of them that can serve as a reference source or treatise on specific doctrines (though we hope that we can offer some enlightening background and commentary on at least a few of those doctrines). We are simply trying to generate enough raw data from which to induce a tentative definition of deference and to derive a vocabulary to explain and elaborate upon that definition. We find deference appearing in virtually every possible context, from fact-finding to law determination to policy making to trial management to intergovernmental relations. In Chapter 3, we will see if this variegated set of contexts can yield a definition of deference that one can recite while standing on one foot. For now, we are content with getting a handle on the practices.

## 1.  Deference in Fact-Finding

The most obvious starting point in the United States for a study of deference is judicial deference to adjudicative fact-finders. There are many varieties of adjudicative fact-finders: juries, courts, administrators, and (on very rare occasions, such as impeachment proceedings and perhaps decisions on some private bills) legislatures. In these settings, courts openly describe, and almost always apply, some form of deference to decision-makers at some stage of the adjudicative process.

We should make an important clarification up front. By "adjudicative" fact-finders, we mean actors who find facts in particular, legally binding disputes involving specific parties and events—in lawsuits, administrative proceedings, or impeachment trials. The law involves a great deal of fact-finding that is not "adjudicative" in this sense. Fact-finding is often ancillary to the process of law determination. Legal meaning might, according to various different theories of legal interpretation, be thought to depend on, inter alia, the intentions of a specific set of lawgivers, the legally constructed intentions of a hypothetical lawgiver, the policy consequences of a particular course of action, and so forth. The constitutionality of legislation might depend on the communicative intentions of a text, the motivations of the legislature, the accuracy of legislative assessments of the consequences of actions, judicial judgments about consequences that were not considered by the legislature, and so forth. All of these determinations involve "facts" of one sort or another, but they are general facts about the world rather than specific facts about specific events involving particular litigants. Some kind of deference is sometimes present with respect to these so-called legislative facts,[7] but the deference calculus in this setting can get very complicated. Appellate courts do not ordinarily give much weight to the legislative fact-finding of lower courts; in theory, review of such fact-finding is de novo,[8] though the reality may be more complex than any simple statement can convey.[9] Courts more openly give widely varying levels of deference to legislative judgments about legislative facts; consider, for example, the likely response of courts to a legislature's view about the probable consequences of rent control or an implied warranty of habitability for residential housing versus a legislature's view of the probable consequences of abortion regulations or limits on political speech. The law regarding deference to adjudicative fact-finding is cleaner than it is with respect to legislative fact-finding, and the former therefore provides a better initial window into the meaning and operation of deference as a general concept. There is also an incalculable amount of official fact-finding that occurs outside the context of legally binding proceedings; we leave that universe to another project.

The judicial treatment of adjudicative fact-finding depends very much on who is finding the facts. When juries find facts in civil trials, the US Constitution specifies for federal courts that "no fact tried by a jury, shall be otherwise reexamined in any Court of the United States, than according to the rules of the common law."[10] As a matter of original meaning, there is a good case to be made that this provision forecloses judicial review of jury verdicts unless there is literally no evidence in the record to support that verdict, which would amount to a rule of conclusive or absolute deference to jury fact-finding.[11] Ever since the late nineteenth century, however, the principle has been differently, and less strictly, formulated as permitting judicial overturning of jury verdicts whenever, but only whenever, no *reasonable* jury could have found the facts as it did. The Supreme Court said in 1871:

> Formerly it was held that if there was what is called a *scintilla* of evidence in support of a case the judge was bound to leave it to the jury, but recent decisions of high authority have established a more reasonable rule, that in every case, before the evidence is left to the jury, there is a preliminary question for the judge, not whether there is literally no evidence, but whether there is any upon which a jury can properly proceed to find a verdict for the party producing it, upon whom the *onus* of proof is imposed.[12]

More recent decisions couch this analysis in the language of jury reasonableness: "the trial judge must direct a verdict if, under the governing law, there can be but one *reasonable* conclusion as to the verdict. If *reasonable* minds could differ as to the import of the evidence, however, a verdict should not be directed."[13] Those common law rules, effective as far as we know in every state even without incorporation of the Seventh Amendment as a constitutional rule for state court proceedings, amount to a very strong, though not absolute, principle of judicial deference to civil jury fact-finding.

In criminal cases, due process of law, under both the Fifth and Fourteenth Amendments, places an upper bound on how much deference courts may afford jury fact-finding when it leads to criminal convictions. As the Supreme Court explained:

> [T]he critical inquiry on review of the sufficiency of the evidence to support a criminal conviction must be not simply to determine whether the jury was properly instructed, but to determine whether the record evidence could reasonably support a finding of guilt beyond a reasonable doubt.... [T]he relevant question is whether, after viewing the evidence in the light most favorable to the prosecution, *any* rational trier of fact could have found the essential elements of the crime beyond a reasonable doubt. This familiar standard gives full play to the responsibility of the trier of fact fairly to resolve conflicts in the testimony, to weigh the evidence, and to draw reasonable inferences from basic facts to ultimate facts. Once a defendant has been found guilty of the crime charged, the factfinder's role as weigher of the evidence is preserved through a legal conclusion that upon judicial review *all of the evidence* is to be considered in the light most favorable to

the prosecution. The criterion thus impinges upon "jury" discretion only to the extent necessary to guarantee the fundamental protection of due process of law.[14]

In sum, "[a] reviewing court may set aside the jury's verdict on the ground of insufficient evidence only if no rational trier of fact could have agreed with the jury."[15] This formulation does not materially differ from the formulation for review of civil jury fact-finding, though it has constitutional application to state court criminal proceedings.

Jury fact-finding leading to acquittal in criminal cases comes to court with a specific and quite dramatic lower bound of mandated judicial deference: 100 percent. If the jury finds facts that result in acquittal of a criminal defendant, the government cannot appeal the decision because of the constitutional bar against double jeopardy,[16] which effectively operates as a rule of unconditional deference to the fact-finder in those circumstances. Even if the acquitting jury found facts unreasonably, there is no judicial remedy for the prosecution. The jury receives absolute deference.

In civil bench trials in the federal system, adjudicative findings of fact by the trial judge are reviewed according to a statutorily prescribed deferential standard that is phrased somewhat less generously than is the "reasonable person" jury standard: "Findings of fact [of federal district judges], whether based on oral or other evidence, must not be set aside unless clearly erroneous, and the reviewing court must give due regard to the trial court's opportunity to judge the witnesses' credibility."[17] The Supreme Court has expressly described this standard as one of "deference,"[18] and it has characterized the standard as follows:

> If the district court's account of the evidence is plausible in light of the record viewed in its entirety, the court of appeals may not reverse it even though convinced that had it been sitting as the trier of fact, it would have weighed the evidence differently. Where there are two permissible views of the evidence, the factfinder's choice between them cannot be clearly erroneous.[19]

Put otherwise, reversal is appropriate only when the reviewing court is "left with the definite and firm conviction that a mistake has been committed."[20]

When district judges conduct bench trials in criminal cases, there is, oddly enough, no statutory rule specifying the appropriate standard of appellate review. Courts have interpolated application of the "clearly erroneous" standard from civil bench trials,[21] so in practice the same principle of deference applies to fact-finding in bench trials whether the case is civil or criminal.

Oftentimes, adjudicative facts reach courts after an administrative agency has made factual determinations. Will the court re-find the facts on its own or give a measure of weight to the views of the administrative agency?

The eighteenth- and nineteenth-century answer was mostly the former. As Professor Tom Merrill has noted, "all nineteenth-century review of agency action was, in effect, de novo. Consistent with the de novo nature of review, courts generally gave no deference to agency determinations, whether on issues of law or fact."[22] In the cases of that era, "[t]here was little rhetoric of deference, and even less evidence of it in practice."[23]

That changed in the twentieth century, as courts began to treat administrative fact-finding as akin to fact-finding by civil juries. In 1912, the Supreme Court said of a decision by the Interstate Commerce Commission: "Its conclusion, of course, is subject to review, but, when supported by evidence, is accepted as final; not that its decision, involving, as it does, so many and such vast public interests, can be supported by a mere scintilla of proof, but the courts will not examine the facts further than to determine whether there was substantial evidence to sustain the order."[24] In this context, it was clear that "substantial evidence" meant the kind of evidence necessary to sustain a civil jury verdict. In 1938, the Supreme Court described judicial review of agency fact-finding in exactly the same language that it used to describe review of jury verdicts: "Substantial evidence is more than a mere scintilla. It means such relevant evidence as a reasonable mind might accept as adequate to support a conclusion."[25] Between 1914 and 1940, nearly twenty federal statutes prescribed (either explicitly or implicitly) judicial review of agency fact-finding by a standard of "substantial evidence."[26] by which the legislature most likely meant the same standard as for review of civil juries.[27] That standard was apparently codified as the default rule for review of trial-type, or "formal," agency adjudications in 1946 when the Administrative Procedure Act (APA) provided that reviewing courts should "hold unlawful and set aside agency . . . findings . . . found to be . . . unsupported by substantial evidence."[28] For non-trial-type, or "informal," agency proceedings, the APA told courts to hold unlawful agency findings that were "arbitrary, capricious, an abuse of discretion, or otherwise not in accordance with law."[29] Conceivably, that latter standard could call for even more deference to agencies than to juries (under the twentieth-century rather than the eighteenth-century jury standard), though the distinction might be difficult to draw.

Modern law has modified—or, if one inclines toward original meaning in statutory interpretation, rewritten—the APA's evident review scheme in several important ways. First, the term "substantial evidence" in the APA, and in subsequent statutes such as 1947's Taft-Hartley Act,[30] is now understood to assign on appeal a somewhat lesser quantum of weight to agency factual findings than is given to civil jury verdicts. The practice prior to 1946, as noted above, was to treat agencies much like juries. In 1951, the Supreme Court interpreted (rightly or wrongly is not our concern here) the APA and contemporaneous statutes to be "a response to pressures for stricter and more uniform practice, not a reflection of approval of all existing practices."[31] As a result, said the Court:

> We conclude, therefore, that the Administrative Procedure Act and the Taft-Hartley Act direct that courts must now assume more responsibility for the reasonableness and fairness of Labor Board decisions than some courts have shown in the past. Reviewing courts must be influenced by a feeling that they are not to abdicate the conventional judicial function. Congress has imposed on them responsibility for assuring that the Board keeps within reasonable grounds. That responsibility is not less real because it is limited to enforcing the requirement that evidence appear substantial when viewed, on the record as a whole, by courts invested with the authority and enjoying the prestige of the Courts of Appeals. The Board's findings are entitled to respect; but they must nonetheless be set aside when the record before a Court of Appeals clearly precludes the Board's decision from being justified by a fair estimate of the worth of the testimony of witnesses or its informed judgment on matters within its special competence or both.[32]

While it is not entirely clear what this standard actually means, it seems likely given the context of the decision, which came against the backdrop of decades of treating agencies like juries, that the Court was prescribing a *lesser* measure of deference—though it is impossible to say precisely how much of a lesser measure—to fact-finding by administrative agencies than to fact-finding by juries. Notwithstanding dictum in a 1998 decision recharacterizing the substantial evidence standard as the jury standard,[33] no one who seriously pays attention to US administrative law thinks that federal courts treat agency factual findings the same way that the courts treat jury findings. Courts reverse agencies in circumstances in which they would never think to reverse juries.[34] As one federal court explained in 2007, substantial evidence review of agency fact-finding "is more deferential than the 'clearly erroneous' standard used in reviewing findings of fact by a district judge,"[35] but it also "differs from that applied to jury verdicts"[36] by involving a deeper inquiry into the foundations for, and credibility judgments underlying, agency decisions.

Second, the strong weight of authority in the federal courts holds that the level of deference prescribed by the "arbitrary, capricious, an abuse of discretion, or otherwise not in accordance with law" standard is exactly the same as the level prescribed by the "substantial evidence"[37] standard,[38] though there are occasional outliers who think that substantial evidence review is more rigorous than review under an "arbitrary, capricious, an abuse of discretion, or otherwise not in accordance with law" standard.[39]

There are several contexts in which the US Congress acts in an adjudicative capacity and finds facts as part of that role. As Tuan Samohon explains:

> Article I explicitly authorizes the United States House of Representatives to adjudicate when it acts on a case-by-case basis to impeach officers. Similarly, Article I authorizes the United States Senate to try cases when it sits as a court of impeachment to try and perhaps convict. More generally, the House and Senate acting together adjudicate when they fact gather, engage in "legislative adjudication," and deliberate the equities of a private bill for the benefit of a named individual or individuals.[40]

Those congressional factual findings will not be subject to judicial review in any of their contexts. First, the House finds facts when it decides whether to issue articles of impeachment and the Senate finds facts when it conducts impeachment trials. As a general matter, legislative impeachment decisions are not subject to judicial review.[41] Even if one could find some aspect of the impeachment process that is reviewable (such as whether assignment of the fact-finding role to a committee violates the constitutional requirement that the full Senate try impeachments), that limited review would not extend to the factual findings themselves as opposed to the process by which the Senate conducted its business. Second, Congress also sometimes finds facts when passing on private bills—in determining, for example, whether circumstances warrant indemnification to a government official against whom a judgment was issued in a private damages suit for performance of official functions.[42] No one has a right to a private bill, so there is nothing for a court to review if it does not pass; and no one has standing to challenge the enactment of a private bill if it does pass.[43] We can think of no occasion in which the adjudicative fact-finding (as opposed to the legislative fact-finding) of Congress is likely to be reviewed by a court.

There are also certain kinds of judicial fact-finding that are neither strictly adjudicative nor strictly legislative. The United States, unlike many other countries, does not employ an evidentiary system of free proof in its judicial proceedings. (It does employ something resembling a system of free proof in some of its non-judicial adjudicative fora, such as arbitration and administrative adjudication.[44]) Instead, drawing on the Anglo-American evidentiary tradition, it uses a complex set of exclusionary rules that renders inadmissible much relevant evidence on various policy grounds. There is, for example, a preference for original or duplicates of documents to prove the contents of those documents[45] and a presumptive exclusion of out-of-court statements used to prove the truth of those statements.[46] In applying these exclusionary evidentiary rules, judges must often make factual determinations, regarding what might be termed "evidence facts," that are not subject to the rules for adjudicative fact-finding. For example, the contents of documents can be proved through means other than the original or a duplicate of the document if, inter alia, "all the originals are lost or destroyed, and not by the proponent acting in bad faith."[47] Judges applying this rule might have to determine, as evidence facts, whether or not the original was destroyed, the cause of its destruction, and the mental state of the proponent of the evidence if he or she was the source of destruction.[48] These factual decisions on the admissibility of evidence are normally made without regard to the evidentiary rules themselves. Judges finding evidence facts apply what amounts to a regime of free proof, limited only by evidentiary privileges,[49] though some classes of admissibility decisions are based only on evidence that is itself admissible under the evidence rules and involve only the limited determination whether a reasonable person could, if he or she so wished, find the relevant evidence facts.[50] The mechanics of this complicated scheme do not matter here. What matters is that trial court determinations of evidence facts, whatever form those determinations take, are not reviewed by appellate courts under the "clearly erroneous" standard for adjudicative fact-finding. They are instead reviewed for "abuse of discretion," which involves a large measure of, as the Supreme Court has explicitly described it, "deference that is the hallmark of abuse-of-discretion review."[51] So this too is a practice explicitly described by the courts as deference.

Review of fact-finding thus presents a multiplicity of approaches, all of which are explicitly identified by courts as instances of deference. We will later explore what these approaches might have in common and what might keep them distinct.

## 2. Deference to Agency Legal Interpretations

An obvious next stop in the United States for a study of deference, at least to administrative law scholars such as ourselves, is the so-called *Chevron* deference doctrine. An adequate introduction to the *Chevron* doctrine would require a large segment of a lengthy book[52]; even to broach the subject requires, at a minimum, a lengthy article.[53] We say here only enough about the doctrine to ground an investigation into how US courts employ the concept of deference when applying the doctrine.

Administrative agencies interpret their organic statutes—that is, the congressional acts that create administrative agencies and establish their powers and goals—in the course of exercising their responsibilities. In a legal world in which restrictions on subdelegation of legislative power to executive agents are relaxed or even non-existent,[54] that agency interpretative authority is often very substantial, as many statutes are so open-ended or ambiguous that they give considerable leeway to the interpreter. A notable, and representative, example is US federal regulation of communications, which since 1926 has instructed administrative agencies to regulate radio, telephone, and other communications media in "the public interest"[55] and specifically instructs the Federal Communications Commission to award broadcast licenses "if public interest, convenience, or necessity will be served thereby."[56] Other examples of vaguely worded authority abound: The Environmental Protection Agency (EPA) is told to promulgate air quality standards "the attainment and maintenance of which in the judgment of the Administrator [of the EPA] ... are requisite to protect the public health,"[57] and the Secretary of Labor (through the Occupational Safety and Health Administration) is instructed to set standards for exposure to toxic substances in workplaces "which most adequately assure[], to the extent feasible, on the basis of the best available evidence, that no employee will suffer material impairment of health or functional capacity [from] ... regular exposure to the hazard."[58]

Even statutes that appear to be more detailed often leave considerable room for interpretation. Suppose, for example, that Congress instructs the EPA to implement a permitting program for "new or modified stationary sources"[59] of air pollution, under which producers can operate using "new or modified stationary sources" only if stringent conditions for environmental protection are satisfied. What is a "stationary source"? Does it mean a single integrated unit of production, such as a factory with multiple smokestacks, or does it mean each individual opening from which air pollution can be emitted, so that each smokestack in a factory would be a unique "stationary source"? The question is potentially quite important. If each smokestack is a "stationary source," producers would have to get permits—which might be very difficult and costly, and even impossible under the governing statutory criteria, to obtain—for any action that increased pollution from a single smokestack even if that action reduced the overall level of pollution coming from the plant (e.g., because the factory closed down activity in an inefficient, highly polluting part of its operation and moved that production to more efficient and cleaner units). But if a "stationary source" can mean the entire factory, the agency would be free (and conceivably even obligated) to look to the overall level of pollution from the plant rather than to the pollution levels from each individual unit when deciding whether permits are required. Questions such as this arise in any legal system; no legislature can consistently enact statutes so precise that they cleanly resolve every possible case that can arise under them. Since the administrative agencies applying these statutes always act before their decisions are reviewed by a court, reviewing courts must always ask what weight, if any, they should give to the agencies' view of the law when legal meaning is at issue.

As a general rule, US federal statutory law does not dictate a rule of judicial deference to such agency legal interpretations,[60] though, as we saw in the last section, statutes almost universally prescribe a strong measure of judicial deference to agency factual determinations. On some occasions, to be sure, statutes will fairly obviously limit the judicial role in statutory interpretation. For example, consider a statute that speaks of "unemployment (as determined in accordance with standards prescribed by the Secretary),"[61] which gives an administrator power to determine by regulation the meaning of the term "unemployment." This statute, the Supreme Court concluded, "expressly *delegated* to the Secretary the power to prescribe standards for determining what constitutes 'unemployment' . . . [so that a] reviewing court is not free to set aside those regulations simply because it would have interpreted the statute in a different manner."[62] Relatively few statutes, however, so openly commit legal determinations to the discretion of an agency. Indeed, to the extent that federal statutes speak to the matter at all, they seem to counsel against any such deference on matters of statutory meaning. The Administrative Procedure Act, the central statute in US administrative law, which serves as the default governing statute for all federal agency action, declares that "the reviewing court shall decide all relevant questions of law."[63] While this statement does not explicitly prescribe de novo review, one might reasonably expect such a de novo standard to be the default for court review of an executive decision on questions of legal interpretation; one of the most famous lines in American law is Chief Justice John Marshall's proclamation that "[i]t is emphatically the province and duty of the judicial department to say what the law is."[64]

Nonetheless, from a fairly early date in the emergence of the administrative state, US courts began voluntarily reviewing some agency legal conclusions for reasonableness rather than correctness,[65] at least when those conclusions were closely bound up with factual determinations[66] and sometimes (it was not clear exactly when and why) even if the agency was making so-called pure or abstract legal determinations.[67] As an early decision put it, on some occasions courts should approve agency interpretations of statutes if those interpretations have "a reasonable basis in law."[68] Those occasions were principally "where the question is one of specific application of a broad statutory term in a proceeding in which the agency administering the statute must determine it initially."[69] To be "administering" a statute, the agency surely needs some special relationship to the statute not shared by other agencies; the Internal Revenue Service "administers" the Internal Revenue Code in a way that a rate-setting agency that must interpret and apply the tax code when considering the economic consequences of various actions of regulated industries does not.[70] In circumstances where the court must do more than just find the agency interpretation to be "reasonable," either because the agency does not administer the statute or because the interpretation does not involve "specific application" of statutory terms, mid-twentieth-century law, according to the 1944 decision in *Skidmore v. Swift*,[71] would give some weight to the agency's interpretations if they were grounded in "specialized experience and broader investigations and information than is likely to come to a judge in a particular case."[72] Such interpretations, while not controlling if merely "reasonable," were considered entitled to (perhaps foreshadowing, or even grounding, the language in *Black's* definition of deference) "respect,"[73] so that "[t]he weight of such a judgment in a particular case will depend upon the thoroughness evident in its consideration, the validity of its reasoning, its consistency with earlier and later pronouncements, and all those factors which give it power to persuade, if lacking power to control."[74]

While it is impossible to describe mid-twentieth-century law with any great precision, one of us has previously offered the following summary:

(1) Does the agency administer the statutory provision at issue? If not, then the agency gets, at most, some measure of deference pursuant to *Skidmore v. Swift* if warranted by all of the facts and circumstances. If yes, then ...

(2) Is the agency's legal interpretation a pure, abstract, "ivory tower" legal question that can be asked and answered without knowing anything about the particular dispute before the agency? If no, then the agency presumptively gets a strong measure of deference, tantamount to reasonableness review, unless a constellation of factors counsels otherwise. If yes, then the court presumptively reviews the matter de novo, against subject to a constellation of factors that might counsel otherwise.

(3) Also, if Congress has *expressly* entrusted the law-determination function to the agency, then courts must honor the congressional allocation of authority and give the agency's decision great deference regardless of the classification of the legal question involved.[75]

In *Chevron U.S.A. v. Natural Resources Defense Council, Inc.*,[76] decided in 1984, the EPA interpreted precisely the statutory provision that we described above which established a permitting program for stationary sources of air pollution. The agency determined, after flip-flopping on the question over a period of years, that a "stationary source" could be an entire plant with multiple sources of pollution and not just each individual physical opening out of which pollution emerged. Challengers to the agency decision argued that a "stationary source" meant each individual source and that the statute left no room for placing multiple sources under an imaginary "bubble" and calling them a single source. The federal courts had to decide whether to accept the agency's interpretation of the statutory term "stationary source."

The first federal court to review the agency's decision rejected it, on the ground that a prior decision of that same court already resolved the matter against the agency.[77] (We will later explore whether and how to describe this familiar application of judicial precedent as a form of deference.) A unan-imous US Supreme Court,[78] on an opinion authored by Justice John Paul Stevens, reversed the lower court and upheld the agency decision. The Court's opinion contained language seeming to say that federal courts, when conducting review of a federal administrative agency's action, must *always* defer to the agency's legal interpretation of the federal law that it administers when certain conditions were met: (1) statutory meaning is unclear, (2) there is therefore room for disagreement about proper interpretation, and (3) the agency's answer is based on a permissible—i.e., reasonable—construction of the statute. In some of the most frequently quoted language in all of US law, the Court said:

> When a court reviews an agency's construction of the statute which it administers, it is confronted with two questions. First, always, is the question whether Congress has directly spoken to the precise question at issue. If the intent of Congress is clear, that is the end of the matter; for the court, as well as the agency, must give effect to the unambiguously expressed intent of Congress. If, however, the court determines Congress has not directly addressed the precise question at issue, the court does not simply impose its own construction on the statute, as would be necessary in the absence of an administrative interpretation. Rather, if the statute is silent or ambiguous with respect to the specific issue, the question for the court is whether the agency's answer is based on a permissible construction of the statute.[79]

The language in *Chevron* did not distinguish between "pure" or "mixed" questions of law, as arguably did the pre-existing doctrine of administrative review, but seemed, on its face, to be categorical. It is nonetheless clear that the Court in *Chevron* did not mean to prescribe any change in pre-existing standards of judicial review; Justice Stevens himself made that clear at his first opportunity to clarify the opinion that he authored.[80] The Court viewed the *Chevron* case, if it actually viewed the case as anything other than a narrow and technical decision involving a specific problem in environmental law, as a straightforward application of its prior decisions, under which agency decisions even on "pure" questions of law might sometimes merit defer-ence if a wide range of factors counseled it. As the Court explained later in its opinion: "In these cases the Administrator's interpretation represents a reasonable accommodation of manifestly competing interests and is entitled to deference: the regulatory scheme is technical and complex, the agency considered the matter in a detailed and reasoned fashion, and the decision involves reconciling conflicting policies."[81] An honest reading of the opinion indicates that deference results from factors specific to the particular decision at hand (note the colon in the quoted passage) rather than from any universalizable principle about agency interpretations in general.

Some lower courts, however, seized on the *Chevron* language to construct an elaborate edifice of wide-ranging deference to administrative legal determinations, and the Supreme Court eventually accepted the lower courts' expansive version of *Chevron* through a process of accretion and default.[82] As a consequence, the so-called *Chevron* doctrine of deference to agency interpretations of ambiguous statutory provisions that the agency administers has been among the centerpieces of American administrative law since the mid-1980s. The term *"Chevron* deference" even merits its own entry in *Black's Law Dictionary.*[83]

So what, exactly, does this doctrine instruct reviewing courts to do with agency legal interpretations that fall within the criteria for application of the doctrine? That is less clear than one might expect from a doctrine as well known and long established as the doctrine of *Chevron* deference. Indeed, the contours of the doctrine are so uncertain that some commentators, and some federal judges, have openly called for the doctrine's abandonment on the ground, inter alia, that the doctrine is so vague as to be unworkable.[84]

The canonical formulation, drawn from the *Chevron* decision, seems to suggest that courts should approach agency legal interpretations in much the way that *Black's Law Dictionary* understands deference: with a presumption of correctness. How strong a presumption is unclear; the *Chevron* decision unhelpfully said that agency determinations should be upheld if they are "permissible," but later decisions have clarified that the appropriate adjective is "reasonable." As the Court said in 2013, "[s]tatutory ambiguities will be resolved, within the bounds of reasonable interpretation, not by the courts but by the administering agency."[85] On closer examination, however, the meaning of *Chevron* deference gets more opaque, from several different directions.

First, when a court determines that a statutory provision is ambiguous and the agency's interpretation is reasonable, the court does not merely address that decision with *Black's* "polite and respectful attitude or approach." The court is legally obliged under those circumstances to accept the agency's decision, and a court that fails to accept the decision will be reversed on appeal by a higher court if one exists. (If the Supreme Court treats an agency's decision in a fashion that seems legally inappropriate, there is not much that anyone can do about it.) In this respect, the definition in *Black's* fails to capture the extent of the reviewing court's legal obligation under *Chevron* to give way to agency decisions.

On the other hand, there are parts of the review process for which the definition in *Black's* seems to overstate the extent of the reviewing court's obligation under *Chevron*. Courts only review agency decisions for reasonableness rather than correctness if courts first determine that the statute is ambiguous. If the meaning of the statute is "clear," whatever the term "clear" turns out to mean, then courts adopt that clear meaning without regard to the agency's views. This is why *Chevron* is often described as a "two-step" inquiry: At "step one," the court first determines, without considering the agency's views, whether the statute has a clear meaning; and only if the statute does not have a clear meaning does the court proceed to "step two," in which the agency wins if its interpretation is "reasonable." When courts reach "step two" of the process, agencies win almost 95 percent of the time, while agencies win only about 40 percent of the time when courts end the inquiry at "step one" of *Chevron*.[86] If courts are deferring to agencies at step one of *Chevron*, that deference is not apparent.

The sharp division in both the language and results of deference between steps one and two of *Chevron* is puzzling once one recognizes that the distinction between the two steps is artificial. Courts reviewing agency decisions are not ordinarily faced with two separate decisions from the agency: one deciding that the statute is ambiguous rather than clear and the other adopting one from among a range of (so the agency believes and hopes the court will conclude) reasonable alternative interpretations. While agencies will sometimes adopt that two-tiered inquiry at the stage of initial decision,[87] it makes no sense for them to do so; *Chevron* is a doctrine about judicial review of agency decisions, not a stand-alone theory of statutory interpretation to be employed by agencies in the first instance. Most of the time, agencies simply present an interpretation of the statute for a court to review. A *Black's*-style deferential approach would give that interpretation a presumption of correctness, understanding that the presumption will be overcome if the agency interpretation is contrary to clear statutory meaning. There are some scholars, including one of the present authors, who argue that *Chevron* actually does involve precisely that single, unitary inquiry about reasonableness[88]; and one now-deceased Supreme Court justice agreed with that view, writing: "The dissent finds it 'puzzling' that we invoke this proposition (that a reasonable agency interpretation prevails) at the 'outset,' omitting the supposedly prior inquiry of ' "whether congress has directly spoken to the precise question at issue." ' But surely if Congress has directly spoken to an issue, then any agency interpretation contradicting what Congress has said would be unreasonable."[89] Nonetheless, the two-step formulation is standard in judicial decisions and finds a measure of academic support.[90]

Second, this one-step-or-two-step question has an additional implication that highlights an ambiguity in the ostensible object of deference: Does deference describe, as *Black's* suggests, an attitude toward the decision under review or does deference describe the *consequence* of a substantive decision about the law reached independently by the court? The result in either case is the same, but the mental operation described by deference is slightly different depending on how one identifies the object.

If deference is an attitude toward the decision of the prior actor, one would expect the *Chevron* inquiry to be framed as a single step: Is the decision under review reasonable, even if the court, left to its own devices, would reach a different conclusion than did the agency? Deference in some fashion would be present throughout the judicial decision-making process. The standard two-step formulation of *Chevron* deference, however, suggests a different mental operation. The first inquiry is what the statute means. Under a two-step formulation, the court makes that decision *without* an attitude of respect for or deference to the agency decision. The court simply decides what it thinks about the statute. As the Supreme Court said in 2018, "we owe an agency's interpretation of the law no deference unless, after 'employing traditional tools of statutory construction,' we find ourselves unable to discern Congress's meaning."[91] Numerous other decisions—too large a number even for a string citation—say the same thing.[92] It is thus standard practice to view the first step of *Chevron* as a preliminary decision whether to defer to the agency rather than a decision itself informed by deference. The trick is that the court's first-step, non-deferential thoughts about the statute are not supposed to be directed to the *correct* meaning of the statute but to the *clear* meaning of the statute. If the court finds that there is no *clear* meaning of the statute, that finding is equivalent to (another way of stating that) the statute is ambiguous.[93] At that point, the court enters a deferential posture and yields to any agency interpretation of the ambiguous statute that is reasonable.

One should not make too much of this fine distinction as a matter of doctrine. Under a two-step approach, the court does indeed assume an attitude of deference toward the decision under review, but only after first reaching a particular legal conclusion about the meaning of the statute—namely, that there is no clear meaning of the statute. We highlight this subtlety only to bring to the fore the conceptual importance of focusing on *exactly what aspect of the prior decision* might be the object of deference. Treatments of prior decisions can seem deferential or non-deferential depending on how one characterizes the aspect of the prior decision under review. We will say more about this (we think) very significant idea later.

Third, once one reaches the second step of *Chevron* and deference to the agency's interpretation is deemed appropriate, what exactly does that deference involve? Respect? Obeisance? Something resembling "clearly erroneous" review? Perhaps remarkably, the case law provides no good answers. There is no canonical decision that systematically sets out what it means for an agency interpretation to be "reasonable." We know that very few agency decisions are found to be unreasonable. One study finds that when courts of appeals reach *Chevron* step two, the agency wins 93.8 percent of the time.[94] One of us has described the practice of federal courts at step two thusly:

Courts generally affirm agencies at step two in cursory fashion, *see, e.g., Air Transport Ass'n of America v. FAA,* 169 F.3d 1 (D.C.Cir.1999), and often with no more than a single conclusory sentence. *See, e.g., Automated Power Exchange, Inc. v. FERC,* 204 F.3d 1144 (D.C.Cir.2000); *Natural Resources Defense Council v. EPA,* 749 F.3d 1055, 1060 (D.C.Cir.2014). For a particularly dramatic example, see *Adirondack Medical Center v. Sebelius,* 740 F.3d 692 (D.C.Cir.2014) (spending seven pages on step one of *Chevron* and one sentence on step two). Frequently, the court will simply apply its step-one analysis: The same reasons why the agency does not lose at step one generally establish that its interpretation is at least reasonable. *See, e.g., Competitive Enterprise Inst. v. United States Dep't of Transportation,* 863 F.3d 911, 917 (D.C.Cir.2017) ("Petitioners present no arguments under *Chevron's* second step beyond those already discussed as part of step one. The *Chevron*-one analysis supports a reasonableness finding."). Cases that affirm agencies after more than a cursory discussion of step two typically do so by concluding that the agency's interpretation is *better* than competing interpretations, *see, e.g., County of Los Angeles v. Shalala,* 192 F.3d 1005,

1007-20 (D.C.Cir.1999), which sheds little light on what constitutes a "reasonable" interpretation.

In the infrequent cases in which agencies lose at step two, the agency interpretations typically either fail completely to advance the goals of the underlying statute, *see Chemical Manufacturers Ass'n v. EPA*, 217 F.3d 861 (D.C.Cir.2000), or are so bizarre that close analysis is unnecessary. *See NRDC v. Daley*, 209 F.3d 747 (D.C.Cir.2000); *Whitecliff, Inc. v. Shalala*, 20 F.3d 488 (D.C.Cir.1994). For example, in the first case in the Supreme Court in which an agency lost at step two, *AT & T Corp. v. Iowa Utilities Board*, 525 U.S. 366, 119 S.Ct. 721, 142 L.Ed.2d 835 (1999), the agency effectively construed an important statutory requirement out of existence.[95]

We have no good language to describe the kind of deference that this represents. Indeed, it is not even clear what criteria courts employ to determine the reasonableness of the agency's action. Is it conformance to the statute's language and structure? The policy consequences of the agency's decision? The thoroughness of the agency's reasoning and process of consideration? The law as of yet has no good answers.

Thus, one of American law's most conspicuous and explicit doctrines of deference leaves as many questions open as it answers, even after more than three decades of voluminous doctrinal development. Perhaps this is emblematic of why the systematic study of deference has not caught on. Nonetheless, *Chevron* deference must serve as one of the key data points in an inductive approach to defining deference.

There are several doctrines that the courts identify as instances of deference that are at least cousins to *Chevron* deference. One concerns agency interpretations of the agency's own regulations rather than the underlying statute. In 1945, the Supreme Court declared that a federal agency's interpretation of its own regulation is "of controlling weight unless it is plainly erroneous or inconsistent with the regulation."[96] That position was reaffirmed by the Court in 1997 in *Auer v. Robbins*,[97] a case in which the agency's interpretation of its regulation was put forward for the first time in a legal brief. As the Court explained: "Petitioners complain that the Secretary's interpretation comes to us in the form of a legal brief; but that does not, in the circumstances of this case, make it unworthy of deference. The Secretary's position is in no sense . . . advanced by an agency seeking to defend past agency action against attack. There is simply no reason to suspect that the interpretation does not reflect the agency's fair and considered judgment on the matter in question."[98] This doctrine of giving great weight to agency interpretations of their regulations has come to be called *"Auer* deference."[99] One Justice described it as "*Chevron* deference applied to regulations rather than statutes. The agency's interpretation will be accepted if, though not the fairest reading of the regulation, it is a plausible reading—within the scope of the ambiguity that the regulation contains."[100] Some lower courts have suggested that *Auer* deference is "even greater than our deference to an agency's interpretation of ambiguous statutory terms,"[101] though other courts have resisted drawing any distinction between the two standards.[102] This doctrine is something of an oddity. Normally, ambiguities in a legal instrument are construed *against* the drafter; *Auer* deference rewards the drafter of ambiguities by allowing it to twist those ambiguities in its own favor at a later date. A number of Supreme Court Justices, including the author of *Auer v. Robbins*, have expressed grave doubts about the continuing vitality of *Auer* deference.[103] Indeed, on December 10, 2018, the Supreme Court agreed to reconsider the *Auer* doctrine by granting certiorari in *Kisor v. Wilkie*[104] to address the question: "Whether the Court should overrule *Auer* and *Seminole Rock*."[105] Many observers (including us) thought it unlikely that the Court would hear that case unless it was prepared to abandon deference to agency interpretations of their own regulations. Nonetheless, the Court in *Kisor*, by a narrow majority, elected to retain *Auer* deference, albeit in a limited form. As five Justices put it: "The deference doctrine we describe is potent in its place, but cabined in its scope."[106] Some measure of deference to an agency's interpretation of its regulations is warranted, said the Court, because "the agency that promulgated a rule is in the 'better position [to] reconstruct' its original meaning,"[107] "resolving genuine regulatory ambiguities often 'entail[s] the exercise of judgment grounded in policy concerns,'"[108] and a presumption of deference "reflects the well-known benefits of uniformity in interpreting genuinely ambiguous rules."[109] This regime of deference, however, does not universally apply to all agency interpretations of their regulations. As the Court explained:

> But all that said, *Auer* deference is not the answer to every question of interpreting an agency's rules. Far from it . . . .[T]he possibility of deference can arise only if a regulation is genuinely ambiguous. And when we use that term, we mean it—genuinely ambiguous, even after a court has resorted to all the standard tools of interpretation. Still more, not all reasonable agency constructions of those truly ambiguous rules are entitled to deference. As

just explained, we presume that Congress intended for courts to defer to agencies when they interpret their own ambiguous rules. But when the reasons for that presumption do not apply, or countervailing reasons outweigh them, courts should not give deference to an agency's reading, except to the extent it has the "power to persuade." We have thus cautioned that *Auer* deference is just a "general rule"; it "does not apply in all cases." *Christopher*, 567 U.S. at 155, 132 S.Ct. 2156. And although the limits of *Auer* deference are not susceptible to any rigid test, we have noted various circumstances in which such deference is "unwarranted." In particular, that will be so when a court concludes that an interpretation does not reflect an agency's authoritative, expertise-based, "fair[, or] considered judgment."[110]

With those limitations, said the Court, *stare decisis* warrants retention of the *Auer* deference framework.[111]

Four concurring Justices would have abandoned *Auer* entirely. Indeed, given the constraints on the framework laid out in the majority opinion, the concurrence described the majority opinion's treatment of *Auer* as "more a stay of execution than a pardon,"[112] in which "the doctrine emerges maimed and enfeebled—in truth, zombified."[113] Chief Justice Roberts, while joining most of the majority opinion, added the following intriguing commentary:

> I write separately to suggest that the distance between the majority and Justice GORSUCH is not as great as it may initially appear. The majority catalogs the prerequisites for, and limitations on, *Auer* deference: The underlying regulation must be genuinely ambiguous; the agency's interpretation must be reasonable and must reflect its authoritative, expertise-based, and fair and considered judgment; and the agency must take account of reliance interests and avoid unfair surprise. Justice GORSUCH, meanwhile, lists the reasons that a court might be persuaded to adopt an agency's interpretation of its own regulation: The agency thoroughly considered the problem, offered a valid rationale, brought its expertise to bear, and interpreted the regulation in a manner consistent with earlier and later pronouncements. Accounting for variations in verbal formulation, those lists have much in common.
>
> That is not to say that *Auer* deference is just the same as the power of persuasion discussed in *Skidmore v. Swift & Co.*, 323 U.S. 134, 65 S.Ct. 161, 89 L.Ed. 124 (1944); there is a difference between holding that a court ought

to be persuaded by an agency's interpretation and holding that it should defer to that interpretation under certain conditions. But it is to say that the cases in which *Auer* deference is warranted largely overlap with the cases in which it would be unreasonable for a court not to be persuaded by an agency's interpretation of its own regulation.[114]

Perhaps this signals that *Auer* deference has been overruled in all but name and that a full-fledged overruling is virtually inevitable. Until that happens, however, *Auer* deference continues, at least formally, to be a part of US administrative law, and it will continue to be an important part of the modern history of deference in all events.

As was noted earlier, there are many contexts involving agency statutory interpretation to which the *Chevron* doctrine does not apply, either because the agency does not administer the statute in question or because the agency's interpretation was not promulgated with the force of law under circumstances indicating that Congress intended the agency to have interpretative authority.[115] In those cases in which *Chevron* is inapplicable, courts will not necessarily review the agency's decision de novo, if by "de novo" one means "without regard to the agency's decision." They will sometimes choose to give a measure of weight to the agency decision if, all things considered, the court believes that the agency decision merits weight. This has come to be called "*Skidmore* deference,"[116] named for the 1944 decision in *Skidmore v. Swift*. This deference doctrine will assume seemingly outsized importance in the next chapter when we attempt to define deference, so it requires some explanation.

The Fair Labor Standards Act (FLSA) requires overtime pay for employees who work more than forty hours per week.[117] *Skidmore* concerned firefighters who were present in their fire hall for some evenings outside their normal paid workweek. For most of that extra time, they did not have much to do; "[t]he men used their time in sleep or amusement as they saw fit, except that they were required to stay in or close by the fire hall and be ready to respond to alarms."[118] They got paid for responding to alarms but not for the time spent in the fire hall waiting for calls. Seven employees sued for overtime pay under the FLSA, claiming that their waiting time counted as work time under the statute. The FLSA provides for direct actions in court by employees without any prior agency action. "Congress did not utilize the services of an administrative agency to find facts and to determine in the first instance whether particular cases fall within or without the Act. Instead, it put this responsibility on the courts."[119] But while the Administrator of the Department of Labor's Wage and Hour Division had no authority over damages actions for back pay under the FLSA, the Administrator opined in published bulletins and informal rulings that such waiting time could, in some circumstances, count as work time under the statute; and, in an amicus brief in the *Skidmore* case, the Administrator suggested that on-call time not spent sleeping or eating should qualify for overtime pay under the specific facts of *Skidmore*. Because the agency does not "administer" the statute for these purposes, the agency would not be entitled to *Chevron* deference in modern times, and it was not in 1944 entitled to pre-*Chevron* deference for agency applications of statutory terms to particular facts. The Supreme Court's treatment of the agency's views in *Skidmore* has become a very important part of modern administrative law, in addition to a very important part of the fabric of federal court deference, and it deserves to be quoted at length:

> There is no statutory provision as to what, if any, deference courts should pay to the Administrator's conclusions. . . . They are not, of course, conclusive, even in the cases with which they directly deal, much less in those to which they apply only by analogy. They do not constitute an interpretation of the Act or a standard for judging factual situations which binds a district court's processes, as an authoritative pronouncement of a higher court might do. But the Administrator's policies are made in pursuance of official duty, based upon more specialized experience and broader investigations and information than is likely to come to a judge in a particular case. They do determine the policy which will guide applications for enforcement by injunction on behalf of the Government. Good administration of the Act and good judicial administration alike require that the standards of public enforcement and those for determining private rights shall be at variance only where justified by very good reasons. The fact that the Administrator's policies and standards are not reached by trial in adversary form does not mean that they are not entitled to respect. . . .
>
> We consider that the rulings, interpretations and opinions of the Administrator under this Act, while not controlling upon the courts by reason of their authority, do constitute a body of experience and informed judgment to which courts and litigants may properly resort for guidance. The weight of such a judgment in a particular case will depend upon the thoroughness evident in its consideration, the validity of its reasoning, its

consistency with earlier and later pronouncements, and all those factors which give it power to persuade, if lacking power to control.[120]

*Skidmore* deference, as so described, does not correspond to any particular degree or quantum of deference but varies with the facts and circumstances of each particular act of interpretation. It nonetheless qualifies as a bona fide legal doctrine because it requires reviewing courts at least to consider agency interpretations even if they ultimately choose to give them no weight.[121] That feature of *Skidmore* will loom large later in this book.

For many years after 1944, *Skidmore* receded into the background. It rose to the forefront of doctrine again in 2000, in another FLSA case, when the Supreme Court denied *Chevron* deference to a Department of Labor opinion letter but concluded that *Skidmore* deference was appropriate:

> Interpretations such as those in opinion letters—like interpretations contained in policy statements, agency manuals, and enforcement guidelines, all of which lack the force of law—do not warrant *Chevron*-style deference. Instead, interpretations contained in formats such as opinion letters are "entitled to respect" under our decision in *Skidmore v. Swift & Co.*, but only to the extent that those interpretations have the "power to persuade."[122]

Justice Antonin Scalia strongly objected to the use of *Skidmore* in a post-*Chevron* world, calling it "an anachronism, dating from an era in which we declined to give agency interpretations (including interpretive ruless, as opposed to 'legislative rules') authoritative effect."[123] Justice Scalia was simply wrong to think that *Chevron* categorically required deference to every agency legal interpretation; even the strongest form of *Chevron* excluded from its scope interpretations of statutes that were not administered by the agency, such as interpretations of government-wide statutes like the Administrative Procedure Act or the Federal Tort Claims Act. There always was and always will be a set of agency interpretations to which no version of *Chevron* applies, and there is nothing in the nature of *Chevron* that forces other kinds of deference, such as *Skidmore*, out of those *Chevron*-free zones. In any event, Justice Scalia's concerns were rejected even more resoundingly in 2001 in *United States v. Mead Corp.*, when the Supreme Court denied *Chevron* deference to a (legally binding) adjudicative determination by the US Customs Service but then remanded the case to the lower court to make a "*Skidmore* assessment . . . in the first instance."[124] The Court reiterated that such an assessment turns on "the merit of the writer's thoroughness, logic and expertness, its fit with prior interpretations, and *any other sources of weight.*"[125] Justice Scalia redoubled his objections:

> And finally, the majority's approach compounds the confusion it creates by breathing new life into the anachronism of *Skidmore*, which sets forth a sliding scale of deference owed an agency's interpretation of a statute that is dependent "upon the thoroughness evident in [the agency's] consideration, the validity of its reasoning, its consistency with earlier and later pronouncements, and all those factors which give it power to persuade, if lacking power to control"; in this way, the appropriate measure of deference will be accorded the "body of experience and informed judgment" that such interpretations often embody. . . . *Skidmore* deference is an empty truism and a trifling statement of the obvious: A judge should take into account the well-considered views of expert observers.
>
> It was possible to live with the indeterminacy of *Skidmore* deference in earlier times. But in an era when federal statutory law administered by federal agencies is pervasive, and when the ambiguities (intended or unintended) that those statutes contain are innumerable, totality-of-the-circumstances *Skidmore* deference is a recipe for uncertainty, unpredictability, and endless litigation.[126]

The majority was unmoved by Justice Scalia's concerns:

> Although we all accept the position that the Judiciary should defer to at least some of this multifarious administrative action, we have to decide how to take account of the great range of its variety. If the primary objective is to simplify the judicial process of giving or withholding deference, then the diversity of statutes authorizing discretionary administrative action must be declared irrelevant or minimized. If, on the other hand, it is simply implausible that Congress intended such a broad range of statutory authority to produce only two varieties of administrative action, demanding either *Chevron* deference or none at all, then the breadth of the spectrum of possible agency action must be taken into account. Justice Scalia's first priority over the years has been to limit and simplify. The Court's choice has

been to tailor deference to variety. This acceptance of the range of statutory variation has led the Court to recognize more than one variety of judicial deference.[127]

The end result is that "*Skidmore* deference" is a vibrant part of modern US administrative law. A simple WESTLAW search of "Skidmore /2 deference" on November 14, 2018, yielded 485 cases from the federal courts of appeals, 408 cases from the federal district courts, and 1,235 secondary sources that employ the terms in proximity

Bookmark this sentence: Any descriptive account of US federal court deference that does not include *Skidmore* deference is radically incomplete.

## 3. Deference in Constitutional Law

When US constitutional scholars think of deference, they are likely to think of James Bradley Thayer. In 1893, Thayer wrote one of the most famous and influential articles in all of American constitutional law, entitled *The Origin and Scope of the American Doctrine of Constitutional Law*.[128] Thayer's central claim is that, as a matter of both historical description and normative prescription, courts with the power of judicial review should exercise it only when, in the words of an early state court decision in Pennsylvania, "the violation of the constitution is so manifest as to leave no room for reasonable doubt."[129] As Thayer put it:

> If their duty [as reviewing courts] were in truth merely and nakedly to ascertain the meaning of the text of the constitution and of the impeached Act of the legislature, and to determine, as an academic question, whether in the court's judgment the two were in conflict, it would, to be sure, be an elevated and important office, one dealing with great matters, involving large public considerations, but yet a function far simpler than it really is. Having ascertained all this, yet there remains a question—the really momentous question—whether, after all, the court can disregard the Act. It cannot do this as a mere matter of course,—merely because it is concluded that upon a just and true construction the law is unconstitutional. . . . It can only disregard the Act when those who have the right to make laws have not merely made a mistake, but have made a very clear one,—so clear that it is not open to rational question.[130]

This doctrine is often called "Thayerian deference."[131] Much more commonly, it is called the "presumption of constitutionality,"[132] which is identifiable as an instance of deference. As Justice Scalia put it, "we ordinarily give some deference, or a presumption of validity, to the actions of the political branches."[133] Under either label, the doctrine prescribes deference to the constitutional views of legislatures and executives that have enacted statutes. (As we will later see, Thayer himself tried to limit his principle of deference to decisions by *federal* officials, leaving the courts more free to substitute their judgment for that of *state* officials, but it is hard to see a textual rather than policy-based foundation for that distinction.) The legislature and executive presumably believe that the statutes they enact are constitutional. Under Thayerian deference, or the presumption of constitutionality, that judgment is overturned by courts only in the case of very clear error. Thayer would characterize the inquiry as akin to a "beyond a reasonable doubt" standard; other forms of the presumption of constitutionality may not be as strong.

To be sure, the relationship between Thayerian deference and the presumption of constitutionality is likely more nuanced, at least in the present day, than we have thus far suggested. One scholar has suggested, with some force, that Thayerian deference to legislative interpretations of the Constitution is now effectively passé. On this account, the presumption of constitutionality no longer amounts to a presumption about legal meaning but instead assumes the existence of factual conditions necessary to satisfy the preconditions for constitutionality under judicially determined constitutional meanings:

> Under Thayerian deference, the courts ask whether the Constitution is reasonably subject to the interpretation put on it by the legislators. Under the presumption [of constitutionality], by contrast, courts do not consider the rationality of the legislature's interpretation. Instead, a court applies its own interpretation of the Constitution, and it asks whether there is a conceivable set of facts that would justify the law given that interpretation. Thus, the current presumption affords some degree of judicial deference to the legislature while at the same time allowing the judiciary to retain control over the interpretation of the Constitution.[134]

Descriptively, there is much to be said in favor of this account. Writing in 1893, Thayer could look back at many judicial pronouncements declaring something like his clear-error rule about constitutional meaning. (Whether the pre-1893 practice actually conformed to those pronouncements across a wide range of cases is a different question that we do not pursue here.) Had he written half a century later, however, Thayer would have faced a different legal environment, with very different judicial attitudes about legislatures and executives and their relationship to courts.

In *Cooper v. Aaron* in 1958, facing resistance from state officials to the Supreme Court's decisions ordering desegregation of public schools,[135] the Court declared "that the federal judiciary is supreme in the exposition of the law of the Constitution, and that principle has ever since been respected by this Court and the Country as a permanent and indispensable feature of our constitutional system. It follows that the interpretation of the Fourteenth Amendment enunciated by this Court in the *Brown* case is the supreme law of the land."[136] This is very far from a Thayerian declaration of deference by the Court to the views of legislatures and executives (*Cooper* specifically involved action by a state executive, but there is no reason to think that the Court would have felt differently about resistance from a state, or for that matter a federal, legislature). Rather, it is a declaration that legislatures and executives must defer—indeed, must defer absolutely—to the views of the Court on questions of constitutional meaning. The terms of debate thus shifted dramatically from *Marbury v. Madison*,[137] where the issue was whether the Court must defer absolutely to the views of the legislature and executive or whether the Court has any power, in any circumstances, to exercise legal judgment independent of the political branches. The Court in *Marbury* asserted its power and duty to make legal determinations even in the face of prior determinations by Congress and the President, but nothing in *Marbury* specified in terms the manner in which that power and duty would be exercised. It is at least consistent with, if not in any way dictated by, *Marbury* to suggest a Thayerian rule of deference in executing the judicial power. Nothing in *Marbury* even remotely suggests interbranch judicial supremacy in constitutional interpretation. Indeed, if it is a hard question whether courts *may* exercise judgment independent of the political branches, it is surely an easy question—with an easy answer of "no"—whether courts are *supreme* over the political branches in legal interpretation. By 1958, however, it was very hard to see any principle of Thayerian deference in the attitude of the Court. (Again, Thayer himself would distinguish court review of state decisions from review of federal decisions, but the courts since 1958 have not drawn that distinction.)

To be sure, the Court in 1958 was faced with open state resistance, not just to the Court's abstract views on the meaning of the Fourteenth Amendment but to specific judgments applying that meaning to a particular set of facts. Deference to court judgments is quite a different matter than deference to abstract court interpretations.[138] The broader language in *Cooper* was thus dictum—and it would have amounted to circular and self-referential reasoning even if it was holding; surely the Court cannot justify its own supremacy by announcing and relying on its own supremacy. Nonetheless, the decision has set—or at least represented—the tone for US federal judicial relations with political actors, both state and federal, for the past half-century and more. While the Court still occasionally speaks as though deference to legislative and executive interpretations of the Constitution is the order of the day, those statements usually come at the end of a decision explaining why the legislative or executive judgment is wrong and will not be followed notwithstanding all due deference.[139] Presidents and congresses have found it politically expedient to let the Court claim and exercise this supreme interpretative power,[140] and they accordingly defer to the views of courts rather than vice versa. Thayerian deference in its strong form rather plainly does not describe the actual practice of modern constitutional litigation, even if it ever correctly described the actual practice of the first century of the United States. Indeed, "pleas for consistent Thayerian deference have gone unheeded by every justice on the modern Supreme Court."[141]

Thayerian deference is nonetheless a theoretically important construct that continues to attract the attention of scholars and makes at least token appearances in judicial opinions. Whatever one's views about its merits, it at least deserves serious consideration: If courts are willing to defer to administrative agencies' constructions of statutes that those agencies administer, why would they not be willing to defer to legislative constructions of constitutional provisions that those legislatures administer? If agencies get deference in the interpretation of statutes that define those agencies' own powers,[142] why wouldn't Congress (or the President) get deference in the interpretation of constitutional provisions that define Congress's (or the President's) powers? We leave for another day, however, any discussion of whether Thayerian deference is a good or bad way to conduct judicial review, either as a matter of constitutional interpretation or of legal policy.[143] Our goal here is only to describe the way that the contemporary legal landscape employs the idea of deference in the context of constitutional interpretation.

Thayerian deference may not be much of a part of that landscape, but the presumption of constitutionality in its narrower, fact-assuming sense assuredly is. In many contexts, courts routinely assume the existence of facts necessary for legislation to satisfy constitutional standards. This happens most notably when courts assess whether legislation has a "rational basis." In those circumstances, primarily but not exclusively when legislation is challenged as a violation of due process of law or the equal protection of the laws, the announced standard is to ask "if there is any reasonably conceivable state of facts that could provide a rational basis for the classification."[144] To be sure, there is a large class of cases in which courts, seeking to protect interests that find favor with the judiciary, examine legislative judgments and classifications with considerably more rigor than this rational basis standard would prescribe,[145] but "where 'ordinary commercial transactions' are at issue, rational basis review requires deference to reasonable underlying legislative judgments."[146] In essence, rational basis review does more than just instruct courts to defer heavily to legislative findings of so-called legislative facts and the corresponding legislative assessment of how those legislative facts affect constitutional meaning. That would be akin to deferring to administrative agencies when those agencies construct legal meaning inductively through applying statutes to particular facts. Rational basis review, by contrast, does not require the court to ascertain that the legislature has actually found any facts. It tells courts to uphold legislative enactments if a hypothetical legislature *could* have made the necessary factual findings, even if the real legislature did no such thing. As a result, in its application to interests that do not fall into the favored category of "fundamental" or "protected" interests, rational basis review is "tantamount to no review at all."[147] As one commentator has aptly described rational basis review:

> Absent some reason to apply heightened scrutiny, courts afford a great deal of deference to legislative judgments. Under the familiar "rational basis" test—which is the default standard for equal protection and substantive due process claims—courts insist on little more than a plausible connection between legislative means and ends. The government need not produce any evidence to support a classification. And it does not matter if all available evidence suggests the legislature was mistaken. A statute may be upheld based on *any* conceivable basis, including one that the legislature never considered.[148]

This strong form of deference has its share of critics,[149] but it is a fixture in the present legal firmament.

A full account of judicial deference to legislative and executive actors would require a separate volume, not a few pages of summary. Much depends on the level of government; Thayer, for example, was much more enthusiastic about deference to the federal Congress than he was about deference to state legislatures.[150] Courts often (though not always) take a different view of deference when foreign affairs or national security claims are involved,[151] and the scales are often weighted in times of war. There are too many different manifestations of deference in constitutional law to catalogue here. Indeed, an apt account of modern constitutional review might run something like this: Courts do not defer at all to legislative or executive judgments of constitutional meaning, but they defer almost conclusively to legislative (though not to executive) findings of legislative facts and the application of those legislative facts to particular circumstances . . . unless they really don't want to do so. For our purposes of seeking material for inductive generalizations, it is enough to note the general and abstract phenomenon of Thayerian deference and move on.

The United States, of course, is not the only country in which courts must assess the actions of legislatures and executives. Any national court system with provisions for judicial review will face some such set of cases, and international tribunals increasingly find themselves called upon to evaluate the actions of national legislatures and executives. The same questions about the nature and scope of deference that infuse US constitutional law arise in those contexts as well.

There is no reason to expect the answers to be the same, or even similar, in each context. The US doctrine, after all, arises in a specific legal and political context which includes a written Constitution that has more than two centuries of history, and more than two centuries of accumulated interpretations and applications, behind it. International tribunals, by contrast, frequently operate with relatively vague charters that say little about deference or scope of review, do not have well-established traditions of interpretation or application, and must deal with member nations with widely varying legal cultures. Nonetheless, at least some of those bodies have developed doctrines that are classifiable as instances of deference.

Perhaps the most obvious deference doctrine applied by international tribunals is the "margin of appreciation," under which international tribunals declare and define abstract rights but give individual nations considerable leeway in how to implement those rights in their particular circumstances and cultures.[152] This idea was clearly expressed by the European Court of Human Rights (ECtHR) in 1976, when it ruled that the United Kingdom could (at least at that time and place) prohibit and seize as obscene books that presented sexual material to young children.[153] Application of the United Kingdom law against obscene publications was challenged as a violation of Article 10 of the Convention for the Protection of Human Rights and Fundamental Freedoms, which provides:

1. Everyone has the right to freedom of expression. This right shall include freedom to hold opinions and to receive and impart information and ideas without interference by public authority and regardless of frontiers. This Article (art. 10) shall not prevent States from requiring the licensing of broadcasting, television or cinema enterprises.

2. The exercise of these freedoms, since it carries with it duties and responsibilities, may be subject to such formalities, conditions, restrictions or penalties as are prescribed by law and are necessary in a democratic society, in the interests of national security, territorial integrity or public safety, for the prevention of disorder or crime, for the protection of health or morals, for the protection of the reputation or rights of others, for preventing the disclosure of information received in confidence, or for maintaining the authority and impartiality of the judiciary.[154]

The court upheld the state's action with the following explanation:

[T]he machinery of protection established by the Convention is subsidiary to the national systems safeguarding human rights. . . . The Convention leaves to each Contracting State, in the first place, the task of securing the rights and liberties it enshrines. The institutions created by it make their own contribution to this task but they become involved only through contentious proceedings and once all domestic remedies have been exhausted.

These observations apply, notably, to Article 10 para. 2 (art. 10-2). In particular, it is not possible to find in the domestic law of the various Contracting States a uniform European conception of morals. The view taken by their respective laws of the requirements of morals varies from time to time and from place to place, especially in our era which is characterised by a rapid and far-reaching evolution of opinions on the subject. By reason of their direct and continuous contact with the vital forces of their countries, State authorities are in principle in a better position than the international judge to give an opinion on the exact content of these requirements as well as on the "necessity" of a "restriction" or "penalty" intended to meet them. . . .

Consequently, Article 10 para. 2 (art. 10-2) leaves to the Contracting States a margin of appreciation. This margin is given both to the domestic legislator ("prescribed by law") and to the bodies, judicial amongst others, that are called upon to interpret and apply the laws in force.

Nevertheless, Article 10 para. 2 (art. 10-2) does not give the Contracting States an unlimited power of appreciation. The Court, which, with the Commission, is responsible for ensuring the observance of those States' engagements, is empowered to give the final ruling on whether a "restriction" or "penalty" is reconcilable with freedom of expression as protected by Article 10. The domestic margin of appreciation thus goes hand in hand with a European supervision.[155]

This is obviously a doctrine of deference, though the degree of deference is limited and variable with circumstances. We do not here explore this doctrine in sufficient detail to include it in our database for deriving an inductive definition of deference; there is a voluminous literature, which we do not engage, on the mechanics and merits of the margin of appreciation doctrine as applied by the ECtHR and other tribunals.[156] Our point here is only that questions of deference are endemic to systems of constitutional review, no matter how those systems choose to allocate authority across institutions. The United States has its own set of answers to those questions, but the questions are universal.

## 4. Federal Court Deference to Executive Policymaking

The presumption of constitutionality as applied to legislation is essentially a deferral to Congress in the realm of policymaking. Unless one has a very strong inclination to natural law, under which legislatures may only properly announce and clarify pre-existing norms,[157] policymaking is what legislatures do, so there is some obvious logic to affording those institutions a measure of deference. But executives also make numerous decisions that cannot be reduced simply to fact-finding, law determination, and the application of law to facts. If a President chooses whether to issue a pardon, the President acts pursuant to legal authority granted in the Constitution, but that legal authority does not specify the appropriate grounds for issuance of a pardon. The President thus exercises what can only be described as policy judgment—or, if one prefers, discretion—in executing the pardon power.

Much, and perhaps even most, executive action takes this form. The essence of executive power is to execute—to carry into effect—legal norms.[158] But not all legal norms are so crisp that their execution is merely ministerial; even under a regime that strictly enforces a principle against subdelegation of legislative authority, there is sure to be some fuzziness along the boundary between executive and legislative power that leaves some room for executive discretion in law execution. In a regime that broadly permits legislative subdelegation, executive discretion effectively determines the substantive content of the law; the executive assumes the legislature's lawmaking function within the scope of the subdelegation. And even if the legislative norm is so clear that any interpretative discretion is insignificant, there remains issues of the form and timing of execution. Through what means will the laws be executed? How will limited resources be allocated among possible acts of execution? To what extent should executive action look forward to new activities or backward to correcting or perfecting acts already taken? There is always going to be a degree of discretionary executive policymaking as an essential component of the exercise of executive power.

To what degree is executive policymaking subject to judicial review, and with what measure of deference, if any, will the courts exercise any such power?

The former question would need to be the subject of a separate book. In *Marbury v. Madison* in 1803, the Supreme Court apparently disclaimed authority to examine discretionary executive actions that did not affect private rights:

By the constitution of the United States, the President is invested with certain important political powers, in the exercise of which he is to use his own discretion, and is accountable only to his country in his political character, and to his own conscience. . . .

. . . [W]hatever opinion may be entertained of the manner in which executive discretion may be used, still there exists, and can exist, no power to control that discretion. The subjects are political. They respect the nation, not individual rights, and being entrusted to the executive, the decision of the executive is conclusive. . . .

The conclusion from this reasoning is, that where the heads of departments are the political or confidential agents of the executive, merely to execute the will of the President, or rather to act in cases in which the executive possesses a constitutional or legal discretion, nothing can be more perfectly clear than that their acts are only politically examinable. But where a specific duty is assigned by law, and individual rights depend upon the performance of that duty, it seems equally clear that the individual who considers himself injured, has a right to resort to the laws of his country for a remedy.[159]

Of course, the last line in the quoted passage makes clear that judicial review of some kind *is* available when private rights are at issue. This hard line between reviewable and unreviewable actions depended on a number of background assumptions that no longer hold two centuries later. One concerns the evolving relationship between courts and other actors described earlier in this chapter. Another concerns the definition of "individual rights." The understanding of private rights—or "life, liberty, or property,"[160] as the Constitution identifies them—was in some important respects narrower in 1803 than under current law, and those differences have important implications for the constitutionally proper scope of executive power. One of us has explored some of those implications at length elsewhere.[161] The two of us have previously suggested that *all* executive action, including the kind of action that *Marbury* assumed was unreviewable, is subject to constitutional constraints that impose fiduciary duties on public officials,[162] though whether and how those constraints are reviewable through judicial and/or political mechanisms is a delicate question. We leave such delicate questions aside for the moment. Suffice it to say that a broad range of executive policymaking is today considered amenable to judicial review. The more pertinent question for now is how rather than whether that review takes place.

The vast majority of executive decisions are not made by the President personally. They are made by subordinate officials executing functions vested by statute, where the statutes openly grant vast discretion to the administrative officials both to enforce and to promulgate legal norms. This structure is neatly encapsulated by the phrase "the administrative state." As that administrative state has mushroomed in size and complexity over the past century, courts and legislatures have had to think carefully about how and when courts would supervise executive decisions that are not reducible to factual and legal determinations and therefore amount to exercises of discretion or policymaking authority.

The legislative answer in the United States, announced in general terms in the Administrative Procedure Act in 1946 and repeated many times since in agency organic statutes, has been to prescribe review of such judgments to ensure that they are not "arbitrary, capricious, an abuse of discretion, or otherwise not in accordance with law."[163] There is some ambiguity in this legislative prescription. The terms "arbitrary" and "capricious" in 1946 were closely associated with the kind of "rational basis" review afforded legislative judgments, in which case agency decisions could be upheld based on assumed or postulated facts without regard to whether the agency actually found the relevant facts when making its decision.[164] On the other hand, the term "abuse of discretion" is familiar from appellate review of trial court decisions, and while such review is highly deferential, it requires the appellate body to understand and evaluate the actual reasons for decision applied by the trial court. Review for "abuse of discretion" requires that discretion actually be exercised. Whatever might be the correct answer as a matter of original statutory meaning, as a matter of doctrine the Supreme Court in 1983 explicitly rejected an equation of legislative and administrative policymaking: "We do not view as equivalent the presumption of constitutionality afforded legislation drafted by Congress and the presumption of regularity afforded an agency in fulfilling its statutory mandate."[165] Unlike legislatures, agencies must articulate the legal, factual, and policy bases for their decisions, and the courts are not supposed to uphold agency actions on bases not at least implicitly relied upon by the agencies.[166] Once those reasons are articulated, however, review of the policymaking component of those decisions is generally deferential: "a court is not to substitute its judgment for that of the agency."[167] If the agency decision involves highly technical matters, as do many decisions, judicial deference is likely to be at its peak: "A court generally must be 'at its most deferential' when reviewing scientific judgments and technical analyses within the agency's expertise."[168] To be sure, there can be agency decisions so absurd that even a deferential standard cannot save them, and a court will therefore conclude that the agency "has failed to exercise its discretion in a reasoned manner."[169] But such decisions are hard to find. Even when an agency decision appears on its face to be manifestly absurd, courts will normally send the decision back to the agency for a fuller explanation rather than simply pronounce the agency decision absurd and invalid.[170] If we are right that the federal Constitution is a fiduciary instrument that incorporates by reference background principles of fiduciary law,[171] there may be a constitutional grounding for an even stricter review that focuses more on the substance of the agency decision,[172] but that is a story for another time. The focus of modern judicial review of agency policy-making is on the agency's *decision-making process* rather than on the result, though an absurd result may be a warning sign that something went seriously wrong with the process. Within that focus, however, review is intense and at best only moderately deferential. Courts seek to ensure that agencies took a "hard look"[173] at the problems before them. Courts are vigorous in requiring agencies to identify the steps in their reasoning process, and they are often persnickety about what counts as an adequate path of reasoning.

Parallel stories of legal development of administrative review can surely be told in virtually every country that has a developed administrative state, though we are not the ones to tell those stories (at least not in this volume). For example, one could trace the evolution of judicial review of administrative action in England through stages of development not unlike the moves in the United States. At roughly the same time that the United States was enacting the Administrative Procedure Act, which authorized judicial review of agency discretion that was "arbitrary, capricious, an abuse of discretion, or otherwise not in accordance with law," the Kings Bench Division decided *Associated Provincial Picture Houses, Ltd. v. Wednesbury Corp.*[174] A series of laws permitted movie theaters to operate on Sundays, but subject to conditions imposed by local authorities. Wednesbury authorized the plaintiff to operate on Sundays if no children under the age of fifteen were admitted, and the operator objected that the condition was unlawful. The terms of the relevant statute were open-ended and conferred seemingly unlimited discretion on the permitting authority: "The authority having power, in any area to which this section extends, to grant licences under the Cinematograph Act, 1909, may, notwithstanding anything in any enactment relating to Sunday observance, allow places in that area licensed under the said Act to be opened and used on Sundays for the purpose of cinematograph entertainments, subject to such conditions as the authority think fit to impose."[175] The court upheld the permitting conditions. Lord Greene expressed the limited scope of judicial review of such action in language that has come to be called "*Wednesbury* deference":

What, then, is the power of the courts? They can only interfere with an act of executive authority if it be shown that the authority has contravened the law. It is for those who assert that the local authority has contravened the law to establish that proposition. On the face of it, a condition of the kind imposed in this case is perfectly lawful. It is not to be assumed prima facie that responsible bodies like the local authority in this case will exceed their powers; but the court, whenever it is alleged that the local authority have contravened the law, must not substitute itself for that authority. It is only concerned with seeing whether or not the proposition is made good. When an executive discretion is entrusted by Parliament to a body such as the local authority in this case, what appears to be an exercise of that discretion can only be challenged in the courts in a strictly limited class of case. . . . The exercise of such a discretion must be a real exercise of the discretion. If, in the statute conferring the discretion, there is to be found expressly or by implication matters which the authority exercising the discretion ought to have regard to, then in exercising the discretion it must have regard to those matters. Conversely, if the nature of the subject matter and the general interpretation of the Act make it clear that certain matters would not be germane to the matter in question, the authority must disregard those irrelevant collateral matters.

. . . .

The court is entitled to investigate the action of the local authority with a view to seeing whether they have taken into account matters which they ought not to take into account, or, conversely, have refused to take into account or neglected to take into account matters which they ought to take into account. Once that question is answered in favour of the local authority, it may be still possible to say that, although the local authority have kept within the four corners of the matters which they ought to consider, they have nevertheless come to a conclusion so unreasonable that no reasonable authority could ever have come to it. In such a case, again, I think the court can interfere. The power of the court to interfere in each case is not as an appellate authority to override a decision of the local authority, but as a judicial authority which is concerned, and concerned only, to see whether the local authority have contravened the law by acting in excess of the powers which Parliament has confided in them.[176]

This formulation is familiar from several other contexts. The requirement that agency action be substantively reasonable—or, more to the point, not wholly unreasonable—has very old origins in English administrative law, going back at least to 1598, when Lord Coke said of a statute that allowed the Commissioner of Sewers to implement water-control measures "as case shall require, after your wisdoms and discretions" and to impose costs on land-owners to pay for those measures as the Commissioner "shall deem most convenient to be ordained"[177]:

> [N]otwithstanding the Words of the commission give Authority to the commissioners to do according to their Discretions, yet their Proceedings ought to be limited and bound with the Rule of Reason and law. For Discretion is a Science or Understanding to discern between Falsity and Truth, between Wrong and Right, between Shadows and Substance, between Equity and colourable Glosses and Pretences, and not to do according to their Wills and private Affections.[178]

We have elsewhere discussed at some length this "principle of reasonable-ness," its origins in the law of agency, its development through the eighteenth century, and its implications for US constitutional and administrative law.[179] The idea that discretionary authority must be exercised with some measure of substantive reasonableness, absent specific instructions to the contrary in the authorizing instrument, is a straightforward application of traditional agency law in both private and public settings. The only question is how unreasonable action must be in order to fall outside the zone of authorized discretion. *Wednesbury* suggests that it must be truly absurd, akin to the pre-modern meaning of "arbitrary" or "capricious" characteristic of US "rational basis" review. We leave to others the story of how modern law has developed "variable" *Wednesbury* deference, in which action involving important rights receives stricter (though not necessarily US-style "strict") scrutiny; how such review relates to proportionality review; and how different Commonwealth countries have approached these questions.[180] As with the margin of appre-ciation, our point is only to highlight (or acknowledge) that the problems posed by deference are universal even if the doctrines and answers are not.

Another context called to mind by *Wednesdbury* is the standard formu-lation for hard-look review in US law, articulated by the Supreme Court in 1983:

> The scope of review under the "arbitrary and capricious" standard is narrow and a court is not to substitute its judgment for that of the agency.

Nevertheless, the agency must examine the relevant data and articulate a satisfactory explanation for its action including a "rational connection between the facts found and the choice made." In reviewing that explanation, we must "consider whether the decision was based on a consideration of the relevant factors and whether there has been a clear error of judgment." Normally, an agency rule would be arbitrary and capricious if the agency has relied on factors which Congress has not intended it to consider, entirely failed to consider an important aspect of the problem, offered an explanation for its decision that runs counter to the evidence before the agency, or is so implausible that it could not be ascribed to a difference in view or the product of agency expertise.[181]

Apart, perhaps, from the reference to a "clear error of judgment," this formulation bears striking resemblance to the *Wednesbury* standard: the focus is on ensuring that agencies consider, and consider only, relevant factors. In practice, review under this standard in the United States is considerably more vigorous than the standard's rhetoric would suggest, but that may be true in England as well. Again, we leave that topic to others who are better informed than we.

## 5. Federal Court Deference to State Courts

From the founding of the United States onward, federal courts have had some power to review the judgments of state courts in certain cases. Section 25 of the Judiciary Act of 1789 provided for federal appellate jurisdiction over state court decisions in which the state court ruled against a claimed federal right.[182] This provision was replaced by a similar provision in 1867, which provided that state court judgments ruling against federal rights "may be re-examined and reversed or affirmed in the Supreme Court of the United States .[183] Importantly, the 1867 law omitted a provision that had been in the Judiciary Act of 1789 specifying, after limiting jurisdiction to matters decided by state courts against federal rights: "No other error shall be assigned or regarded as a ground of reversal in any such case as aforesaid, than such as appears on the face of the record, and *immediately respects the before mentioned questions of validity* or construction of the said constitution, treaties, statutes, commissions, or authorities in dispute."[184] Modern law has no limitations on federal jurisdiction over state court judgments presenting federal questions, saying merely: "Final judgments or decrees rendered by the highest court of a State in which a decision could be had, may be reviewed by the Supreme Court by writ of certiorari where the validity of a treaty or statute of the United States is drawn in question or where the validity of a statute of any State is drawn in question on the ground of its being repugnant to the Constitution, treaties, or laws of the United States, or where any title, right, privilege, or immunity is specially set up or claimed under the Constitution or the treaties or statutes of, or any commission held or authority exercised under, the United States."[185]

Go back to 1867. Without the proviso specifically limiting federal court review of state judgments only to federal issues, which did not make its way into the 1867 amendment, suppose that a state court judgment ruling against a federal right involves, as part of the case, a construction of that state's own law. (For example, in order to hold that a challenged state law is constitutional, the state court must determine what the state law actually means.) Could the US Supreme Court decide the case by determining that the state court misinterpreted its own state's law?

Based solely on the language of the 1867 jurisdictional act, there is no apparent reason why not. Once the Supreme Court has jurisdiction over the case, it seemingly can decide any matter properly before it, whether it involves a question of federal law or state law. Congress could have written the statute to limit the grounds of decision solely to matters of federal law, as it had explicitly done in 1789, but the 1867 statute as written does not seem to contain any such limitation. Of course, the question would remain whether the federal court *should* give some measure of weight to the state court's view of the state law, but the federal court would have the *power* to review the state court interpretation of state law in some fashion.

Nonetheless, in 1874 in *Murdock v. City of Memphis*,[186] the Supreme Court concluded that (a post-Civil War!) Congress could not possibly have intended federal courts to examine the state law determinations of (post-Civil-War!) state courts: "The State courts are the appropriate tribunals, as this court has repeatedly held, for the decision of questions arising under their local law, whether statutory or otherwise. And it is not lightly to be presumed that Congress acted upon a principle which implies a distrust of their integrity or of their ability to construe those laws correctly."[187] Consequently, said the Court, on matters of state law, "we must receive the decision of the State courts as conclusive."[188] So framed, the decision prescribes a rule of absolute federal court deference to state court decisions involving state law. Scholars disagree about whether the decision correctly interpreted the relevant jurisdictional statute,[189] but everyone agrees that the "principle continues to govern the Court today, and it reinforces the view that state courts are the final arbiters of the meaning of state law."[190]

Except in some cases the principle does not govern and state courts are not the final arbiters of the meaning of state law. The hard-line, unconditionally deferential bar of *Murdock* has not held up over time. It is easy to see why not. Suppose that a state court rules, as a matter of state law, that a party's federal claim brought in state court was procedurally defective, so that no judgment on the merits of the federal claim is necessary or appropriate. Suppose further that the state court interpretation of state law on which this decision is based is objectively absurd. The absolutely deferential rule of *Murdock* forecloses federal courts from re-examining the state court's ruling on state procedural law, which then effectively means that the federal claim never gets to federal court through the state court system. What happens, in other words, when federal courts looking at state courts discover a "distrust of their integrity"?

The case that broke the camel's back was *NAACP v. State of Alabama ex rel. Patterson*.[191] In the late 1950s, the State of Alabama, as with much of the American South at that time, was actively resisting desegregation, as was described in detail by the NAACP in its brief to the Supreme Court.[192] Alabama sought to shut down the National Association for the Advancement of Colored People, which had been operating as a foreign (New-York based) corporation in Alabama since 1918. Alabama claimed that the NAACP had failed to comply with foreign corporate registration requirements; the NAACP agreed that it had not registered but insisted that it was exempt from those requirements. As part of that litigation in state court, the state demanded production of numerous records, including a list of all NAACP members in the state. Fearing obvious reprisals against its members, the organization refused to produce its membership list, and the state courts imposed large civil contempt fines. The NAACP sought review of those contempt orders in state court, but the Alabama Supreme Court declined review because it said that the NAACP had pursued the wrong procedural mechanism for review (it used certiorari rather than mandamus). The NAACP then sought review in the US Supreme Court, claiming that the production orders violated the constitutional associational rights of its members.

The case is doctrinally noteworthy for two reasons. First, it announced a constitutional "right of association" under the First and Fourteenth Amendments—a right nowhere textually specified.[193] Second, and more importantly for our purposes, it articulated a federal court power to reject state court interpretations of state law. The NAACP had followed what appeared to be the procedural path to review set out by prior Alabama cases. The Alabama Supreme Court, however, construed its procedural laws to foreclose the path taken by the NAACP. Dismissal of the NAACP's challenge to the contempt order thus did not appear to rest on interpretation or application of any federal law, leaving nothing for the federal courts to do or say. Any comments on the underlying federal merits of the NAACP's claims that Alabama was denying its members their freedom of association would be a classic "advisory opinion" that would not affect the outcome of the underlying state litigation.[194] In order to avoid this result, the Supreme Court concluded that the Alabama courts had—one strongly suspects deliberately—misapplied their own law: "We are unable to reconcile the procedural holding of the Alabama Supreme Court in the present case with its past unambiguous holdings as to the scope of review available upon a writ of certiorari addressed to a contempt judgment. . . . [W]e can discover nothing in the prior state cases which suggests that mandamus is the exclusive remedy for reviewing court orders after disobedience of them has led to contempt judgments."[195] Previous US Supreme Court decisions had held, quite sensibly, that federal courts get to determine whether a federal claim was actually involved in the case[196] and whether factual findings by state courts that avoided federal claims were supported by evidence,[197] but it is a different matter for a federal court to say that a state court misinterpreted its own laws, whether statutory or case-created. Nor does it appear as though the US Supreme Court gave any deference to the views of the Alabama Supreme Court about how to understand prior Alabama case law. The US Supreme Court simply made its own judgment about the best reading of Alabama law. There is nothing inevitable about that attitude; it is possible to think that federal courts should review state court interpretations of state law but do so by giving considerable weight to the prior state court determination.[198] Under the circumstances present in NAACP, it is not surprising that the US Supreme Court did not take that deferential approach.

To be clear: We are not arguing here whether the US Supreme Court was right or wrong in its decision in NAACP.[199] Our goal here is only to identify the use and limits of deference by federal courts in various contexts.

There are many contexts in which federal courts must assess how to deal with prior state court decisions. The Contracts Clause, for example, provides that "[n]o State shall . . . pass any . . . Law impairing the Obligation of Contracts."[200] In order to apply this clause under current doctrine (which may not reflect the clause's original meaning), a federal court must address three questions: "whether there is a contractual relationship, whether a change in law impairs that contractual relationship, and whether the impairment is substantial."[201] The question whether a contract exists, which one might suppose is a question of state law, is considered by the Supreme Court to be "a federal question for purposes of Contract Clause analysis."[202] Nonetheless, says the Court, "[w]e 'accord respectful consideration and great weight to the views of the State's highest court,' though ultimately we are 'bound to decide for ourselves whether a contract was made.'"[203] The Court thus defers to state court determinations, but only in a limited fashion.

There are various other doctrines that reflect some measure of deference to state court determinations. Some of those doctrines are statutory. Federal courts entertaining petitions for writs of habeas corpus from prisoners in state custody after a determination on the merits in a state court may not grant the writ "unless the adjudication of the claim—(1) resulted in a decision that was contrary to, or involved an *unreasonable application of, clearly established* Federal law, as determined by the Supreme Court of the United States; or (2) resulted in a decision that was based on an *unreasonable* determination of the facts in light of the evidence presented in the State court proceeding."[204] This statute effectively prescribes a substantial measure of deference to prior state court determinations, though because habeas proceedings are not review proceedings, the language of deference is not precisely applicable. Many statutes forbid federal court intervention in state court proceedings in particular circumstances or through particular means. "The Anti-Injunction Act, the Three-Judge Court Act, the statutory branch of the habeas corpus exhaustion requirement, the Tax Injunction Act, and the Johnson Act constitute a statutory network of legislatively directed limitations on the exercise of federal court power to disrupt state proceedings or interfere unduly with state policies."[205] These statutes amount to legislatively prescribed absolute deference within their spheres of operation.

On other occasions, the federal courts have devised their own schemes of deference to decisions of state courts. These schemes go under the umbrella term "abstention." These are instances in which federal courts appear to have statutory jurisdiction over a matter but decline to exercise it—at a particular time and in a particular manner—in favor of proceedings in a state court.

Professor Martin Redish, who is a brutal critic of these various schemes, summarizes them as follows:

> The *Younger v. Harris* abstention doctrine provides that a federal court may not enjoin an ongoing state criminal proceeding, even to protect federal constitutional rights. The Supreme Court has also applied the doctrine to the issuance of declaratory relief and to certain state civil proceedings that implicate important state concerns.
>
> In *Burford v. Sun Oil Co.*, the Supreme Court ordered abstention in order to prevent federal judicial interference in complex state administrative schemes. The Court also found abstention appropriate in *Louisiana Power & Light Co. v. City of Thibodaux*, a case concerning the validity of state expropriation of property. Finally, though the presence of a parallel proceeding in a state court generally does not justify the dismissal of a federal suit, in *Colorado River Water Conservation District v. United States* the Court held that "exceptional" circumstances may justify a stay.[206]

The Supreme Court has justified these doctrines (rightly or wrongly we do not say[207]) in terms of deference: "Federal courts abstain out of deference to the paramount interests of another sovereign, and the concern is with principles of comity and federalism."[208] The Court has explicitly described abstention as "federal-court deference."[209] In this context, deference does not mean giving some measure of weight to a prior actor's views when making one's own decision. It means electing not to decide the matter at all.

As with *Skidmore* deference, there is an important point here to keep in mind: Any definition of deference that does not include complete abstention from at least some decisions will not accurately describe what federal courts call deference.

* * *

This short study does not begin to cover exhaustively the many usages of the term "deference" in American law. It does not even cover exhaustively all of the usages of the term in the federal courts. We have not said anything, for example, about the extent to which federal courts defer to private actors. While there are contexts in which such deference arises,[210] that is a matter that is of much more significance for state courts. Corporate law, for example, is largely about the extent to which courts will defer to the decisions of corporate directors. When federal courts decide such cases, they are applying state law. While we think that there are important lessons to be drawn from corporate law for contemporary public law (after all, corporate law *was* public law until relatively recently, and governmental bodies are corporations), we leave that subject for future projects.[211] Nor does our current discussion say much about the ways in which "deference" is employed in other countries, especially civil law countries; we leave that topic for a future project. But we think we have presented enough at least to begin an inquiry into an appropriate definition for the term. In the next chapter, we try to draw out the central ideas represented by deference, to identify the various grounds for deference that are invoked by legal systems, and to explore how the term has been understood by other scholars and actors.

## Notes

1. Today, major units of government are commonly described as "branches." Eighteenth-century terminology in the United States, however, used the term "branch" to describe the different houses of a multicameral legislature and used the term "departments" to describe the larger units—legislative, executive, judicial—of government. *See* Steven G. Calabresi & Kevin H. Rhodes, *The Structural Constitution: Unitary Executive, Plural Judiciary*, 105 HARV. L. REV. 1153, 1156 n. 6 (1992). Notwithstanding our fondness for the eighteenth century, we generally speak of the legislative, executive, and judicial "branches" in this book because we believe this usage to be more familiar to modern readers. But on occasion, we revert (defer?) to eighteenth-century practice and speak of the legislative, executive, and judicial "departments." No significance should be attached to our choice of usage in any given context.
2. We previously elaborated on these reasons for a court-centric approach in Gary Lawson & Guy Seidman, *Deference and National Courts in the Age of Globalization: Learning, Applying, and Deferring to Foreign Law*, *in* 2 IUS DICERE IN A GLOBALIZED WORLD 431 (Chiara Antonia d'Allesandro & Claudio Marchese eds., 2018).
3. We believe that the President of the United States is constitutionally unitary in this respect, though many scholars (and judges) disagree, and modern practice in the United States does not reflect a strictly unitary conception of the executive. *See* Gary Lawson & Guy Seidman, *The Jeffersonian Treaty Clause*, 2006, U. ILL. L. REV. 1, 22–43.
4. THE FEDERALIST No. 37, at 183 (James Madison) (G. W. Carey & J. McClellan eds., 2001). For an intriguing account of one aspect of decisional fragmentation in the US executive department, see Rebecca Ingber, *The Obama War Powers Legacy and the Internal Forces that Entrench Executive Power*, 110 AM. J. INT'L L. 680 (2016).
5. MICHAL BOBEK, COMPARATIVE REASONING IN EUROPEAN SUPREME COURTS 20 (2013).

6. *See* GARY LAWSON, FEDERAL ADMINISTRATIVE LAW 748–851 (8th ed., 2019).

7. Professor Kenneth Davis is often credited with pioneering the classification of legal facts as adjudicative or legislative. *See* Kenneth Culp Davis, *An Approach to Problems of Evidence in the Administrative Process*, 55 HARV. L. REV. 364, 404 (1942).

8. *But see* Caitlin E. Borgmann, *Appellate Review of Social Facts in Constitutional Rights Cases*, 101 CALIF. L. REV. 1185 (2013) (arguing that the rules for review of trial court findings of adjudicative facts apply as well to trial court findings of legislative facts).

9. *See* Kenji Yoshino, *Appellate Deference in the Age of Facts*, 58 WM. & MARY L. REV. 251 (2016).

10. U.S. CONST. amend. VII.

11. *See* Ellen E. Sward, *The Seventh Amendment and the Alchemy of Fact and Law*, 33 SETON HALL L. REV. 573 (2003).

12. Improvement Co. v. Munson, 81 U.S. (14 Wall.) 442, 448 (1871).

13. Anderson v. Liberty Lobby, Inc., 477 U.S. 242, 250–52 (1986) (emphasis added) (citation omitted).

14. Jackson v. Virginia, 443 U.S. 307, 318–19 (1979).

15. Cavazos v. Smith, 565 U.S. 1, 2 (2011).

16. *See* U.S. CONST. amend. V ("nor shall any person be subject for the same offense to be twice put in jeopardy of life or limb").

17. Fed. R. Civ. Proc. 52(a)(6).

18. Anderson v. City of Bessemer City, N.C., 470 U.S. 564, 574, 575 (1985).

19. *Id.* at 574.

20. United States v. United States Gypsum Co., 333 U.S. 364, 395 (1948).

21. *See, e.g.,* United States v. Fernandez, 887 F.2d 564, 567 (5th Cir. 1984).

22. Thomas W. Merrill, *Article III, Agency Adjudication, and the Origins of the Appellate Review Model of Administrative Law*, 111 COLUM. L. REV. 939, 953 (2011).

23. *Id.* at 951.

24. ICC v. Union Pac. R.R. Co., 222 U.S. 541, 547–48 (1912).

25. Consolidated Edison Co. of N.Y. v. NLRB, 305 U.S. 197, 217 (1938).

26. *See* E. Blythe Stason, *"Substantial Evidence" in Administrative Law*, 89 U. PA. L. REV. 1026, 1026–28 (1941).

27. *See id.* at 1038, 1056.

28. 5 U.S.C. § 706(2)(E) (2012). More precisely, this standard applies to factual findings in cases "reviewed on the record of an agency hearing." *Id.* Determining when a statute requires an "on the record" hearing is sometimes a difficult task, especially with regard to agency adjudication. *See* LAWSON, *supra* note 6, at 352–68.

29. 5 U.S.C. § 706(2)(A) (2012).

30. 29 U.S.C. § 160(e) (2012) (prescribing for courts reviewing decisions of the National Labor Relations Board that "findings with respect to questions of fact if supported by substantial evidence on the record considered as a whole shall be conclusive").

31. Universal Camera Corp. v. NLRB, 340 U.S. 474, 489 (1951).

32. *Id.* at 490.

33. *See* Allentown Mack Sales & Serv., Inc. v. NLRB, 522 U.S. 359, 366–67 (1998) ("We must decide whether . . . [the agency's] conclusion is supported by substantial evidence on the record as a whole. . . . Put differently, we must decide whether on this record it would have been possible for a reasonable jury to reach the Board's conclusion"). This language was not surprising. The opinion in *Allentown Mack* was authored by Justice Antonin Scalia. Ever since his days as a court of appeals judge, Justice Scalia, who strongly preferred clear and easily administered rules to multiple standards, did not like the idea of slotting a deference doctrine somewhere below the jury standard. *See* Association of Data Processing Serv. Orgs., Inc. v. Board of Governors of the Fed. Reserve Syste. 745 F.2d 677, 685 (D.C. Cir. 1984) ("There is surely little appeal to an ineffable review standard that lies somewhere in-between the quantum of factual support required to go to a jury (the traditional 'substantial evidence' test) and the 'preponderance of the evidence' standard that would apply in *de novo* review"). Professor Lawson is quite certain (because he specifically asked Justice Scalia about it in the late 1980s) that Justice Scalia thought it contrary to rule-of-law values to introduce into scope-of-review doctrines non-traditional standards that would allow judges to exercise more discretion when reviewing agency findings. Yet that kind of intermediate standard-slotting is precisely what *Universal Camera* was obviously trying to introduce. *See* Peter L. Strauss, *In Search of* Skidmore, 83 FORDHAM L. REV. 789, 793–94 (2014). Judge Scalia in 1984 could do nothing about it; Justice Scalia in 1998 thought he would take a shot at (in his mind) simplifying the doctrine. Casual empiricism suggests that his effort was not successful; courts often cite Justice Scalia's dictum in *Allentown Mack*, but it is very difficult to claim that they are applying its substance. *See* LAWSON, *supra* note 6, at 543–44.

34. This is not a proposition that we can empirically demonstrate. But even a casual reading of decisions applying substantial evidence standards to agency fact-finding shows it to be true. *See, e.g.*, Kimm v. Department of the Treasury, 61 F.3d 888 (Fed. Cir. 1995).

35. Chen v. Mukasey, 510 F.3d 797, 801 (8th Cir. 2007).

36. *Id.*

37. It is a bit, but only a bit, misleading to speak of "the" substantial evidence standard, as though there is only one such standard. The term "substantial evidence" shows up in many statutes. In theory, it could mean something different in each statute. In practice, courts tend to construe the term presumptively to have the same meaning in all of its applications, as did the Supreme Court in *Universal Camera*. But that equivalence is only a presumption, which can be overcome in appropriate cases. *See* Corrosion Proof Fittings v. EPA, 947 F.2d 1201, 1213–14 (5th Cir. 1991). The same is true in principle of the "arbitrary, capricious, an abuse of discretion, or otherwise not in accordance with law" standard, which appears both in the APA and in numerous organic statutes. The courts evidently consider the meaning of that standard to be presumptively invariant in different statutory contexts, though nothing in the nature of statutory interpretation or administrative law dictates that result.

38. *See, e.g.*, Association of Data Processing Serv. Org., 745 F.2d at 683–86.

39. *See, e.g.,* Browning-Ferris Indus. of South Jersey, Inc. v. Muszynski, 899 F.2d 151, 164 (2d Cir. 1990).

40. Tuan N. Samohon, *Characterizing Power for Separation-of-Powers Purposes*, 52 U. RICH. L. REV. 569, 579 (2018).

41. *See* Nixon v. United States, 506 U.S. 224 (1993).

42. *See, e.g.,* Act for the Relief of George Little, ch. 4, 6 Stat. 63 (1807). This statute indemnified a naval captain who had been found liable in damages for obeying a presidential order that turned out to be unauthorized by statute. *See* Little v. Barreme, 6 U.S. (2 Cranch) 170 (1804). This kind of case-by-case indemnification by private bill was very common in the founding era. *See* James E. Pfander & Jonathan L. Hunt, *Public Wrongs and Private Bills: Indemnification and Government Accountability in the Early Republic*, 85 N.Y.U.L. REV. 1862 (2010).

43. *See Note: Private Bills in Congress*, 79 HARV. L. REV. 1684, 1685 (1966).

44. *See, e.g.,* 5 U.S.C. § 556(d) (2012) (prescribing in formal agency adjudication that "[a]ny oral or documentary evidence may be received, but the agency as a matter of policy shall provide for the exclusion of irrelevant, immaterial, or unduly repetitious evidence"). There are some administrative contexts in which something resembling the judicial rules of evidence apply, *see, e.g.,* 29 U.S.C. § 160(b) (2012) (providing that unfair labor practice proceedings before the National Labor Relations Board "shall, so far as practicable, be conducted in accordance with the rules of evidence applicable in the district courts"), but those contexts exist only because of specific statutes targeted at specific agency proceedings.

45. *See* Fed. R. Evid. 1102–03.

46. *See* Fed. R. Evid. 802.

47. Fed. R. Evid. 1104(a).

48. *See, e.g.,* Fed. R. Evid. 1108; Seiler v. Lucasfilm, Ltd., 808 F.2d 1316 (9th Cir. 1986).

49. *See* Fed. R. Evid. 104(a).

50. *See* Fed. R. Evid. 104(b), 602, 901(a), 1008.

51. General Elec. Co. v. Joiner, 522 U.S. 136, 143 (1997).

52. *See* LAWSON, *supra* note 6, at 586–748.

53. *See* Gary Lawson & Stephen Kam, *Making Law Out of Nothing At All: The Origins of the* Chevron *Doctrine*, 65 ADMIN. L. REV. 1 (2013).

54. On the demise of the constitutional principle against sub-delegation in the United States, see GARY LAWSON & GUY SEIDMAN, "A GREAT POWER OF ATTORNEY: UNDERSTANDING THE FIDUCIARY CONSTITUTION 104–26 (2017). For a perspective on US law from outside the United States, see BOGDAN IANCU, LEGISLATIVE DELEGATION: THE EROSION OF NORMATIVE LIMITS IN MODERN CONSTITUTIONALISM (2012).

55. *See* Randolph J. May, *The Public Interest Standard: Is It Too Indeterminate to Be Constitutional?*, 53 FED. COMM. L.J. 427 (2001).

56. 47 U.S.C. § 307(c) (2012).

57. 42 U.S.C. § 7409(b)(1) (2012).

58. 29 U.S.C. § 655(b)(5) (2012).

59. 42 U.S.C. § 7502(b)(6) (1982).

60. *See, e.g.,* Skidmore v. Swift, 323 U.S. 134, 139 (1944) ("There is no statutory provision as to what, if any, deference courts should pay to the Administrator's [legal] conclusions").

61. 42 U.S.C. § 607(a) (1976).

62. Batterton v. Francis, 432 U.S. 416, 4265 (1977).

63. 5 U.S.C. § 706 (2012).

64. Marbury v. Madison, 5 U.S. (1 Cranch) 137, 177 (1803).

65. For careful study of how a doctrine of deference emerged prior to and shortly after enactment of the Administrative Procedure Act, see Aditya Bamzai, *The Origins of Judicial Deference to Executive Interpretation,* 126 YALE L.J. 908 (2017).

66. *See, e.g.,* Gray v. Powell, 314 U.S. 402 (1941).

67. *See, e.g.,* FEC v. Democratic Senatorial Campaign Comm., 454 U.S. 27 (1981).

68. NLRB v. Hearst, 322 U.S. 111, 131 (1944).

69. *Id.*

70. The notion of an agency "administering" a statute is technical but has no precise definition. It roughly means statutes for which specific agencies have distinctive responsibility. Agencies apply and enforce many statutes that they do not "administer" in this specialized sense. Both before and after the *Chevron* decision, federal courts treated agency interpretations of statutes that the agencies "administered" differently from statutes that they did not "administer."

71. 323 U.S. 134 (1944).

72. *Id.* at 139.

73. *Id.* at 140.

74. *Id.*

75. LAWSON, *supra* note 6, at 585; Lawson & Kam, *supra* note 53, at 22–23.

76. 467 U.S. 837 (1984).

77. *See* Natural Res. Defense Council, Inc. v. Gorsuch, 685 F.2d 718, 725–27 (D.C. Cir. 1982).

78. Because of recusals, only six of the nine Justices participated in the decision.

79. *See Chevron,* 467 U.S. at 842–43 (footnotes omitted).

80. *See* INS v. Cardoza-Fonseca, 480 U.S. 421, 445–48 (1987). For an analysis of Justice Stevens's attempt to clarify his prior language in *Chevron,* see Lawson & Kam, *supra* note 53, at 66–68.

81. 467 U.S. at 865.

82. For a lengthy, case-by-case account of this process of creation and acceptance, see Lawson & Kam, *supra* note 53.

83. BLACK'S LAW DICTIONARY, Chevron *Deference* (10th ed., 2014).

84. *See, e.g.,* Michigan v. EPA, 135 S. Ct. 2699, 2712 (2015) (Thomas, J., concurring); Jack M. Beermann, *End the Failed* Chevron *Experiment Now: How* Chevron *Has Failed and Why It Can and Should Be Overruled,* 42 CONN. L. REV. 779 (2010).

85. City of Arlington, Tex. v. FCC, 569 U.S. 290, 296 (2013).

86. *See* Kent Barnett & Christopher J. Walker, Chevron *in the Circuit Courts,* 116 MICH. L. REV. 1, 6, 34 (2017).

87. For a critical account of one such example of agency two-step reasoning at the stage of initial statutory interpretation, see Gary Lawson, *Dirty Dancing—The FDA Stumbles with the* Chevron *Two-Step*, 93 CORNELL L. REV. 927 (2008).

88. *See* Gary Lawson, *Proving the Law*, 86 Nw. U.L. REV. 859, 884 n.78 (1992); Matthew C. Stephenson & Adrian Vermeule, Chevron *Has Only One Step*, 95 VA. L. REV. 597 (2009).

89. *See* Entergy Corp. v. Riverkeeper, Inc., 556 U.S. 208, 218 n.4 (2009) (opinion by Scalia, J.).

90. *See* Kenneth A. Bamberger & Peter L. Strauss, Chevron's *Two Steps*, 95 VA. L. REV. 611 (2009).

91. SAS Inst., Inc. v. Iancu, 138 S.Ct. 1348, 1358 (2018) (quoting *Chevron*).

92. *See, e.g.*, Epic Systems Corp. v. Lewis, 138 U.S. 1612, 1630 (2018) ("deference is not due unless a 'court, employing traditional tools of statutory construction,' is left with an unresolved ambiguity" (quoting *Chevron*); Texas v. United States, 328 F.Supp.3d 662, 713 (S.D. Tex. 2018) (" 'If the intent of Congress is clear, that is the end of the matter; for the court, as well as the agency, must give effect to the unambiguously expressed intent of Congress'; if so, the court owes no deference to the agency") (quoting *Chevron*).

93. If the reader is wondering what it means for the meaning of a statute to be "clear," the courts have no good answer. It might mean that the meaning of the statute is *obvious*. It might mean that the meaning of the statute, while perhaps not obvious, emerges, after possibly long and careful study, with a certain degree of clarity in which one can have a high degree of confidence. Or it could involve some combination of the two. There is, as of yet, no definitive statement in any federal court decision of which we are aware that resolves this matter—or even acknowledges that it is something needing resolution. For an extensive discussion of the case law's seeming obliviousness to this issue, *see* LAWSON, *supra* note 6, at 659–89. At least one federal judge of some renown is acutely aware of the problem. *See* Brett M. Kavanaugh, *Book Review*, 129 HARV. L. REV. 2118, 2153 (2016) ("there is no particularly principled guide for making that clarity versus ambiguity decision, and no good way for judges to find neutral principles on which to debate and decide that question").

94. *See* Barnett & Walker, *supra* note 86, at 6.

95. LAWSON, *supra* note 6, at 689–90.

96. Bowles v. Seminole Rock & Sand Co., 325 U.S. 410, 414 (1945).

97. 519 U.S. 452, 461 (1997).

98. *Id.* at 462.

99. *See, e.g.*, Decker v. Northwest Envtl. Def. Ctr., 568 U.S. 597, 614 (2013) (citation omitted); Christopher v. SmithKline Beecham Corp., 567 U.S. 142, 159 (2012).

100. *Decker*, 568 U.S. at 617 (Scalia, J., concurring in part and dissenting in part) (citation omitted).

101. C.F. Commc'ns Corp. v. FCC, 128 F.3d 735, 738 (D.C. Cir. 1997). *See also* Consarc Corp. v. Iraqi Ministry, 27 F.3d 695, 702 (D.C. Cir. 1994) (agency regulatory interpretation "receives an even greater degree of deference than the *Chevron* standard").

102. *See, e.g.*, Paralyzed Veterans of Am. v. D.C. Arena L.P., 117 F.3d 579, 584 (D.C. Cir. 1997), *overruled on other grounds*, Perez v. Mortgage Bankers Ass'n, 135 S.Ct. 1199 (2015).

103. *See* United Student Aid Funds, Inc. v. Bible, 136 S.Ct. 1607, 1608 (2016) (Thomas, J., dissenting from the denial of certiorari) (collecting prior opinions from Justices Alito, Roberts, Scalia, and Thomas expressing doubts about the validity of *Auer* deference).

104. 2018 WL 6439837.

105. Petition for a Writ of Certiorari, *Kisor v. O'Rourke*, No. 18-15, at i.

106. 139 S.Ct. 2400, 2408 (2019).

107. *Id.* at 2412.

108. *Id.* at 2413.

109. *Id.*

110. *Id.* at 2414 (citations omitted).

111. *Id.* at 2422–23.

112. *Id.* at 2425 (Gorsuch, J., concurring).

113. *Id.*

114. *Id.* at 2424–25 (Robert, C.J., concurring in part).

115. *See* United States v. Mead Corp., 533 U.S. 218 (2001). On the many preconditions for *Chevron* deference, see LAWSON, *supra* note 6, at 606–58.

116. *See, e.g.*, E. I. Du Pont De Nemours & Co. v. Smiley,138 S.Ct. 2563, 2563(2018) (Gorsuch, J., respecting the denial of certiorari); Vance v. Ball State Univ., 570 U.S. 421, 462 (2013) (Ginsburg, J., dissenting); Riegel v. Medtronic, Inc., 552 U.S. 312, 326 (2008); Kristin E. Hickman & Matthew D. Krueger, *In Search of the Modern Skidmore Standard*, 107 COLUM. L. REV. 1235 (2007).

117. 29 U.S.C. § 207(a) (2012).

118. 323 U.S. at 136.

119. *Id.* at 137.

120. *Id.* at 139–40.

121. *See, e.g.*, United States v. Mead Corp., 533 U.S. 218, 238–39 (2001) (remanding a case to the lower court "[s]ince the *Skidmore* assessment called for here ought to be made in the first instance by the Court of Appeals").

122. Christensen v. Harris Co., 529 U.S. 576, 587 (2000) (citations omitted).

123. *Id.* at 589 (Scalia, J., concurring in part and concurring in the judgment).

124. *Mead Corp.*, 533 U.S. at 238–39.

125. *Id.* at 235 (emphasis added).

126. *Id.* at 250 (Scalia, J., dissenting).

127. *Id.* at 235–37 (footnotes omitted).

128. James B. Thayer, *The Origin and Scope of the American Doctrine of Constitutional Law*, 7 HARV. L. REV. 129 (1893).

129. Commonwealth ex rel. O'Hara v. Smith, 4 Binn. 117, 123 (1811).

130. Thayer, *supra* note 119, at 143–44.

131. A simple WESTLAW search for "Thayerian deference" on October 20, 2018 turned up 75 entries for the term in law review articles.

132. A simple WESTLAW search of "presumption of constitutionality" on October 20, 2018 turned up 1,557 entries in cases and 4,492 entries in law reviews and other secondary sources.

133. *See, e.g.*, Morrison v. Olson, 487 U.S. 654, 704 (1988) (Scalia, J., dissenting).

134. F. Andrew Hessick, *Rethinking the Presumption of Constitutionality*, 85 NOTRE DAME L. REV. 1447, 1460 (2014).

135. *See* Brown v. Board of Educ., 347 U.S. 483 (1954).

136. Cooper v. Aaron, 358 U.S. 1, 18 (1958).

137. 5 U.S. (1 Cranch) 137 (1803).

138. Or so one of us has argued at some length. *See* Gary Lawson & Christopher D. Moore, *The Executive Power of Constitutional Interpretation*, 81 IOWA L. REV. 1267 (1996).

139. *See, e.g.*, City of Boerne v. Flores, 521 U.S. 507, 536 (1997).

140. *See* KEITH E. WHITTINGTON, POLITICAL FOUNDATIONS OF JUDICIAL SUPREMACY: THE PRESIDENCY, THE SUPREME COURT, AND CONSTITUTIONAL LEADERSHIP IN U.S. HISTORY (2006).

141. Jonathan F. Mitchell, *Reconsidering* Murdock: *State-Law Reversals as Constitutional Avoidance*, 77 U. CHI. L. REV. 1335, 1340 (2010).

142. *See* City of Arlington v. FCC, 569 U.S. 290 (2013).

143. One of us thinks it is bad on both fronts. *See* Gary Lawson, *Thayer v. Marshall*, 88 NW. U.L. REV. 221 (1993) (Thayerianism is bad as a matter of constitutional interpretation); Gary Lawson, *Interpretative Equality as a Structural Imperative (or "Pucker Up and Settle THIS!")*, 20 CONST. COMMENTARY 379 (2003) (Thayerianism is bad as a matter of legal policy).

144. FCC v. Beach Commc'ns, Inc., 508 U.S. 307, 313 (1993).

145. *See* Randy E. Barnett, *Scrutiny Land*, 106 MICH. L. REV. 1479 (2008).

146. Armour v. City of Indianapolis, Ind., 566 U.S. 673, 680 (2012).

147. *Beach Commc'ns*, 508 U.S. at 323 n.3 (Stevens, J., concurring).

148. Maria Ponomarenko, *Administrative Rationality Review*, 104 VA. L. REV. 1399, 1400–1401 (2018).

149. *See, e.g.*, Evan Bernick, *Subjecting the Rational Basis Test to Constitutional Scrutiny*, 14 GEO. J.L. & PUBL. POL'Y 347 (2016); Clark Neily, *Litigation Without Adjudication: Why the Modern Rational Basis Test Is Unconstitutional*, 14 GEO. J.L. & PUB. POL'Y 537 (2016); Tara A. Smith, *A Conceivable Constitution: How the Rational Basis Test Throws Darts and Misses the Mark*, 59 S. TEX. L. REV. 77 (2017). We have elsewhere argued that the rational basis test may underestimate the kind of scrutiny that is appropriate for evaluating the actions of legislative and executive agents under the Constitution. *See* Gary Lawson & Guy I. Seidman, *By Any Other Name: Rational Basis Inquiry and the Federal Government's Fiduciary Duty of Care*, 69 FLA. L. REV. 1385 (2017).

150. Thayer, *supra* note 128, at 154–55.

151. *See, e.g.*, Trump v. Hawaii, 138 S. Ct. 2392, 2418–21 (2018).

152. *See* Ran Hirschl, *Opting Out of "Global Constitutionalism,"* 12 L. & ETHICS OF HUMAN RIGHTS 1, 3 (2018) ("The 'margin of appreciation' principle—essentially a

judicial doctrine whereby supra-national courts allow states to have a measure of diversity in their interpretation of human rights treaty obligations, based on local traditions, heritage, and context—is repeatedly invoked by the European Court of Human Rights (ECtHR) in its politically-sensitive rulings.").

153. Handyside v. United Kingdom, 1 Eur. Ct. H.R. 737 (1976).

154. Convention for the Protection of Human Rights and Fundamental Freedoms art. 10, Nov. 4, 1950, 213 U.N.T.S. 221.

155. Handyside v. United Kingdom, ¶¶ 48–50.

156. Just within the WESTLAW law review database, a simple search for "margin of appreciation" on December 29, 2018, yielded almost 2,000 articles. For a description, and defense, of the margin of appreciation doctrine as a form of deference, *see* Andrew Legg, The Margin of Appreciation in International Human Rights Law: Deference and Proportionality (2012).

157. One of us does have such inclinations, but that is a story for another day.

158. *See* Saikrishna Prakash, *The Essential Meaning of Executive Power*, 2003 U. Ill. L. Rev. 701.

159. *Marbury*, 5 U.S. at 165–66.

160. U.S. Const. amend. V.

161. Gary Lawson, *Take the Fifth . . . Please! The Original Insignificance of the Fifth Amendment's Due Process of Law Clause*, 2017 B.Y.U. L. Rev. 611.

162. *See* Lawson & Seidman, *supra* note 149. Do these fiduciary constraints apply even to seemingly wholly discretionary matters such as exercises of the pardon power? In all likelihood, yes. *See* Ethan J. Leib & Jed Handelsman Shugerman, *Fiduciary Constitutionalism: Two Legal Conclusions*,—17 Geo. J.L. & Pub. Pol'y 463— (2019).

163. 5 U.S.C. § 706(2)(A) (2012).

164. *See* Lawson, *supra* note 6, at 751.

165. Motor Vehicle Mfrs. Ass'n of the United States v. State Farm Mut. Auto. Ins. Co., 463 U.S. 29, 43 n.9 (1983). Are presidential decisions in the form of executive orders more like legislation or like agency activity in this respect? Oddly enough, there is no explicit doctrinal answer. For a discussion, see David M. Driesen, *Judicial Review of Executive Orders' Rationality*, 98 B.U. L. Rev. 1013 (2018).

166. *See* SEC v. Chenery Corp., 318 U.S. 80 (1943); Lawson, *supra* note 6, at 516–18.

167. *Motor Vehicle Mfrs. Ass'n*, 463 U.S. at 43.

168. Tri-Valley Cares v. United States Dep't of Energy, 671 F.3d 1113, 1124 (9th Cir. 2012) (quoting Baltimore Gas & Elec. Co. v. NRDC, Inc., 462 U.S. 87, 103 (1983)). For a critical assessment of this doctrine of heightened deference to agency technical or scientific judgments, *see* Emily Hammond Meazell, *Super Deference, the Science Obsession, and Judicial Review as Translation of Agency Science*, 109 Mich. L. Rev. 733 (2011).

169. Judulang v. Holder, 565 U.S. 42, 53 (2011).

170. *See, e.g.*, Puerto Rico Sun Oil Co. v. United States EPA, 8 F.3d 73 (1st Cir. 1993).

171. *See* Lawson & Seidman, *supra* note 54.

172. *See* Lawson & Seidman, *supra* note 149.

173. The term "hard look" is generally associated with Greater Boston Television Corp. v. FCC, 441 F.2d 841, 851–53 (D.C. Cir. 1971), though the term first appeared as a description of a form of judicial review two years earlier in Pikes Peak Broad. Co. v. FCC, 422 F.2d 671, 682 (D.C. Cir. 1969). Under this standard, the court is supposed to ensure that the agency took a "hard look" at the problems before it. In order to make that assessment, the court must itself take a "hard look" at those problems in order to know what a "hard look" would involve. You cannot evaluate someone's approach to a problem without yourself understanding the problem and the range of possible approaches.

174. [1948] 1 K.B. 223.

175. Sunday Entertainments Act 1932, ch. 51, s.1(1).

176. 1 K.B. at 228–29, 233–34.

177. 23 Hen. 8, c. V, s.3(2–3) (1531).

178. Rooke's Case, 5 Co. Rep. 99b (1598).

179. *See, e.g.,* Gary Lawson & Guy I. Seidman, *Necessity, Propriety, and Reasonableness,* *in* GARY LAWSON, GEOFFREY P. MILLER, ROBERT G. NATELSON & GUY I. SEIDMAN, THE ORIGINS OF THE NECESSARY AND PROPER CLAUSE 120 (2010).

180. *See, e.g.,* Michael Taggart, *Proportionality, Deference,* Wednesbury, 2008 N.Z. L. REV. 423.

181. *Motor Vehicle Mfrs. Ass'n,* 463 U.S. at 43 (citations omitted).

182. An Act to Establish the Judicial Courts of the United States, ch. XX, § 15, 1 Stat. 73, 85–86 (1789). The constitutionality of this provision was upheld by the Supreme Court in 1816. *See* Martin v. Hunter's Lessee, 14 U.S. (1 Wheat.) 304, 351 (1816).

183. *See* Act of Feb. 5, 1867, ch. XXVIII, § 2, 14 Stat. 25, 26 (1867).

184. 1 Stat. at 86–87 (emphasis added).

185. 28 U.S.C. § 1257 (2012).

186. 87 U.S. (20 Wall.) 590 (1874).

187. *Id.* at 626.

188. *Id.* at 635.

189. *Compare* MICHAEL S. GREVE, THE UPSIDE-DOWN CONSTITUTION 484 n.44 (2012) (*Murdock* was probably wrongly decided); Mitchell, *supra* note 141, at 1345 (*Murdock* "was unsupported by constitutional or statutory text, structure, or history") *with* Michael G. Collins, *Reconstructing* Murdock v. Memphis, 98 VA. L. REV. 1439, 1445 (2012) ("*Murdock*'s understanding that Congress did not wish the Court to be able routinely to review questions of state law in cases within their appellate jurisdiction was likely right").

190. Collins, *supra* note 189, at 1441.

191. 357 U.S. 449 (1958).

192. *See* Brief for Petitioner, No. 91, *NAACP v. State of Alabama ex rel. Patterson,* at 12–17, 1957 WL 55387.

193. *See NAACP,* 357 U.S. at 460.

194. This so-called independent and adequate state ground doctrine was well established in 1958, *see* Klinger v. State of Mo., 80 U.S. (13 Wall.) 257 (1871); Fox Film Corp.

v. Muller, 296 U.S. 207 (1935), and remains so today. *See* Michigan v. Long, 463 U.S. 1032 (1983).

195. *NAACP*, 357 U.S. at 456–57.

196. *See, e.g.*, Boyd v. State of Neb. ex rel. Thayer, 143 U.S. 135, 180 (1892).

197. *See, e.g.*, Ward v. Board of County Comm'rs of Love County, Okla., 253 U.S. 17, 22–23 (1920).

198. *See* Mitchell, *supra* note 141.

199. Professor Lawson, for whatever it is worth, thinks that the US Supreme Court was clearly right. Absent a proviso of the kind present in the 1789 Judiciary Act, he can see no good reason why federal courts cannot and should not decide state law questions once a properly presented case is before those courts. No legal rule commands deference to prior state court determinations of state law, and while there might be good grounds for some kind of deference in normal circumstances, the conditions in Alabama in 1958 were anything but normal. (And those who know Professor Lawson know that he is not inclined to take positions simply because they sound politically correct.)

200. U.S. Const. art. I, § 10, cl. 1.

201. General Motors Corp. v. Romein, 503 U.S. 181, 186 (1992).

202. *Id.* at 187.

203. *Id.* (quoting Indiana ex rel. Anderson v. Brand, 303 U.S. 95, 100 (1938)).

204. 28 U.S.C. § 2254(d) (2012).

205. Martin H. Redish, The Federal Courts in the Political Order: Judicial Jurisdiction and American Political Theory 53 (1991) (footnotes omitted).

206. *Id.* at 49. For the Supreme Court's summary of some of its abstention doctrines, most notably *Younger* abstention, *see* Sprint Commc'ns, Inc. v. Jacobs, 571 U.S. 69, 72–73, 78 (2013).

207. To be sure, one of us has previously said that *Younger* abstention "is difficult to understand and even more difficult to justify, whether as a matter of constitutional law, statutory interpretation, political theory, or common sense." Steven G. Calabresi & Gary Lawson, *Equity and Hierarchy: Reflections on the Harris Execution*, 102 Yale L.J. 255, 258 (1992). He is no more sanguine about the other abstention doctrines—unless they are reconceptualized as exercises of equitable discretion. *See id.* at 258–66 (arguing that many of the results reached through abstention can be justified as straightforward refusals to grant discretionary equitable relief).

208. Quackenbush v. Allstate Ins. Co., 517 U.S. 706, 723 (1996).

209. Middlesex Co. Ethics Comm. v. Garden St. Bar Ass'n, 457 U.S. 423, 434 (1982).

210. *See* Paul Horwitz, *Three Faces of Deference*, 83 Notre Dame L. Rev. 1061 (2008).

211. For some preliminary explorations, *see* Gary Lawson & Guy Seidman, *An Enquiry Concerning Constitutional Understanding,*—17 Geo. J.L. & Pub. Pol'y 491 (2018)

# 3

# Defining Deference

In ordinary conversation, when one says to another, "I defer to your judgment"—regarding, for example, where to go to dinner tonight—that normally means that the deferring party is *yielding entirely* to the judgment of the other party. It does not normally mean that the deferring party will take into account the other party's views, give them some measure of weight, and then factor those views into an all-things-considered judgment about the best course of action. In these kinds of conversations, deference is an all-or-nothing affair that involves one party choosing to step aside entirely in favor of another.

By that standard, relatively few of the examples of practices identified by the federal courts as deference that we discussed in the previous chapter would actually count as deference. Judicial deference to the factual findings of juries that lead to acquittals in criminal cases would count; in those circumstances, courts yield entirely (by constitutional command) to the views of another actor. The various abstention doctrines would count as well. When federal courts abstain, they remove themselves (by judicial choice) entirely from the decision-making process and leave the matter—i.e., defer in the ordinary-language sense—to state actors. It is true that deference of the kind represented by abstention is temporary; a federal court that abstains, at a particular point in time, from interference in an ongoing state criminal proceeding might later take a very active, and decidedly non-deferential, role in reviewing the final results of that proceeding if there is a federal constitutional issue raised. But in law, as in comedy, timing is often everything. Parties care not just about *what* judicial relief they can get but also about *when they can get it.* It matters a great deal to a death-row inmate, for example, whether judicial relief in his case is an order of release prior to execution or a judgment for wrongful death paid post-execution to the inmate's family. Less dramatically, a major issue in the law of procedural due process under the Fifth and Fourteenth Amendments is *when* various procedures must be provided to parties who are being deprived by the government of life, liberty, and property. Relatively modest procedures before a deprivation

*Deference.* Gary Lawson and Guy I. Seidman, Oxford University Press (2020). © Oxford University Press.
DOI: 10.1093/oso/9780190273408.001.0001

takes place might be more valuable to a party than are spectacularly elaborate procedures after the deprivation has already happened.[1] So abstention-grounded deference can make a big difference to parties even if the stepping aside is only temporary. Our key point here is simply that such absolute deference corresponds to the ordinary-language meaning of deference. Federal courts sometimes give way entirely to the views of other actors, removing themselves completely—whether by legal command or by choice, and at specified times—from the decision-making process, while describing what they are doing as deference.

The other instances of judicial behavior that the federal courts identify as deference, of course, do not appear to take this all-or-nothing ordinary-language form. Instead, those instances treat a prior actor's decision as something relevant to the decision-making process, but the form and degree of relevance varies with the context. *Skidmore* deference is perhaps at one pole; the prescription in that circumstance is for a reviewing court to give an agency's legal interpretation whatever weight the interpretation merits, all things considered. The only strict requirement is that the prior decision at least be considered, even if the ultimate judgment upon consideration is to give the prior decision no weight whatsoever. One might place at another pole judicial deference to jury fact-finding that does not result in a criminal acquittal. The jury's findings carry so much weight that a reviewing court will reach a contrary conclusion only if no reasonable person could have behaved as did the jury. Perhaps judicial deference to legislative determinations of legislative facts or policy judgments is even more extreme, as courts will defer not merely to actual legislative judgments but even to hypothetical legislative judgments that never happened, and reversal of those judgments in ordinary circumstances not involving "fundamental" rights is virtually impossible. Various other doctrines labeled by the courts as instances of deference fall somewhere in between these poles.

These doctrines all have in common that they do not seem to conform to the ordinary-language meaning of deference with which we began this discussion. Indeed, on occasions courts will turn this meaning entirely on its head and speak as though the ordinary-language idea of complete submission *cannot* be considered deference at all because *only* the giving of (non-infinite) weight to another's decision counts as deference. *Batterton v. Francis*,[2] for example, involved an agency regulation setting forth criteria for determining when someone is considered unemployed for purposes of a federal welfare program. The regulation was issued pursuant to a statute that referred to "unemployment (as determined in accordance with standards prescribed by the Secretary),"[3] with no further elaboration of the Secretary's authority. The Supreme Court took this statute to be a legislative determination that the Secretary rather than the courts was the primary, if not quite the exclusive, entity charged with prescribing criteria for the term "unemployment."[4] As a result, said the Court, "[t]he regulation at issue in this case is therefore entitled to more than mere deference or weight."[5] The use of the phrase "mere deference or weight" suggests a meaning of deference that is relatively modest, and certainly far more modest than complete submission; it fully equates deference with weight to the exclusion of the term's ordinary-language meaning. The more potent force given to the agency's decision—which could be set aside, according to the Court, "only if the Secretary exceeded his statutory authority or if the regulation is 'arbitrary, capricious, an abuse of discretion, or otherwise not in accordance with law' "[6]—evidently did not qualify as "mere" deference.

Of course, one should never make too much of scattered comments in US judicial decisions. Many of those comments are written by law clerks barely out of law school, often under serious time pressure, and often subject only to minimal editing and supervision by judges. The judges, for their part, are not always selected for their jurisprudential sophistication and keen attention to the precise use of terms. The idea that US judicial opinions universally represent carefully crafted works by sober and thoughtful jurists poring over the significance of each line is somewhere between delusional and pathetic. Sometimes the words are carefully chosen, but much of the time they are ill-considered or barely considered, if they are considered at all. The limited point here, which is supported by far more than isolated lines in random opinions, is only that US courts often, and perhaps even primarily, use the term "deference" to describe a sliding scale of weight rather than the kind of yielding likely to be meant in ordinary conversation.

To be sure, there is a way to reconcile the law's usage and ordinary usage. Whether one can be said to give some measure of weight or to yield entirely to another's decision depends on how one characterizes the action that one is contemplating taking and the decision that one is reviewing. Consider a court reviewing a civil jury verdict that is challenged as being unsupported by adequate facts in the record. If the question is, "What are the adjudicative facts in this case that the law should take as authoritative for purposes of assigning legal consequences?," a reviewing court must give great—not quite dispositive but great—weight to the jury's determinations. That is clearly how the law typically frames the inquiry. The reviewing court "finds" facts in a sense while taking the jury's findings of those facts as a very strong, near-but-not-wholly-irremovable, anchor. But if the question is instead posed as, "How should the case be decided—and by whom?," the decision process can be described in a more complex way that leaves no room for anything between de novo review and complete abnegation. One could think of the court deciding for itself—entirely for itself, with no weight given to the views of the jury—whether there is enough evidence in the record to pass a certain minimum threshold fixed by the law in support of certain factual findings. If the court says no, the jury's verdict is reversed if the verdict requires those findings. If the court says yes, it defers—in the absolute sense—to the jury's verdict. Thus, one can describe the process entirely without reference to the idea of weight; all decisions involve either de novo determinations or complete abnegation. Indeed, one can see how deference-as-weight is unnecessary to this process by observing that a reviewing court could, in theory, decide whether the record contains a required minimum level of support for a verdict *without knowing what that verdict was.* Imagine a system in which courts automatically review all jury verdicts, regardless of which way they come out, and are asked only the hypothetical question whether the record evidence could, in principle, support verdicts in either or both directions. Under these assumptions, one would never give weight to actual verdicts because one would never know them. If that is so, the verdict itself need play no epistemological role in the court's threshold determination. And once the threshold is cleared, there is no longer any room for further judicial review, and the jury decision stands without additional inquiry, weighted or otherwise. Any review process under any standard can be broken down into similar components, in which the first stage of the analysis ("is there enough of whatever the law is seeking to pass a certain threshold of acceptability?") is conducted by a court de novo and the second stage is one of absolute rather than gradational deference. In this respect, one can describe deference entirely in terms of assignments of responsibility for different parts of a decision, in which each actor performs his assigned tasks without reference to the views of the other actors. Sometimes that assigned task is simply to identify outer boundaries for decision rather than to make the actual decision.

We actually think that, as a matter of first principles, there is much to be gained from viewing decision processes in this all-or-nothing fashion. It focuses attention on the allocation of decision-making authority and forces legal designers to confront the real issues involved: What, exactly, do legal designers want specific legal actors to decide? Who gets to decide what? It is well recognized that "[s]cope of review . . . is the principal means by which adjudicative decisional power and responsibility are divided between the trial and appellate levels,"[7] as well as between courts and other actors, so directing attention toward rather than away from this basic feature of legal design seems sensible.

Others have shared this intuition about the proper conceptual use of deference as a binary, all-or-nothing choice that is really just a way of representing an allocation of decision-making responsibility among multiple actors. The issue came to light in *Metropolitan Life Insurance Co. v. Glen*,[8] decided by the US Supreme Court in 2005. It will take a moment to set the stage for how that intuition was expressed (in words that seem to have been quite carefully considered by the judges involved, as these things go) and by whom.

*Metropolitan Life* concerned judicial review of decisions of administrators of benefit plans subject to federal regulation under the Employment Retirement Income Security Act of 1974 (ERISA). The administrators of those plans are fiduciaries for the beneficiaries, so plan administrators must conform their decisions to the basic requirements of trust law.[9] In accordance with those requirements, decisions of administrators who are vested with discretion by the relevant plan are normally reviewed by courts for abuse of discretion (while administrators with no discretion under the plan have their decisions reviewed de novo). The majority of the Court in *Metropolitan Life* concluded that when plan administrators vested with discretion had a conflict of interest—in this case, the plan that decided whether the claimant was eligible for benefits would itself have to pay the benefits if the claimant was found eligible—courts would continue to review decisions deferentially but would take into account the conflict of interest as one of many factors that determine whether discretion was abused.[10] The claimant had argued that deference to plan administrators ran along a sliding scale and that factors such as a conflict of interest on the part of the administrator should reduce the degree or amount of deference afforded those administrators: they claimed that "under ERISA, deference should decrease in proportion to the quantum of evidence that the conflict might have affected the outcome."[11] The majority specifically denied that its decision affected the scope of review of, or degree of deference to, administrator decisions: "We do not believe that *Firestone's* statement implies a change in the *standard* of review, say, from deferential to *de novo* review. Trust law continues to apply a deferential standard of review to the discretionary decisionmaking of a conflicted trustee, while at the same time requiring the reviewing judge to take account of the conflict when determining whether the trustee, substantively or procedurally, has abused his discretion."[12]

Chief Justice Roberts, in a concurring opinion, worried that the majority was, in fact if not in intention, altering the degree of deference to be afforded plan administrators, reasoning that "[t]he majority's approach would allow the bare existence of a conflict to enhance the significance of other factors already considered by reviewing courts, even if the conflict is not shown to have played any role in the denial of benefits. The end result is to *increase the level of scrutiny* in every case in which there is a conflict—that is, in many if not most ERISA cases—thereby *undermining the deference* owed to plan administrators when the plan vests discretion in them."[13] Chief Justice Roberts clearly envisioned a sliding scale of deference and saw the Court's opinion as moving the relevant point on the scale, just as the claimants had urged the Court to do.

Justice Scalia, for his part, rejected the whole idea that deference was even in principle something that could slide. For him, and for Justice Thomas who joined his dissenting opinion, deference was necessarily all or nothing: "Of course when one is speaking of deferring to the judgment of another decisionmaker, the notion that there are degrees of deference is absurd. There are degrees of *respect* for the decisionmaker, perhaps—but the court either defers, or it does not. 'Some deference,' or 'less than total deference,' is no deference at all."[14] Professor Paul Daly (of whom we will hear much more in the next chapter of this book) agrees, maintaining that "the decision to defer or not will inevitably be binary in nature."[15] Thus, some very smart people in the law who have thought very deeply about deference for a long time doubt whether it makes sense to discuss degrees of deference, or deference as a sliding scale, or more versus less deference. For them, deference in the law means exactly what deference means in ordinary conversation. You either give way entirely—though you may be giving way only over a portion of an integrated decision-making process and thus may still be deciding at least part of the matter for yourself—or you are not deferring.

If this book was normative rather than descriptive, we would consider devoting some attention to developing a model of decision-making along these lines that looked directly to the allocation of decision-making authority rather than obscuring those allocations within a graded model of deference. That is likely how we would approach the matter as legal designers as well. For two equally fundamental reasons, however, we continue to employ the deference-as-continuum model in this book rather than trying to create a vocabulary that matches the all-or-nothing intuition.

First, the (re)characterization of deference as an all-or-nothing proposition works well for scope-of-review doctrines that are fixed by law, in which actors are effectively seeking to ascertain their assigned roles in a layered decision-making process. It works less well when courts elect, for whatever reasons, to look outside themselves for help in resolving questions that everyone agrees are questions for courts to resolve. De novo review does not necessarily mean review cut off from all contact with the world outside the mind of the judge; it simply means review that does not, as a matter of legal command, have to give weight to the particular decision under review. As we will explain in more detail shortly, a court engaged in "de novo" review could conceivably choose to give some measure of weight to the views of other actors, including the actors whose decision is under review, for any number of reasons that are entirely consistent with a legal prescription of de novo review. In those situations, it is much harder to break down the decision process into distinct roles, declare review to be either de novo or wholly absent, and move on, as much of that activity can only be described in terms of a sliding scale of weight. Because those situations are very common, a large-scale reconfiguration of the language of deference in the law seems unwise.

Second, even in the context of legally prescribed scope-of-review standards, we do not harbor ambitions of changing the design or direction of legal systems. As a matter of brute fact, the US legal system does not generally refer to its legally prescribed review processes as fine-tuned allocations of non-deferential decision-making authority in the fashion that we have proposed, but instead often speaks of review as involving the weighted authority of other decisions. Justice Scalia may not have liked that very much (and Justice Thomas may still not like it very much), but there were many things about the operation of the US legal system that Justice Scalia did not very much like. It is not surprising that a sliding-scale view of deference rather than a view grounded in allocations of non-deferential decision-making authority would make his hit list. Justice Scalia valued rules as the basis for decision above almost all else,[16] and a sliding-scale view of deference is decidedly un-rule-like. Of course, allocations of decision-making authority might also be un-rule-like, depending on how they are formulated, but they at least offer the possibility of being crafted as rules. But Justice Scalia pretty clearly lost this particular battle about the usage of language regarding deference in US law. Nothing other than a view of deference as weighted or sliding explains the law's vast array of standards of review that span a broad spectrum which contains far more points than "de novo" and "absolute deference."

Indeed, the most noteworthy feature of the doctrines that are described by courts as doctrines of deference is the almost dizzying variation in the extent or degree to which someone else's decision will hold sway. The range of weight that runs from *Skidmore* to abstention is very broad. This variation has important definitional consequences. In particular, if the law's practice does not always conform to the ordinary-language understanding of deference or Justice Scalia's ideal conception, neither does it always (or even often) conform to the understanding reflected in *Black's Law Dictionary*'s definition of deference. That definition, recall, tries to peg deference as a "presumptive[]" acceptance of another's decision. In one sense, that formulation is imprecise enough to capture a wide range of practices. Presumptions can be strong or weak, and *Black's* wisely does not attempt to fix a uniform strength for a supposedly unitary presumption. In another sense, however, *Black's* misses badly at describing both poles of the range of legal practice. *Skidmore* requires respectful consideration; it does not require presumptive acceptance, absent a showing of all-things-considered factors that warrant such a presumption in a specific case. Under *Skidmore,* courts must *consider* the agency's decision because it is the agency's decision, but courts do not have to presume that the agency's decision is right. Abstention, at the other pole, requires complete acquiescence; it does not require presumptive acceptance subject to override based on specific factual showings. And the deference given to legislative findings of legislative facts or non-acquitting jury findings of adjudicative facts, while not absolute, seems stronger than anything reasonably conveyed by the term "presumptive[]."

So the definition in *Black's* does not capture the attitudinal range of the federal courts represented by the idea of deference. Some practices identified as deference by federal courts involve granting a much heavier weight to the prior decision than merely saying that it "should be presumptively accepted" and some involve a much lesser weight.

There is also a second respect in which the *Black's* definition does not accurately describe the practice of federal courts. The *Black's* definition grounds deference in "[a] polite and respectful attitude or approach, esp. toward an important person or venerable institution." That sometimes corresponds to the practice in federal courts and sometimes does not. *Skidmore* deference is probably the classic instance of deference grounded in respect for the views of the prior actor, and the super-strong deference represented by abstention has some elements of this rationale as well. But other forms of deference do not necessarily have anything to do with respect. Federal courts do not necessarily defer to the factual findings of juries because they respect those juries. They defer because they are ordered to do by the US Constitution. A particular court may think that a particular jury is an utterly contemptible group of losers, but the jury still counts as a jury, and its factual findings still get the deference due a jury's findings under the constitutional scheme. Similarly, if *Chevron* deference is considered binding on the lower federal courts as a matter of precedent, then those courts must defer to the legal views of administrative agencies even if the courts doubt the agencies' competence or even honesty. The factual findings of a federal trial judge are entitled to deference on appeal whether or not the appellate court has any respect for or polite feelings toward that particular trial judge.

This discussion points to several paths that might help clarify the meaning of deference. The first path (we will get to the second a few pages hence) is to try to frame an account of deference at a higher level of generality than did *Black's*. Given the wide variations in the degree of weight provided to different decisions in the federal court system, it seems unlikely that a definition that tries to peg deference at some specific level of weight—even a level as vague as presumptive acceptance—will prove to be the most useful definition. Nor will it be descriptively accurate to try to limit deference to a particular rationale, such as respect. Deference in the federal courts comes from many different sources and rationales. Nor does it seem as though deference is limited to a particular institution to whom deference is owed; Congress, the President, other courts, administrative agencies, and state actors, among others, all receive deference in some form at some times. A descriptively accurate definition will have to be framed in terms that might, at first glance, seem so broad as to be unhelpful.

Accordingly, we tentatively propose, subject to further examination and possible revision (spoiler alert: the definition in this precise form will not survive even this chapter), a definition of deference as: *The choice by a legal actor to give some measure of consideration or weight to the decision of another actor in exercising the deferring actor's function.* When the relevant legal actor is a federal court, this definition leaves room for everything from *Skidmore* to abstention, because it does not try to specify in advance how much weight the prior decision will or should receive, why the prior decision receives it, or who made the prior decision. In that sense, it is robustly descriptive of the practices of the federal courts. Whether it can be robustly descriptive, or useful analytically, with respect to legal actors other than federal courts is something we take up in a subsequent chapter. For now, we consider it only in the context of federal courts, because that is the source from which we drew the data when inducing our definition.

There is another sense, however, in which our definition is deliberately and consciously misdescriptive of federal court practices. We describe deference as a *choice*. At least some of the practices labeled as deference by the federal courts are mandated by positive law. Deference in those circumstances does not involve a choice by the deferring actor, other than a choice to obey concededly binding positive law. We will get to that misdescription, and our reasons for knowingly embracing it in our initial definition, in due course.

For the moment, however, consider by way of comparison with both our tentative definition of deference and the definition in *Black's* a far more elaborate—and meandering and verbose—definition put forward by another legal dictionary: the recently reissued *Bouvier Law Dictionary*.

## 1. Back to the Future

The *Bouvier Law Dictionary* is a story unto itself. In 1839, John Bouvier published a two-volume legal dictionary in the United States because he wanted to provide a source to other lawyers for bar exam preparation in light of his own experience ("To THE difficulties which the author experienced on his admission to the bar, the present publication is to be attributed") and because then-existing law dictionaries were oriented toward English law, with a focus on English law's feudal foundations which had little application to the United States ("Th[ose works] were written for another country, possessing laws different from our own . . . [and] most of the matter in the English law dictionaries will be found to have been written while the feudal law was in its full vigor, and not fitted to the present times, nor calculated for present use, even in England").[17] The *Bouvier Law Dictionary* was the first truly American law dictionary.

Up through the 1930s, it was the favored law dictionary of the US Supreme Court,[18] though it has since been overwhelmingly overtaken in citation count by *Black's*.[19] It was certainly dominant in the 1860s, which perhaps makes it relevant for understanding the original meaning of Civil War-era enactments.[20] The work has recently been reissued and updated by Wolters Kluwer, one of the leading legal publishers of today, which touts it as "[d]erived from the famous 1853 law dictionary used by Daniel Webster, Abraham Lincoln, and Justice Oliver Wendell Holmes, Jr."[21] A hundred years ago, we would probably be leading off our discussion here with *Bouvier* while perhaps dropping, at most, passing references to *Black's*.

In contrast to the terse treatment of deference given by *Black's*, the *Bouvier* dictionary, as reissued in modern times,[22] has much to say about deference:

[D]deference (defer)

To yield to someone or something else, at least for a time. Deference is an act of restraint by a person or entity with the authority or power to act but who chooses not to do so in order to abide the result of another's action, or at least to await the completion of another's action to determine whether to act. Deference in law is essential to the functioning of the legal system, in which a single legal determination depends on a division of labor, so that a legal official tasked with one component of a decision must defer to other officials in their respective tasks. The allure of deference in allowing the official to evade responsibility for a decision or action committed to the office, however, endangers the legal system at least as much as the risk of failures of deference. The proper limit of deference may be the same as the proper scope of discretion, but deference, inherently, must fall within the scope of discretion: an official may only defer when the official has the power to act. As such, deference does not ultimately foreclose the possibility of action, as the deferring official retains an obligation to act if the official to which deference is given fails to act or acts unlawfully in some manner.

Deference, in general, is appropriate by one official or entity toward another, when the law creating their officers delegates a particular task or experience to one and not the other. Courts defer to one another in this way, as well as to legislatures and executives, and legislatures and executives defer to one another and to the courts. This is both the essence of separation of powers and the basis of a reasonable division of labor among the creation, execution, and interpretation of law—recognizing that such categories are never perfect.

Courts in the United States defer routinely to one another, so that trial courts defer to courts of appeal and supreme courts on matters of the interpretation of law, and appellate courts defer to trial courts on matters of trial discretion, such as the admission or significance of evidence. Judges defer to juries on matters found by the jury as fact, and juries defer to judges on matters of law. In addition, federal courts defer to Congress on matters of legislative authority to the agencies, which are created by legislation, to execute and interpret the legislative matters committed to the agency. Both executives and legislatures defer to courts on constitutional matters and on matters in which the courts have a customary expertise or commitment, such as their own rules.[23]

There is obviously considerably more substance to this definition than there is to the single-sentence definition of deference in *Black's* or to our own brief (tentative) definition. That is not surprising; *Bouvier* was designed to be both a legal dictionary and a legal encyclopedia that would explicate as well as define terms. There is a great deal in the *Bouvier* definition/explication of deference that requires some unpacking, and that unpacking process promises to yield some useful insights about the nature and use of deference in the law.

Two important features of the *Bouvier* definition of deference emerge from the entry's first two sentences. Initially, in the first sentence, *Bouvier* sees deference simply as an act of yielding to another, with no attempt to specify the magnitude or degree of that yielding. We agree that this non-specific account is appropriate given the vast range of practices that fall under the umbrella of deference. All of those practices involve some kind of yielding, but the character and degree of that yielding differs so much across contexts that trying to prescribe a uniform magnitude, even with a vague term such as "presumptively accepted," is unlikely to capture all that is important to capture. The second sentence reflects a view of deference as "an act of restraint by a person or entity with the authority or power to act but who *chooses* not to do so in order to abide the result of another's action." Deference, according to this understanding, is a choice. It is a *discretionary* decision to "yield to someone or something else at least for a time." If one does not make the choice, says this passage in *Bouvier,* one cannot really be said to be deferring. By this reckoning, "deference" that is compelled by some authoritative legal source or actor is not really deference. One cannot defer on a decision that one has no power to make in the first instance.

That limitation of deference to voluntary, or discretionary, actions is, of course, flatly inconsistent with much of the second and third paragraphs of the *Bouvier* entry, which discuss deference in the contexts of appellate review and review of jury verdicts. Much of this deferring activity, at least in the federal courts, is prescribed by positive law, either by the Constitution or statutes. Judges do not choose to defer to juries; judges are ordered by the Constitution to defer to juries. Appellate judges do not choose to defer to trial judges in adjudicative fact-finding; they are ordered to do so by the Federal Rules of Civil Procedure. It is obviously possible to describe this kind of legal prescription as a form of deference, but the initial instinct of *Bouvier* was not to do so. As our own first tentative definition of deference illustrates, and as we will later explain, *Bouvier's* initial instinct is ours as well. That instinct simply could not be maintained consistently throughout the dictionary's entry, because the practices that seem to need description do not all conform to that instinct.

Much of the rest of the *Bouvier* definition of deference does not really define the term but instead outlines some of the *reasons* why a court might defer (whatever deferring ultimately turns out to mean) to another actor. At first glance, that seems backward; it is impossible to analyze the reasons for deference without first knowing for what one is giving reasons. You have to know what deference is before you can know whether and when there are any good reasons to do it. Strictly speaking, a definition of deference must precede the articulation of rationales for the practice. Nonetheless, it turns out to be very difficult to give a good explanatory account of the varied activities that are sometimes labeled deference without understanding why those practices exist and persist.

This leads to the second path mentioned earlier that might help us refine a definition of deference: Maybe doing it backward will help one move forward, as the rationale for the practice may help explain its scope and limits. Accordingly, let us for the moment broaden our account of deference a bit to include all of the practices given that label by courts, including those that are not acts of choice by the courts, in order to explore the various reasons why those practices might be followed. Perhaps those reasons will shed light on the practice itself.

## 2. Gimme Just One Reason: Mandatory Deference

We have already seen one reason why a court might give way to another actor: Perhaps it has been ordered to do so by higher authority. The US Constitution orders courts to give way to factual findings by juries—to give way absolutely and unconditionally for judgments of acquittal in criminal cases and to give way subject to "reasonable person" review in other cases. If a federal jury acquits a criminal defendant, the judge cannot (lawfully) alter the verdict and executive officials cannot (lawfully) confine the defendant. This conclusion is legally commanded without reference to the particular features, circumstances, or quality of any particular jury. "Even if the judge, the lawyers, the Attorney General, and the President all believe—and even believe correctly—that the jury was incompetent, stupid, and biased and has blatantly disregarded the law, including the applicable law of the Constitution, the acquittal still stands. Acquittals by criminal juries are legally conclusive, not because of any case-specific determinations of the wisdom or competence of the particular jury in the case, but simply because the Constitution says that acquittals by criminal juries are legally conclusive."[24] Deference attaches by operation of law from the mere *status* of the decision-maker. The same holds true for deference to civil jury fact-finding that is commanded by the Seventh Amendment: "[a]gain, this legal rule does not depend on particular facts about particular juries; a jury verdict is entitled to a measure of legal weight simply because the Constitution commands deference to jury verdicts."[25]

Statutory law often similarly operates to command deference to particular actors, generally because of the status or position of those actors rather than because of any particular facts about the abilities of those actors. The Federal Rules of Civil Procedure order appellate courts categorically to give a specified measure of deference to the adjudicative fact-finding of federal trial courts, limiting reversal to those findings which are "clearly erroneous."[26] Numerous federal statutes prescribe various measures of deference that reviewing courts must, as a matter of positive law, give to the findings and conclusions of administrative agencies. Indeed, virtually all (we are tempted to say "all" but want to hedge just in case there is an odd exception that we have missed) federal judicial review of agency fact-finding is governed by statutes. Many of these statutes are organic statutes that specifically prescribe a standard of review for a specific agency or agency action. For example, in unfair labor practice proceedings, findings of the National Labor Relations "with respect to questions of fact if supported by substantial evidence on the record considered as a whole shall be conclusive,"[27] and courts reviewing decisions of the Merit Systems Protection Board "shall review the record and hold unlawful and set aside any agency action, findings, or conclusions found to be—(1) arbitrary, capricious, an abuse of discretion, or otherwise not in accordance with law; (2) obtained without procedures required by law, rule, or regulation having been followed; or (3) unsupported by substantial evidence."[28] These kinds of organic statutes are commonplace. In the absence of a specific organic statute, the Administrative Procedure Act fills in the gap by authorizing judicial invalidation of agency factual findings in formal proceedings if they are "unsupported by substantial evidence"[29] and in informal proceedings if they are "arbitrary, capricious, an abuse of discretion, or otherwise not in accordance with law."[30] Whatever the precise meaning of these statutory terms may be, they clearly prescribe something considerably less rigorous than de novo review—and prescribe it as a matter of positive law.

Congress almost never prescribes a deferential standard of review for review of agency legal determinations, though it sometimes expressly mandates de novo review, as it has in the Freedom of Information Act.[31] A rare exception is the Dodd-Frank Wall Street Reform and Consumer Protection Act of 2010. A lengthy provision in the statute defines the power of the federal Comptroller of the Currency to preempt state consumer financial laws. Courts may review such preemptive determinations by the Comptroller, and in so doing "shall assess the validity of such determinations, depending upon the thoroughness evident in the consideration of the agency, the validity of the reasoning of the agency, the consistency with other valid determinations made by the agency, and other factors which the court finds persuasive and relevant to its decision."[32] This provision rather plainly—and deliberately[33]— codifies the standard set forth in Skidmore v. Swift. The legislation also declares that "the deference that a court affords to a Federal agency with respect to a determination made by such agency relating to the meaning or interpretation of any provision of this subchapter that is subject to the jurisdiction of such agency shall be applied as if that agency were the only agency authorized to apply, enforce, interpret, or administer the provisions of this subchapter."[34] This provision is clearly designed to avoid a lower-court-created doctrine that sometimes denies Chevron deference to agencies when more than one agency administers a statute.[35] In that respect, it is a requirement that courts employ Chevron, even in circumstances where their own court-created doctrine would prescribe otherwise. Even more intriguingly, the statute instructs courts deciding preemption cases: "No regulation or order of the Comptroller of the Currency prescribed under subsection (b) (1)(B), shall be interpreted or applied so as to invalidate, or otherwise declare inapplicable to a national bank, the provision of the State consumer financial law, unless substantial evidence, made on the record of the proceeding, supports the specific finding regarding the preemption of such provision in accordance with the legal standard of the decision of the Supreme Court of the United States in *Barnett Bank of Marion County, N.A. v. Nelson, Florida Insurance Commissioner,* et al., 517 U.S. 25 (1996)."[36] The *Barnett*[37] case set forth a (well-established) standard for determining when state laws are preempted by federal acts:

> This question is basically one of congressional intent. Did Congress, in enacting the Federal Statute, intend to exercise its constitutionally delegated authority to set aside the laws of a State? If so, the Supremacy Clause requires courts to follow federal, not state, law.
>
> Sometimes courts, when facing the pre-emption question, find language in the federal statute that reveals an explicit congressional intent to pre-empt state law. More often, explicit pre-emption language does not appear, or does not directly answer the question. In that event, courts must consider whether the federal statute's "structure and purpose," or nonspecific statutory language, nonetheless reveal a clear, but implicit, pre-emptive intent. A federal statute, for example, may create a scheme of federal regulation "so pervasive as to make reasonable the inference that Congress left no room for the States to supplement it." *Rice v. Santa Fe Elevator Corp.,* 331 U.S. 218, 230 (1947). Alternatively, federal law may be in "irreconcilable conflict" with state law. *Rice* v. *Norman Williams Co.,* 458 U.S. 654, 659 (1982). Compliance with both statutes, for example, may be a "physical impossibility," *Florida Lime* & *Avocado Growers, Inc.* v. *Paul,* 373 U.S. 132, 142-143 (1963); or, the state law may "stan[d] as an obstacle to the accomplishment and execution of the full purposes and objectives of Congress." *Hines* v. *Davidowitz,* 312 U.S. 52, 67 (1941).[38]

In other words, *Barnett* held that preemption is appropriate only when Congress intends it. The review provision in the Dodd-Frank Act aims to prescribe the standard of review for the obviously legal question[39] whether a federal act preempts a state statute, although it does so by characterizing that obviously legal question as one of *fact* subject to "substantial evidence" review. Fortunately, our point here is not to analyze whether any particular congressional statutes prescribing standards of judicial review for agency legal determinations make any sense but simply to highlight how unusual they are. Professor Kent Barnett, one of America's most perspicacious administrative law scholars, declared in 2014 that "these statutory provisions are, to the best of my knowledge, the first that expressly instruct or allow courts to defer to an agency's statutory interpretations."[40]

One of us actually has grave doubts about the constitutional power of Congress, as a matter of original meaning, to impose standards of review on courts by statute,[41] but the validity of these statutes under current doctrine (which bears only a tangential relationship to original meaning) is beyond rational question. And if the Supreme Court is able to specify methodologies for deciding cases that are binding on lower federal courts, one might say that deference doctrines such as *Chevron* and *Skidmore*, to the extent that they emanate from the Supreme Court, are imposed on lower courts by law much as are the statutory or constitutionally based deference doctrines.

If one believes that courts must obey binding positive law, the existence of such binding positive law is a very good reason why a court might defer to the views of another actor. Such deference, however, is not really an act of *choice* on the part of the reviewing court, except in the limited sense that courts must choose to follow the law. Does it really make sense to describe this kind of legally compelled yielding as *deference*?

We doubt that it makes sense; "[i]t is not appropriate to speak of deference when one has been ordered to act."[42] If we were constructing an ideal legal vocabulary from the ground up, we would probably describe choices to yield as deference and use another term, such as "preclusion" or "partial preclusion" or perhaps (following Professor Paul Horwitz, of whom we will speak much more in a later chapter) "obedience"[43] to describe yielding by command. The courts, of course, use deference to describe both chosen and commanded yielding, so a purely descriptive project must accept that fact and move on. On the basis of that acceptance, given that our project is first and foremost descriptive, our tentative definition of deference must therefore be amended to read: *The giving by a legal actor of some measure of consideration or weight to the decision of another actor in exercising the deferring actor's function,* without attempting to specify under what circumstances or constraints the consideration or weight is given.

Frankly, we do not believe that much turns on whether we employ this more descriptively accurate definition or our more limited definition that considers only *discretionary* decisions as acts of deference. After all, we have passed over very quickly the basic fact that judges who are commanded to defer must *choose* to obey the command. Perhaps we passed it over too quickly, so we will state it openly: Judges must *choose* to defer to what positive law proclaims to be an authoritative source of law. There may (or may not) be consequences for a judge who chooses not to follow positive law, but it is a choice that the judge (and anyone else deferring in any context) must make.

In that sense, deference and choice are always and inextricably linked. There is no deference without a choice to defer.

There does, however, seem to be something categorically different about yielding to another actor because you are ordered to do so by someone whose authority you recognize and yielding to another actor because you choose, without legal compulsion, to do so. We have a hard time articulating precisely why this difference seems important, but we both think it is important in some fashion, and we are not surprised that others share that intuition (though we will not be surprised if some people do not). Accordingly, we think there is some value in differentiating deference by command from deference by (in the narrower sense of the term) choice.

One of us has previously used the label "legal deference" to describe the act of yielding to another because of the commands of positive law.[44] On reflection, this is probably not the best label, because all deference in the law is legal in some fashion. A better term is probably "mandatory deference," leaving the term "discretionary deference" to describe (for lack of a better word) discretionary—again in the narrower sense that assumes that obedience to positive law is not really discretionary—decisions to yield, to some degree, to the views of another. We think that this usage of mandatory and discretionary deference is preferable to introducing an entirely new word, such as "obedience" or "preclusion," though we think it for no better reason than that legal practice at least sometimes speaks of instances of mandatory deference as instances of deference and reflecting that practice, for our project, is a positive good. Accordingly, that is how we will use the terms "mandatory deference" and "discretionary deference" in the rest of this book. Deference, as an unqualified concept, encompasses both of those subcategories.

Legal designers might have many reasons for constructing a regime of mandatory deference in any given context. Judges who do not face mandatory deference might employ those same reasons in support of a discretionary decision to defer. It is therefore appropriate to explore possible reasons for deference other than, and that might lay behind, the commands of positive law to get a full sense of how and why deference functions in the legal system.

### 3. Why Choose to Defer?

We can identify at this point at least four classes of reasons that might induce a legal designer to construct a regime of mandatory deference and/

or induce a judge who is not subject to a regime of mandatory deference to *choose* to give consideration or weight to the view of another actor. Those classes involve reasons of (1) legitimation, (2) decisional accuracy, (3) decisional economy, and (4) signaling. The latter reason is unlikely to motivate a legal designer, but, as we will explain more clearly in a subsequent chapter, it might motivate judges making discretionary choices. We make no claim, at any point, to having produced an exhaustive list of possible reasons for discretionary deference. (Another spoiler alert: This list of reasons will in fact expand in the next chapter, when we consider the views of other scholars.) Again, we are simply inducing what we see as the reasons for deference that appear most often in legal practice.

To be very clear: In identifying possible classes of reasons for discretionary deference (or, from the standpoint of a legal designer, constructing a regime of mandatory deference), we are neither endorsing nor criticizing them as reasons, nor are we endorsing or criticizing any specific doctrines that might be grounded, in whole or in part, on any of these reasons. Nor are we attempting to explain or justify specific deference doctrines in terms of any specific set of these reasons. Indeed, the rationales—however persuasive or unpersuasive they may be—behind specific deference doctrines are surely numerous and diverse, combining some or even all of the potential reasons. At the risk of tedium: Our project is descriptive and analytical, not prescriptive or critical. Our modest goal is to provide a framework and vocabulary that can be used, either descriptively or prescriptively, to analyze deference. With that warning in mind. . . .

## 3.1. Legitimation

Start with a sentence from the *Bouvier* account of deference: "Deference, in general, is appropriate by one official or entity towards another, when the law creating their offices delegates a particular task or experience to one and not the other." Strictly understood, this could be seen simply as a manifestation of mandatory deference. If a legal structure assigns a task to specific actors but not to others, it would violate basic principles of structure, or separation of powers, for the "wrong" actor to make the decision (or to make the wrong part of the decision). If it is up to courts and juries to decide whether criminal defendants are guilty, it would be wrong for the executive to fail to defer—absolutely and mandatorily—to judgments of acquittal. If it is up to

Congress and not courts to "declare War,"[45] it would be wrong for courts to fail to defer—absolutely and mandatorily—to procedurally proper congressional declarations of war. Deference in these circumstances flows from, and is necessary to implement, the separation of powers. It is simply a recognition of one's own limited role in a larger legal system.

Structural allocations of power may, however, have implications beyond prescriptions of mandatory deference. Consider a treaty entered into by the United States. Under the Constitution, the treaty-making power is vested in the President and the Senate: The President "shall have Power, by and with the Advice and Consent of the Senate, to make Treaties, provided two thirds of the Senators present concur."[46] Once the treaty is executed, it is a legal document. If questions arise about the treaty's proper interpretation in a case in which the meaning of the treaty matters, it would seem to be a legal question for the court to resolve, just as it is a legal question for the court to ascertain the meaning of any other legal instrument such as a constitution, statute, or contract when the instrument's meaning matters to a case. The power to execute the treaty no more carries with it the power to interpret the treaty with finality once it is executed than does the power to enact statutes carry with it the power to interpret those statutes with finality once they are enacted. The power to execute legal instruments and the power to interpret legal instruments can, of course, go together, but they need not go together. There is nothing in the Constitution that prescribes mandatory deference to the views of the executive—or of the Senate—on the meaning of treaties.[47]

But is there anything in the Constitution's structure that might encourage courts to *choose* to defer to executive (or senatorial) views on the meaning of treaties? Modern courts do so with regularity. According to the Supreme Court, "[i]t is well settled that the Executive Branch's interpretation of a treaty is entitled to great weight."[48] It is less than clear what is meant by "great weight,"[49] but the term clearly falls somewhere on the scale of deference— well above *Skidmore* consideration even if well below deference to juries. Exactly where it might fall—if there even is any "exactly" to be found—is not pertinent here. While it is doubtful whether founding-era actors contemplated any serious measure of deference to the executive in treaty interpretation,[50] judicial deference of some kind to executive treaty interpretation is a fixture in current law.

What would account for this kind of deference, given that it does not follow mandatorily from the Constitution's allocation of functions, which includes the allocation to the federal courts of the "judicial power"? The cases are surprisingly short on explanation. One can readily posit a number of functional considerations that might drive courts to give "great weight" to executive treaty interpretations,[51] most of which focus on the informational advantages that one might think executive agents possess. We will discuss that kind of rationale for deference shortly. Apart from those considerations, however, one might also think that there is something more, for lack of better words, *appropriate* or *legitimate* about executive resolution of treaty ambiguities than about court resolution. Treaties often—not always, but often—involve matters of high importance in international relations. Treaty violations can lead to international sanctions, or even war. While the Constitution does not expressly grant interpretative power over treaties to the executive, or even imply that there is a special treaty carve-out from the usual application of the judicial power, it is not difficult to see why a court might choose to give way to an executive interpretation on questions of foreign affairs, including treaty construction. Yes, treaties are legal instruments and the interpretation of treaties is therefore a judicial function, but they are also foreign policy instruments. When international consequences flow from interpretation, perhaps there are reasons to give a good measure of weight to an institution that is both more accountable to the electorate for those consequences and more capable of explaining and justifying interpretations to foreign partners or adversaries.

The *Bouvier* definition captures this rationale to some extent with its reference to a "division of labor" among institutions. As we have noted, this can be subsumed under the idea of separation of powers, but much of what goes under the heading of "separation of powers" is what we have described as *mandatory* deference that is commanded by positive law rather than the exercise of choice by a legal actor. In the circumstances where choice is possible, separation of powers in a loose, functional sense—what *Bouvier* calls a division of labor—is clearly one of the major justifications behind some decisions by judges that, while they may have the authority to act, it is advisable for them not to employ their own discretion and instead to defer to another official's judgment. While more than one actor may formally have power over a decision, one specific actor, or department, may have, or at least be perceived to have, the greater legitimacy under the constitutional and political order to be the final arbiter on the matter.[52]

This concern about finding the most legitimate decision-maker is surely at least part of the origin of court-created doctrines such as abstention, the political question doctrine, or primary jurisdiction, under which courts choose to defer to their coordinate actors. As with abstention, the political question doctrine involves a refusal by federal courts to exercise granted jurisdiction, on the ground that another department of the national government is better suited to decide the question.[53] "The doctrine of primary jurisdiction concerns whether actions filed directly in court should be referred to an agency for initial consideration."[54] In this respect, it is similar to abstention, except that the body to which the court defers its jurisdiction is a federal administrative agency rather than a state court or state agency. The political question doctrine, when it is not grounded directly in textual allocations of power amounting to mandatory deference, seems plainly to have some grounding in conceptions of legitimacy. Primary jurisdiction, as with abstention, concerns the timing of judicial intervention rather than its force, but some idea of the legitimacy of at least the initial decision-maker for certain decisions surely drives the doctrine in part.

But perhaps the most obvious doctrine for which considerations of legitimation might play an important descriptive and explanatory role is the *Chevron* doctrine. In an ideal world, given the mandatorily prescribed separation of powers in the US Constitution, major legislative decisions will be made by the legislative body. Attempts by the legislature to pawn off its responsibilities on other actors would be blatant subdelegation of authority that is not permissible absent specific authorization in the legislature's constitutive documents or principles.[55] Once the decision has been made to allow subdelegations, however, the next question is *to whom* the authority from those subdelegations flows. If not the legislature, who is next in line as the most plausible lawmaker? As with all questions of second-best, there is not necessarily going to be an airtight argument in favor of any answer, but one can understand why courts, faced with open-ended, and even vacuous, statutes which they will not declare unconstitutional as forbidden subdelegations of legislative authority, might see executive agencies, with at least a minimal level of electoral accountability through the President, as more legitimate surrogate legislatures than themselves. It is impossible to say definitively to what extent this rationale has driven the real-world development of the *Chevron* doctrine, because courts have been remarkably un-self-conscious, or at least remarkably uncommunicative, about their reasons for embracing *Chevron*. Nonetheless, the notion that "[b]ecause agencies are more accountable to the electorate than courts, agencies should have the dominant role in policy making when the choice is between agencies and courts"[56] has been part of the conversation about *Chevron* since the 1980s. Agencies may not be wholly legitimate lawmakers, but they may be less illegitimate than courts, which could counsel in favor of some measure of discretionary deference by courts to agencies when statutes are so ambiguous that they have no meaning (or at least no "clear") meaning.

To be clear, we are not endorsing a practice of legitimation-based deference, either in general or in any specific applications. Indeed, at least one of us has doubts about whether courts can and should take it upon themselves to make judgments about the "legitimacy" of different interpreters when that decision has not been made for them by an authoritative source, and he accordingly doubts, at a minimum, the validity of a political question doctrine that is not grounded squarely and entirely in something that can be identified as constitutionally commanded mandatory deference. The point is only that, as an empirical matter, this notion of more and less legitimate interpreters seems to be among the reasons that sometimes lead courts to defer and might sometimes lead legal designers to impose regimes of mandatory deference. Not always, but sometimes. For ease of exposition, we call deference grounded in whole or in part on this rationale "legitimation deference."

## 3.2. Accuracy

Perhaps the most obvious reason for an actor to choose to defer to another is accuracy. Maybe the other actor is in a better position than is the deferring actor to get the right answer. This could result from the other actor having more knowledge, more expertise or experience, a better perspective from which to glean answers, all of the above, and/or any other consideration that puts one in a position to make good decisions.

A trial judge, for example, presumably develops expertise regarding the real-time application of evidence rules in particular trial contexts.[57] The trial judge also observes the entire trial and can therefore place a specific ruling in the context of a specific trial process, including not only evidence previously introduced but also evidence expected to be introduced as the trial progresses. With respect to matters that involve not (or not just) the abstract meaning of evidence rules but how that meaning maps onto any given concrete application, one might expect appellate judges to give great weight to the views of trial judges—not because they are commanded to do so by authoritative law but simply because it looks like the trial judges are more likely to get it right, at least most of the time. At a minimum, it will often be very difficult to detect errors, when they occur, at the trial level from a bare examination of a printed record. The same considerations likely apply to review of adjudicative fact-finding by trial courts. The trial courts are closer to the action and do it more often than do appellate courts. Maybe that means that they will mostly get it right.

The Supreme Court articulated many of the accuracy-based rationales for deference to trial court adjudicative fact-finding in 1991:

> Those circumstances in which Congress or this Court has articulated a standard of deference for appellate review of district-court determinations reflect an accommodation of the respective institutional advantages of trial and appellate courts. In deference to the unchallenged superiority of the district court's factfinding ability, Rule 52(a) commands that a trial court's findings of fact "shall not be set aside unless clearly erroneous, and due regard shall be given to the opportunity of the trial court to judge of the credibility of the witnesses." In addition, it is "especially common" for issues involving supervision of litigation to be reviewed for abuse of discretion. Finally, we have held that deferential review of mixed questions of law and fact is warranted when it appears that the district court is "better positioned" than the appellate court to decide the issue in question or that probing appellate scrutiny will not contribute to the clarity of legal doctrine.[58]

We can generalize this rationale: Oftentimes, in the exercise of independent, formally de novo, judgment to figure out the best answer to a problem, one will realize that someone else is actually in a better position to reach that best answer. Someone else's decision can be strong, and perhaps even the strongest available, evidence of the right answer. One therefore chooses to defer, not as an abandonment of independent judgment but as the result of an *exercise* of that independent judgment.

This view of de novo review is not universally accepted. *Black's Law Dictionary* defines an "appeal de novo" as "[a]n appeal in which the appellate court uses the trial court's record but reviews the evidence and law *without deference* to the trial court's rulings,"[59] and it defines "de novo judicial review" as "[a] court's *nondeferential* review of an administrative decision, usu. through a review of the administrative record plus any additional evidence the parties present."[60] These definitions suggest that de novo review and deference are wholly incompatible. The Supreme Court has on occasion seemingly said the same thing. *Salve Regina College v. Russell*[61] concerned the long-running question whether federal appellate courts should or could defer to the views of local district judges on the meaning of state law when that state law governs the disposition of federal cases under *Erie Railroad v. Tompkins*.[62] The Court concluded "that a court of appeals should review *de novo* a district court's determination of state law. . . . The obligation of responsible appellate jurisdiction implies the requisite authority to review independently a lower court's determinations."[63] Indeed, the Court even said that "appellate deference to the district court's determination of state law is inconsistent with the principles underlying this Court's decision in *Erie*,"[64] which would seem categorically to place deference in opposition to de novo review. On closer examination, however, we think this seemingly categorical rejection is a bit of an illusion. The Court also said:

> Independent appellate review necessarily entails a careful consideration of the district court's legal analysis, and an efficient and sensitive appellate court at least will naturally consider this analysis in undertaking its review. Petitioner readily acknowledges the importance of a district court's reasoning to the appellate court's review. See Tr. of Oral Arg. 11, 19–22. Any expertise possessed by the district court will inform the structure and content of its conclusions of law and thereby become evident to the reviewing court. If the court of appeals finds that the district court's analytical sophistication and research have exhausted the state-law inquiry, little more need be said in the appellate opinion. Independent review, however, does not admit of unreflective reliance on a lower court's inarticulable intuitions. Thus, an appropriately respectful application of *de novo* review should encourage a district court to explicate with care the basis for its legal conclusions.[65]

Rather plainly, the Court is not telling appellate courts to ignore the lower court's conclusions and start from scratch. It is telling them that de novo review ultimately requires the appellate courts to reach their own conclusions about the right answers, but they may consider the views of others in that decision-making process for whatever those views might be worth.

This latter conception of de novo review is obviously the right one. "De novo review" does not necessarily mean review without reference to anyone else's views. To say that review is de novo is simply to say that there is no *mandatory deference* commanding the judge to yield to another actor to any degree. A court conducting de novo review could, if it wished, start entirely from scratch. But nothing in the concept—or practice—of de novo review *forbids* a judge from yielding if the judge, all things considered, regards yielding as the best way to discharge the judge's responsibility. As Professor Chad Oldfather aptly says of de novo review, "the core idea is that the appellate court owes no *formal* deference to the reasoning or conclusions of the court below. This is not to suggest that the appeals court should not take the lower court's reasoning into account."[66] The judge's responsibility, after all, is to decide cases in accordance with governing law. In order to carry out that function, the judge must necessarily ascertain the content of the governing law. That judicial duty, even if non-delegable, is fully discharged if the judge uncovers the *sources that will disclose* the governing law. It is no more a betrayal of the judicial function to choose to defer to the *wisdom* of another actor than it is to look up the answer in a case reporter or treatise. As long as the "formal" legal rules do not *mandate* any deference, review that is deferential in this limited sense is still properly called de novo review.

One of us has previously called this process of relying on others as part of an independent search for right answers "epistemological deference,"[67] to indicate that deference is serving as a vehicle for ascertaining the best answer from the standpoint of the deferring decision-maker. This is not necessarily the most informative or descriptive label, but a better one does not leap to mind, so we stay with it for now.

Not only is epistemological deference entirely consistent with the judicial function, even when that function formally calls for de novo review, it might actually be *required* by responsible exercise of the judicial function in some circumstances. As one of us, with another co-author, has said:

> A judge's primary obligation is to decide cases in accordance with governing law. The obligation to apply governing law carries with it an obligation to use one's best efforts to determine the governing law that one must apply. Judges thus have an interpretative responsibility to try to get the right answer unless they are told by the Constitution that that responsibility belongs to someone else. Suppose, however, that a judge conscientiously determines that some other actor is better suited than is the judge—by skill, knowledge, temperament, or institutional position—to determine the right answer to a problem. In that circumstance, the judge might well have a legal obligation to defer to the other actor's interpretation, at least to the extent of accepting the other actor's interpretation, unless it is very clearly wrong. Thus, seemingly pragmatic arguments about individual or

institutional competence to reach correct constitutional interpretations can translate into legal arguments because of judges' primary legal obligation to determine correctly the applicable law.[68]

Is there a risk that judges purportedly applying epistemological deference will overshoot the mark and give up too much of their authority to other actors in the misguided belief that they are optimizing the chances of getting right answers? Of course there is. Everything has risks. Anything that can be done, can be done badly. Our point here is not to argue for any particular regime of epistemological deference or to insist that it is legally required in any specific circumstance. It is only to highlight epistemological deference as a prominent, and at least in some contexts entirely sensible, form of deference that might plausibly inform both a judge's discretionary choice to defer and a legal designer's decision to impose mandatory deference.

Indeed, there is a good chance that epistemological deference is at least part of the justification for virtually every deference doctrine one encounters. As a legal designer, surely one will want to construct a system that brings to bear on problems the skills and attention of the people most likely to get right answers, so systems of mandatory deference are surely driven, in some measure, by epistemological concerns. A review system that limits appellate review of on-the-spot factfinders surely draws on notions that people closest to the ground, and in the best position to see witnesses and entire trials unfold, are at least presumptively best situated to find facts. Agencies with demonstrated expertise in some areas surely earn at least a measure of *Skidmore* deference, and such concerns leak into *Chevron* as well.

This does not mean that epistemological deference is, or ought to be, decisive in all circumstances. There can be reasons of legitimation to vest decisional authority in certain actors even when one thinks, on balance, that other actors might be more likely to get "right" answers. Perhaps professional judges will be more likely to find facts that correspond to objective reality than will lay jurors. Perhaps not, of course, but suppose that one believes that legally trained judges are apt to be epistemologically superior to lay jurors. One might still prefer jurors, and thus impose a regime of mandatory deference on judges reviewing the findings of juries, if one thinks that concerns of legitimation—having decision-makers who are not permanently part of the state apparatus—outweigh those epistemological concerns. Again (and again, and again), we are not making any prescriptions here about optimal decision-making structures. We are simply describing the elements of a framework that we think can shed light on the phenomenon of deference. Epistemological deference is obviously an important part of that framework. Indeed, it is doubtful whether it deserves a name at all. "It is simply common sense applied to the task of figuring out right answers."[69]

## 3.3. Cost Savings

Legal systems in advanced countries deal with a staggering volume of cases and issues. Consider a large welfare system, such as Social Security or the system of veterans' benefits in the United States. If each aspect of each decision had to be reviewed de novo by another level, and possibly several other levels, of decision-makers, the system would be swamped. Even within the limits of the court system, one cannot retry every case on appeal. As the Supreme Court said in explaining the rationale behind the "clearly erroneous" standard for review of federal district court adjudicative fact-finding:

> The rationale for deference to the original finder of fact is not limited to the superiority of the trial judge's position to make determinations of credibility. The trial judge's major role is the determination of fact, and with experience in fulfilling that role comes expertise. Duplication of the trial judge's efforts in the court of appeals would very likely contribute only negligibly to the accuracy of fact determination at a huge cost in diversion of judicial resources. In addition, the parties to a case on appeal have already been forced to concentrate their energies and resources on persuading the trial judge that their account of the facts is the correct one; requiring them to persuade three more judges at the appellate level is requiring too much.[70]

Accordingly, one commonplace reason for either discretionary deference or mandatory deference is *cost*: a full system of complete, non-deferential review is simply beyond the capacity of, or at least beyond a sensible allocation of resources within, all but the simplest legal systems. For lack of a better term, we call this kind of deference "economic deference." To be clear, we do not mean by this label to suggest that the standard for this kind of deference is some notion of neoclassical efficiency. The "economic" part simply refers to the costs, however measured or understood, of the *decision-making process*, not some larger notion of social welfare. The idea of cost is meant to be capacious, with no technical meaning underlying the analysis.

"Economic deference results from a cost-benefit analysis that suggests that giving weight to a prior decision is so much easier and cheaper (however 'cheaper' is defined) than reconsidering the matter from scratch that deference to the prior decision is appropriate."[71] On its face, this seems simple, and even simple-minded. In many applications, it is both of those things. But when applied to discretionary deference rather than mandatory deference—when it represents a discretionary decision by a judge rather than a command from a legal designer—it gets complicated very quickly.

It is easy to understand why a legal designer would take significant account of economic deference. Additional levels of decision-making offer potential benefits, in both legitimacy and accuracy, but they also raise the prospect of serious costs, both to the litigants and to the legal system as a whole. It would be astonishing if the benefits always (or never) outweighed the costs; that is why no legal system provides for full reconsideration of every decision made at every level.

It is also easy to understand why judges, in the absence of legal command, might choose to defer in the interests of saving time and resources. Deference makes it harder to overturn a decision. How much harder depends on how much weight is given in the particular case to the prior decision. But as long as the weight is not zero—and if the weight is literally zero in every possible respect (more on what we mean by "every possible respect" in the next chapter), it would be inappropriate to describe what is happening as deference—the existence of deference creates a space in which decisions that might get reversed if given full consideration get affirmed without that full consideration. The absence of full consideration represents the cost savings to the appellate decision-maker. It is generally easier for a judge to decide, for example, whether an agency's factual finding was supported by "substantial evidence"—that is, was not completely ridiculous—than to decide whether the agency got the facts right.[72] To be sure, deference will not always and necessarily make the reviewing court's job easier; it depends on the context and the content of the deference regime. For example, in the United States, judicial review of policymaking by federal agencies involves courts assessing whether agencies took a "hard look" at the problem before them. That review, in turn, requires the court to invest enough resources to ascertain what problem was actually before the agency, what considerations would bear on that problem, and what factors the agency might have overlooked. In an even moderately complex case, this can be a major undertaking.[73] It might be easier for a court simply to decide whether it likes the agency's policy outcome. Nonetheless, over a large range of cases, one would expect deference to lessen rather than increase the difficulty of decision for the reviewing body.

It is quite possible that considerations of economic deference, in addition to the previously identified considerations of legitimacy, drove the development of the otherwise somewhat mysterious *Chevron* doctrine. If one reads the Supreme Court's 1984 *Chevron* decision with no preconceptions or knowledge of modern law, it is very difficult—bordering on impossible—to read the decision to mandate a new regime of judicial review of agency legal determinations. The case reads, and was argued by all of the parties, like a mundane application of then-existing law—and that is certainly how the author of the opinion understood it at the time that it was written and again three years later when he explained exactly how he understood his own opinion.[74] Why would lower courts generate a doctrine—and a doctrine that was sure to generate enormous controversy and that seems to fly in the face of the most obvious epistemological allocation of authority over statutory interpretation—from this unpromising foundation? As a public choice devotee might ask: *Cui bono?*

At least part of the answer may lie in pre-*Chevron* law and economic deference. When *Chevron* was decided in 1984, the law governing judicial review of federal agency legal interpretations was widely perceived to be a mess. Whether it actually *was* a mess is far less clear, but for historical purposes the perception is more important than the reality, if the two indeed differed. The perception was that the question of deference to agency statutory interpretations depended on a multifactor balancing test that considered a wide range of (non-exclusive) features of the agency decisions, any or all of which might tilt the balance, in either direction, for or against deference to the agency's views. This regime was widely decried as confusing and inconsistent.[75] Lower court judges were not shy about expressing their views to the Supreme Court. The D.C. Circuit in 1984, in a decision issued just a few months before the *Chevron* decision came down, wrote:

> [T]he case law under the Administrative Procedure Act has not crystallized around a single doctrinal formulation which captures the extent to which courts should defer to agency interpretations of law. Instead, two "opposing platitudes" exert countervailing "gravitational pulls" on the law. At one pole stands the maxim that courts should defer to "reasonable" agency interpretive positions, a maxim increasingly prevalent in recent decisions. Pulling in the other direction is the principle that courts remain the final

arbiters of statutory meaning; that principle, too, is embossed with recent approval.[76]

This opinion was written by Judge Abner Mikva and joined by then-Judge Antonin Scalia, two of the most important and acute administrative law jurists of the time, and two people who otherwise agreed on relatively little. A decade earlier, Judge Henry Friendly, one of the most respected lower-court judges in the United States, had said much the same thing:

> We think it is time to recognize . . . that there are two lines of Supreme Court decisions on the this subject which are analytically in conflict, with the result that a court of appeals must choose the one it deems more appropriate for the case at hand. Leading cases support [] the view that great deference must be given to the decisions of an administrative agency applying a statute to the facts and that such decisions can be reversed only if without rational basis. . . . However, there is an impressive body of law sanctioning free substitution of judicial for administrative judgment when the question involves the meaning of a statutory term.[77]

Judges who saw this important area of law as confused might well leap at the chance to simplify their lives by adopting a deference regime that universally defers to (a certain class of) agency legal interpretations. While that might entail deferring to some agency decisions for which courts have an epistemological advantage, the cost of case-specific judgments is potentially large, especially when there is very little structure to guide that case-specific process. This is one species of the familiar debate about rules versus standards. Rules are generally cheaper and easier to apply once the rules are properly formulated, but standards are more likely to allow one to reach the "right" result in particular disputes, assuming away resource constraints or anything that might interfere with the optimum application of the standards in a given case. Similarly, deference can be cheaper and easier than non-deferential review over a nontrivial range of cases. The *Chevron* framework, in particular, has an air of simplicity about it. There is no need under *Chevron* to think about whether the question of law is pure or mixed, whether the statute clearly delegates authority to the agency, or how to apply the "sliding scale of deference, taking into account a variety of deference-related factors,"[78] all of which dominated pre-*Chevron* law. One arguably need only ask whether the agency administers the statute, and a measure of deference flows automatically from an answer of yes. For lower courts that had openly complained for years in the pages of the federal reporters that the Supreme Court had not given them a clear scope-of-review doctrine, *Chevron* offered possible reprieve from the darkness.

Whether *Chevron* actually, or could have, delivered on that promise of simplification is another question. It depends on how simple one makes the *Chevron* framework. If *Chevron*'s application requires a detailed, statute-by-statute analysis of whether Congress intended the agency to have primary interpretative authority, as some cases have held, *Chevron* is of little consequence from the standpoint of economic deference. If figuring out whether a statute's meaning is "clear" were no easier (and perhaps harder) than figuring out whether a question of law was pure or mixed, *Chevron* could even make the courts' job harder rather than easier. But intuitively it seems simpler to figure out whether the agency's interpretation is within a range of permissibility than to figure out whether it is right, just as it is generally easier to figure out whether a factual finding is supported by substantial evidence than to figure out whether the factual finding is correct. *Chevron* not only gave courts the promise (which may or may not have been fulfilled in the ensuing decades) of a more rule-like framework for determining whether to defer but also offered the prospect of more deference in more cases. There are very few, if any, occasions in which post-*Chevron* courts will not defer to an agency's legal interpretation when they would have deferred to it under the pre-*Chevron* regime. On the other hand, many "pure" questions of law receive deference under *Chevron* where deference would been very iffy under the pre-*Chevron* framework. More deference, all else being equal, seems to promise lower decision costs for reviewing courts. It is hard to believe that this was not on the minds of the courts that crafted and then solidified the *Chevron* framework.

Once again, we neither endorse nor reject the idea of economic deference, either in general or in specific applications. That is not our job—which is a good thing, because it would be a very difficult job. To what extent are courts justified, in the absence of positive legal command, in sacrificing a measure of decisional accuracy in pursuit of cost savings? This kind of question is immensely complicated: "the 'costs' of not having the right answer vary greatly with the context, as do the costs of determining right answers, the costs of determining the costs of right answers, and the comparative costs of figuring out the right answer and figuring out the answer that is supposedly prescribed by [deference]."[79] This also assumes that judges are calculating costs and benefits with an eye toward fulfilling their appointed functions. It is quite possible to employ economic deference as a form of shirking. It might be easier and cheaper *for the judge* to defer to others even if the overall balance of factors from the standpoint of the legal system as a whole would counsel against it. There is nothing necessarily positive or "efficient" about "economic" deference. It all depends on the perspective, the metric, and the actual decision in any particular case. We offer the notion of economic deference as an analytical tool, not as a how-to guide for judges.

## 3.4. Signaling

Suppose that one is faced with another's decision that is potentially relevant to one's own decision. One has no sense that the other decision-maker has any advantage of legitimacy or knowledge, so neither legitimation deference nor epistemological deference makes sense as a discretionary choice. Assume further that economic deference does not commend itself; the consequences of a wrong answer are not trivial, so deference without investigation of the merits of the answer is risky; and it will require a substantial amount of energy to determine, on the merits, whether the other's view merits any kind of substantive deference. Have we now ruled out deference as a rational strategy?

Not quite. Suppose further that the other decision-makers will simply like you better if you defer to them. It will make them happy, and it will perhaps make them more likely to defer to you in the future and to pay more respect to your decisions. By deferring to them, even if only by taking into account their views, you *communicate* something to them about your relationship and your own decision-making process. As Professor Aileen Kavanagh describes it:

> Sometimes, we defer to others even if we do not respect their judgment. For example, if I want to choose a film to see with a friend, I may defer to her judgment even if I know that her taste in films is poor and is in no way superior to my own. My reason for deferring to her is one of courtesy: I want to show or manifest respect for her, despite the fact that I do not rate her judgment highly. It is a way of signalling my respect for her and how I value our friendship.[80]

There are many contexts in which this kind of signaling could be employed in the law. A court might defer in order to signal to other actors the court's view of those actors' proper roles. It might signal to a legislature the court's view of its own role, either to encourage or discourage certain kinds of legislation affecting the court.[81] It might signal to other legal actors the court's commitment to a particular approach to decision-making. We will explore this latter use of *signaling deference* at some length in a subsequent chapter.

While it would be possible to fold this kind of analysis into a broad idea of economic deference, there is something distinctive about using deference as a communication, or signal, that warrants separate treatment. And if we can fold this signaling function of deference into the category of economic deference, the latter could swallow everything. Some law and economics devotees may encourage and applaud this move, but we are not law and economics devotees. As noted above, we will further develop this signaling notion later in this book.

## 4. A Framework for Deference

We can now at least sketch a framework and vocabulary for analyzing specific problems of deference. As a basic definition of deference, we stick with *the giving by a legal actor of some measure of consideration or weight to the decision of another actor in exercising the deferring actor's function.* We use the term "mandatory deference" to describe giving some measure of consideration or weight to the decision of another actor when such consideration or weight is commanded by positive law that satisfies an adequate rule of recognition regarded by the deferring actor as authoritative, and we use the term "discretionary deference" to describe consideration or weight given to another's decision by choice. The courts do not formally distinguish discretionary deference from mandatory deference, and the same rationales that support discretionary deference in any given case might also induce a legal designer to construct a scheme of mandatory deference in such a case, so we do not claim that there is any kind of legal or metaphysical difference between discretionary and mandatory deference. We use two distinct terms simply because of our intuition that a "choice" to follow binding positive law is different in some important way from a choice to yield to another's decision in the absence of legal command. They seem different both legally and psychologically. If the reader does not share our intuition, not much of consequence will change.

We have identified four classes of reasons that might induce a decision-maker to engage in deference: concerns about legitimacy, concerns about accuracy, concerns about decision costs, and concerns about signaling or communication. We describe deference that is motivated by these concerns as, respectively, legitimation deference, epistemological deference, economic deference, and signaling deference. Any particular act of deference, of course, might well be motivated by some combination of these (and possibly other) reasons, so we offer these as analytical categories, not as boxes into which real-world decisions can be slotted. One is probably unlikely to find any real-world deference decision that cannot be explained at least partially by more than one category of deference. We make no claims that these four reasons are exclusive. We simply offer them as the most common reasons that we observe, in the hope that they provide a set of tools for thinking about deference that can aid both descriptive and prescriptive projects.

One test of the usefulness of our framework is how well it matches up with what other thoughtful scholars have said about deference. If everyone converges on certain key ideas, that is at least some evidence that those ideas deserve consideration. And if there are differences in the way that people define and explain deference, that is an occasion to consider whether one view is more helpful than others or whether these are simply different ways of describing the same phenomenon. We genuinely approached this inquiry with no preconceptions one way or the other on this point. Indeed, we formulated our own tentative views on how to define and analyze deference *before* conducting research on how others approached the subject, precisely because we thought that this method would generate the most interesting information. Accordingly, we now examine how others have thought about deference, and we will consider whether those other thoughts call for any kind of reformulation or clarification of our definition and analytical structure.

## Notes

1. *See* GARY LAWSON, FEDERAL ADMINISTRATIVE LAW 890–91 (8th ed., 2019).
2. 432 U.S. 416 (1977).
3. 42 U.S.C. § 607(a) (1976).

4. *Batterton*, 432 U.S. at 425 ("Congress . . . expressly delegated to the Secretary the power to prescribe standards for determining what constitutes 'unemployment' for purposes of AFDC-UF eligibility. In a situation of this kind, Congress entrusts to the Secretary, rather than to the courts, the primary responsibility for interpreting the statutory term.").

5. *Id*. at 426.

6. *Id*.

7. Martin B. Louis, *Allocating Adjudicative Decision Making Authority Between the Trial and Appellate Levels: A Unified View of the Scope of Review, the Judge/Jury Question, and Procedural Discretion*, 64 N.C. L. Rev. 993, 997 (1986). *See also* Robert Anderson IV, *Law, Fact, and Discretion in the Federal Courts: An Empirical Study*, 2012 Utah L. Rev. 1, 2 ("The federal courts are divided into trial and appellate levels, each with a differentiated role in the adjudicatory process, and the standard of review largely delineates, at least in theory, the line between those roles.") (footnote omitted).

8. 554 U.S. 105 (2005).

9. *See* Firestone Tire & Rubber Co. v. Bruch, 489 U.S. 101, 111–13 (1989).

10. *Metlife*, 554 U.S. at 117.

11. Brief for Respondent 45, No. 06-923, *Metlife v. Glen. See also id*. at 46–50.

12. *Metlife,* 554 U.S. at 115.

13. *Id*. at 120 (emphasis added).

14. *Id*. at 130 n.2 (Scalia, J., dissenting).

15. Paul Daly, A Theory of Deference in Administrative Law: Basis, Application and Scope 25 (2012).

16. *See* Antonin Scalia, *The Rule of Law as a Law of Rules*, 56 U. Chi. L. Rev. 1175 (1989).

17. 1 John Bouvier, Preface to a Law Dictionary Adapted to the Constitution and Laws of the United States of America, and the Several States of the American Union v (1839).

18. *See* Mary Whisner, *Practicing Reference . . . Bouvier's, Black's, and Tinkerbell*, 92 Law Library J. 99, 100 (2000).

19. *See id*. For a detailed study of dictionary citations by Supreme Court Justices, see *United States Supreme Court Justices Citing Dictionaries Through the 1997-1998 Term*, 47 Buff. L. Rev. 397 (1999).

20. *See* Andrew T. Hyman, *The Substantive Role of Congress Under the Equal Protection Clause*, 42 So. U.L. Rev. 79, 114 (2014).

21. http://www.wklegaledu.com/Sheppard-WKBLDDE.

22. Because we are not discussing the original meaning of a term from any specific point in time, it makes no difference which edition of *Bouvier* one wants to employ, so we might as well use the one that is the most accessible in the present day.

23. *The Wolters Kluwer, Bouvier Law Dictionary* 317 (2011).

24. Gary Lawson, *Mostly Unconstitutional: The Case Against Precedent Revisited*, 5 Ave Maria L. Rev. 1, 9 (2007) (footnote omitted). *See also* Rachel E. Barkow, *Recharging the Jury: The Criminal Jury's Constitutional Role in an Era of Mandatory Sentencing*, 152 U. Pa. L. Rev. 33, 48–49 (2003); Margaret H. Lemos, *The Commerce Power and*

*Criminal Punishment: Presumption of Constitutionality or Presumption of Innocence?*, 84 Tex. L. Rev. 1203, 1229–31 (2006).

25. Lawson, *supra* note 24, at 10.

26. Fed. R. Civ. Proc. 52(a).

27. 29 U.S.C. § 160(e) (2012).

28. 5 U.S.C. § 7703(c) (2012).

29. 5 U.S.C. § 706(2)(E) (2012).

30. 5 U.S.C. § 706(2)(A) (2012).

31. 5 U.S.C. § 552(a)(4)(B) (2012) ("the court shall determine the matter de novo").

32. 12 U.S.C. § 25b(5)(A) (2012).

33. *See* Kent Barnett, *Codifying* Chevmore, 90 N.Y.U. L. Rev. 1, 28–32 (2014).

34. 15 U.S.C. § 1681s (2012).

35. *See, e.g.*, Rapaport v. United States Dep't of the Treasury, Office of Thrift Supervision, 59 F.3d 212 (D.C. Cir. 1995).

36. 12 U.S.C. 25b(c) (2012).

37. Barnett Bank of Marion County, N.A. v. Nelson, Fla. Ins. Comm'r, et al., 517 U.S. 25 (1996).

38. *Id.* at 30–31 (citations omitted).

39. By "obviously legal" we mean obviously legal by well-understood conventions regarding the distinction between law and fact. As a matter of first principles, there is much to be said for the proposition that there is no real metaphysical or epistemological distinction between questions of law and questions of fact. Indeed, one of us has said much for it. *See* Gary Lawson, Evidence of the Law: Proving Legal Claims (2017). But as a matter of doctrine and practice, the law/fact distinction is one of the bedrocks of modern legal systems. It is enshrined in numerous statutes, court decisions, and even the US Constitution *See* U.S. Const. art. III, § 2, cl. 2.

40. Barnett, *supra* note 33, at 27.

41. *See* Gary Lawson, *Controlling Precedent: Congressional Regulation of Judicial Decision-Making*, 18 Const. Commentary 191, 215–26 (2001).

42. Andrew Legg, The Margin of Appreciation in International Human Rights Law: Deference and Proportionality 23 (2012).

43. Paul Horwitz, *Three Faces of Deference*, 83 Notre Dame L. Rev. 1061, 1075 (2008).

44. *See* Lawson, *supra* note 24, at 9 ("Legal deference involves giving weight to another actor's decision because some controlling legal authority requires it"). *See also* Gary Lawson & Stephen Kam, *Making Law Out of Nothing at All: The Origins of the* Chevron *Doctrine*, 65 Admin. L. Rev. 1, 10–11 (2013).

45. U.S. Const. art. I, § 8, cl. 11.

46. *Id.*, art. II, § 2, cl. 2.

47. *But see* John Yoo, *Politics as Law?: The Anti-Ballistic Missile Treaty, the Separation of Powers, and Treaty Interpretation*, 89 Calif. L. Rev. 851 (2001). A full treatment of Professor Yoo's idiosyncratic, but characteristically thoughtful, views on treaty interpretation, which have been developed in subsequent years, *see* Julian Ku & John Yoo, Hamdan v. Rumsfeld, *The Functional Case for Foreign Affairs Deference to the*

*Executive Branch*, 23 CONST. COMMENTARY 179 (2006), is well beyond the scope of this book.

48. Abbott v. Abbott, 560 U.S. 1, 15 (2010) (quoting Sumitomo Shoji Am., Inc. v. Avagliano, 457 U.S. 176, 185 (1982)).

49. *See* Scott M. Sullivan, *Rethinking Treaty Interpretation*, 86 TEX. L. REV. 777, 790 (2008) ("The case law of treaty-interpretation deference . . . sheds little light on a structured application of the great weight standard").

50. *See* Robert M. Chesney, *Disaggregating Deference: The Judicial Power and Executive Treaty Interpretations*, 92 IOWA L. REV. 1723, 1741–44 (2007); David Sloss, *Judicial Deference to Executive Branch Treaty Interpretations*, 62 N.Y.U. ANN. SURVEY AM. L. 497 (2007); Sullivan, *supra* note 49, at 787–89.

51. *See* Sullivan, *supra* note 49, at 790–91.

52. *See* Eyal Benvenisti, *Reclaiming Democracy: The Strategic Uses of Foreign and International Law by National Courts*, 102 AM. J. INT'L L. 241, 242 (2008).

53. *See* MICHAEL STOKES PAULSEN, STEVEN G. CALABRESI, MICHAEL W. MCCONNELL & SAMUEL L. BRAY, THE CONSTITUTION OF THE UNITED STATES, 580–600 (2010).

54. *See* LAWSON, *supra* note 1, at 1191.

55. For a detailed defense of this claim in the context of the US Constitution, see GARY LAWSON & GUY SEIDMAN, "A GREAT POWER OF ATTORNEY": UNDERSTANDING THE FIDUCIARY CONSTITUTION 107–26 (2017).

56. Richard J. Pierce, Jr., Chevron *and Its Aftermath: Judicial Review of Agency Interpretations of Statutory Provisions*, 41 VAND. L. REV. 301, 307–8 (1988).

57. One must say "presumably" because some judges might be incompetent and therefore unable or unwilling to develop expertise. We are speaking in generalities, about ideal types, which will be more or less true across individual cases.

58. Salve Regina Coll. v. Russell, 499 U.S. 225 (1991) (citations omitted).

59. BLACK'S LAW DICTIONARY (*appeal de novo*) (2014) (emphasis added).

60. *Id.* (*de novo judicial review*) (emphasis added).

61. 499 U.S. 225.

62. 304 U.S. 64 (1938).

63. *Salve Regina*, 499 U.S. at 231.

64. *Id.* at 234.

65. *Id.* at 232–33.

66. Chad M. Oldfather, *Universal De Novo Review*, 77 GEO WASH. L. REV. 308, 313 (2009) (emphasis added).

67. Gary Lawson & Christopher D. Moore, *The Executive Power of Constitutional Interpretation*, 81 IOWA L. REV. 1267, 1271 (1996).

68. *Id.* at 1278–79.

69. Lawson & Kam, *supra* note 44, at 11.

70. Anderson v. City of Bessemer City, N.C., 470 U.S. 564, 574–75 (1985).

71. Lawson, *supra* note 24, at 11.

72. *See* RICHARD A. POSNER, THE FEDERAL COURTS 176 (1996) ("it is easier to decide whether a finding is reasonable or defensible than to decide whether it is right").

73. When he was a law clerk at the D.C. Circuit, Professor Lawson spent more than half of his year working on exactly two cases reviewing agency action. These were not hot-button cases: One involved crash-test speeds for automobile bumpers and the other involved the ratemaking treatment of tax credits for consolidated energy companies. Each case consumed about three months of clerk time and more than one month of judge time (and one of them consumed an additional three months' time from a prior clerk). If the reader has nothing better to do and wants to examine the gruesome aftermath, these epic cases are enshrined forever in the federal reporter. *See* (or not) City of Charlottesville, Va. v. FERC, 774 F.2d 1205 (D.C. Cir. 1985); Center for Auto Safety v. Peck, 751 F.2d 1336 (D.C. Cir. 1985).

74. *See* Lawson & Kam, *supra* note 44, at 66–69.

75. *See id.* at 6–9.

76. NRDC, Inc. v. EPA, 725 F.2d 761, 767 (D.C. Cir. 1984) (citations omitted).

77. Pittston Stevedoring Corp. v. Dellaventura, 544 F.2d 35, 49 (2d Cir. 1976) (footnote omitted), *aff'd sub nom.* Northeast Marine Terminal Co. v. Caputo, 432 U.S. 249 (1977).

78. American Fed'n of Labor & Congress of Indus. Orgs. v. Donovan, 757 F.2d 330, 341 (D.C. Cir. 1985).

79. Lawson, *supra* note 24, at 11.

80. Aileen Kavanagh, *Deference or Defiance?: The Limits of the Judicial Role in Constitutional Adjudication*, *in* EXPOUNDING THE CONSTITUTION: ESSAYS IN CONSTITUTIONAL THEORY 184, 188 (Grant Huscroft ed., 2008).

81. *See id.* at 189.

# 4

# Other Views of the Cathedral

Although we are not aware of any systematic treatment of the concept of deference, the concept has been employed for so long and by so many people at the retail level that it is impossible to survey the entire universe of discourse on the subject. We have no such ambitions. Our modest goal is to examine what we hope is a representative sample of thoughts about deference to see if any of those thoughts call for reconsideration or elaboration of our own framework. We mean no slight to anyone whose views are not discussed here; our selection of views to address is more random than systematic (and we have reserved discussion of the view of one major scholar—five letters, starts with "S" and ends with "r"—for the next chapter). The selection probably reflects our own scholarly interests more than anything else.

Our discussion is also colored by the nature of our project. Our discussion is driven by our inductive methodology. Our starting point is the set of existing practices that US federal courts describe as deference. We do not seek to derive a concept of deference from first principles and then ask whether courts conform to it. Moreover, the set of practices that we examine covers a wide range of topics, so we are inducing an account of deference at a very high level of generality. If one focuses only on a narrower band of practices, such as judicial review of legislative or executive action affecting fundamental constitutional rights, it is quite possible that one will generate a very different inductive definition than one will draw from a broader database. Some of the scholars who we examine in this chapter explicitly have a narrower focus than do we. It is quite possible that their own accounts of deference are "correct" within their narrower foci but "incorrect" if transplanted to broader contexts. Accordingly, if and when we "reject" the view of others, it is most likely because their views do not fit our project rather than because we see anything objectively "wrong" with what they say. We are trying to find the right tool for the right job.

So let us see whether there is anything in our initial account of deference that needs revision or supplementation in light of the contributions that others have made to a study of deference.

*Deference*. Gary Lawson and Guy I. Seidman, Oxford University Press (2020). © Oxford University Press.
DOI: 10.1093/oso/9780190273408.001.0001

# 1. Paul Daly (et al.)

A book entitled *A Theory of Deference in Administrative Law* sounds like a good place for administrative law scholars (which we both are) to look for alternative views on deference. Canadian legal scholar Paul Daly wrote such a book in 2012, and that is where we begin our examination of other accounts of deference.

As do we, Professor Daly concentrates on deference as it is used by courts while noting that the concept of deference has many broader applications outside the courts, and indeed outside the law.[1] As do we, Professor Daly suspects that, as a matter of first principles, deference might best be understood as a binary choice rather than as a range or a sliding scale,[2] though we think that practice in the US courts forecloses this binary model as a descriptive account of deference. From that point onward, however, his terminology and framework for deference break up the concept along quite different lines than does our own analysis.

Professor Daly begins by examining a definition of deference from another scholar, Brian Foley, which is facially very similar to our own: "Reduced to its most basic form, the deference question concerns the *weight* which courts should attribute to the decisions of non-judicial institutions."[3] We would substitute "consideration or weight" for "weight," would substitute "do or should" for "should," and would not limit the scope of application of the definition to judicial deference to non-judicial institutions, but this definition is certainly in the same family as our own. The key elements are the generality of the definition, which does not depend on the identity of the institution to which deference is given, and its refusal to tie deference down to any specific weight or rationale. Notwithstanding this generality, however, Professor Daly does not endorse Mr. Foley's account as an adequate definition of deference, because he thinks that this definition covers only a subpart of the kind of judicial activity that qualifies as deference. We think, however, that this reads into Mr. Foley's definition—and certainly would read into ours if our own analysis was substituted for Mr. Foley's—a limitation on the definition that simply is not there.

Professor Daly describes deference as set forth in Mr. Foley's definition as "epistemic deference," because it "involves the paying of respect to the decisions of others by means of according weight to those decisions."[4] He worries that this focus on respect-based weight "may cause one to overlook an equally important notion" which he calls *"doctrinal deference."*[5] Doctrinal deference, for Professor Daly, is stronger medicine than epistemic defer-ence: "Rather than *simply* [our emphasis] paying respect to the decisions of another, one might allocate authority to another to make binding decisions. Such authority need not be absolute; its exercise might be subject to limi-tations of, to take a pertinent example, reasonableness."[6] The two catego-ries of epistemic deference and doctrinal deference together comprise what Professor Daly calls "curial deference,"[7] which is, roughly speaking, deference that is relevant to legal actors. Because curial deference is Professor Daly's ul-timate focus, we let him speak for himself about what it means to him:

> The term "curial deference" is preferable to both "deference" and "judi-cial deference." Standing alone, "deference" arguably has inappropriate "overtones of servility, or perhaps gracious concession." Employing the al-ternative "curial deference," by adding an extra word, means that "deference" is less likely to be understood has having connotations of subservience. Moreover, to rule the word "deference" out completely would be to overlook a distinction between "submissive deference" and "deference as respect";
>
> > Deference as submission occurs when the court treats a decision or an aspect of it as nonjusticiable, and refuses to enter on a review of it be-cause it considers it beyond its competence. Deference as respect occurs when the court gives some weight to a decision of a primary decision-maker for an articulated reason, as part of its overall review of the justifi-cation for the decision.
>
> I employ "curial deference" to denote something closer to the latter (though evidently also including doctrinal deference) than to the former. . . . [C]urial deference . . . encompasses both epistemic deference and doctrinal deference.[8]

There is obviously much common ground between our account and Professor Daly's, but each account focuses on different features of defer-ence, for fairly obvious reasons. We are trying to describe the way in which deference is actually applied in a specific legal system, while Professor Daly is trying to establish a normatively appealing structure and accompanying vocabulary as part of a recommendation of best practices for (Canadian) courts. This leads to a number of differences in emphasis.

Most notably, we begin with a much broader understanding of deference as a basic concept than does Professor Daly (which would be a bit ironic if he views our definition, as he did Mr. Foley's, as too narrow in scope). Our baseline definition of deference does not distinguish among the various *reasons* for granting deference, and thus is not limited to what Professor Daly calls epistemic deference but instead tries to describe the activity of deference in all of its manifestations. (As we will shortly explain, we also doubt whether Brian Foley meant to limit his definition only to what Professor Daly calls epistemic deference.) Thus, we think that the broader category of deference, without any adjective, is a good starting point for analysis, from which subsequent subclassifications of deference can then emerge.

As an aside, we do not think that the term "deference" as we employ it necessarily connotes servility or subservience. It can, but it need not. This idea that deference connotes servility is often traced to comments by Lord Hoffman, who wrote in 2004: "although the word 'deference' is now very popular in describing the relationship between the judicial and the other branches of government, I do not think that its overtones of servility, or perhaps gracious concession, are appropriate to describe what is happening."[9] More than a decade earlier, a noted scholar said much the same thing: "The very word *deference* calls up lowering the eyes, baring the covered head, laughing at jokes that are not funny."[10] We think this reads into the language of deference something that is not there. As Professor Aileen Kavanagh aptly said:

> It is certainly the case that when we describe someone as "deferential," it can carry negative connotations of behaving in an obsequious, fawning, or servile way. . . . However, the term deference does not necessarily carry these pejorative overtones. Nor are they central to the meaning of deference. Rather, they refer to being (or appearing) inappropriately deferential. . . . So, the overtones of servility refer to a misuse of an approach to practical reasoning that is often perfectly appropriate and sensible.[11]

We wholly agree. One can easily defer from a position of strength or confidence; only an insecure person always worries about letting others decide from time to time. More to the point, the idea of servility goes to the strength of and reasons for deference, not to the basic practice itself. One can certainly defer servilely, by yielding quickly and without thought because one is intimidated by the other actor, but nothing in the idea of deference calls for this as a general practice. Certainly much of what the US federal courts describe as deference is anything but servile. Because our project aims to describe a broad range of judicial practices, we are reluctant to build adjectival limitations into our definition of deference that are not well grounded in actual usage within the US legal order simply to avoid a possible, clearly mistaken, connotation that the term might hold for some people. Accordingly, we stick with the bare term "deference" as the starting point and go on from there; we assume the risk that someone will wrongly read some notion of servility into that definition.

From a broad initial definition of deference, we then subdivide the field in terms of legal grounds for deference—first into *mandatory deference,* in which the activity of deference results from a decision to follow binding positive law commanding deference, and second into *discretionary deference,* in which the activity of deference results from a voluntary decision by the deferring actor that is not commanded by positive law. Within the subcategory of discretionary deference, we then identify various rationales for choosing to defer when not commanded to do so by positive law, represented most notably by what we call legitimation deference, epistemological deference, economic deference, and signaling deference, with more categories surely out there to be identified. (These rationales could also be employed by legal designers choosing to establish various deference regimes to determine whether and when deference is appropriate.) We do not set forth distinct categories that sort deference by its magnitude or weight. *Skidmore* deference is a kind of deference. Abstention is a kind of deference. They are very different in their consequences in particular cases, but they both deserve to be called deference.

Professor Daly's distinction between deference as a general concept and "curial deference" reflects, we think, a discomfort with a view of deference that would include complete abnegation or "submission" within the concept of deference. Professor Daly therefore seemingly would not consider abstention, for example, as a form of deference, while we have no difficulty extending the range of deference to include complete withdrawal from the decision. Indeed, it is particularly odd to exclude complete withdrawal from the concept of deference when, as we noted at the outset of the last chapter, that is probably the best first approximation of the ordinary language meaning of deference. The linguistically questionable move is to include as deference things *other* than complete withdrawal or submission. We think the move justified in the contexts that we examine in this book because of the actual practices of courts, but we recognize that the linguistic presumption is probably to the contrary. In the end, we prefer our broader definition that includes all poles on the deference continuum simply because it better fits our *descriptive* project. US courts use the term "deference" to describe doctrines such as abstention as well as doctrines such as *Chevron, Skidmore,* and arbitrary or capricious review, and we therefore do as well. That does not make our definition of deference "right" and Professor Daly's "wrong" in any abstract sense. But it does make ours "right" for the limited purpose of describing actual legal practices in the United States and therefore "right" for the limited purposes of this book. Whether it is "right" for any broader purposes remains to be determined.

Professor Daly's distinction between epistemic and doctrinal deference seems at first glance to track our distinction between epistemological and legitimation deference. But that is not really the case. Our set of distinctions based on rationales for deference, which also includes the categories of economic deference and signaling deference, is not really meant to mark out different kinds of deference. It is designed purely as an analytical tool to help understand the how and why of varieties of deference that show up in actual doctrine. The relevant different kinds of deference, for us, are determined by the actual operation of the legal system, not by ideal theory. We identify doctrinal categories of deference doctrinally, meaning empirically through observation, not theoretically. We do not see our various reason-based categories for deference as forming the foundation for an ideal normative structure which then gets imposed on the practices of courts; rather, we observe those reasons in action and thus induce them as an important part of our explanatory project. We use those reasons as categories for analyzing deference because they exist in the legal world that we study and they help explain that world, not because they form a normatively desirable and self-contained conceptual structure. For us, terms like "legitimation deference" and "epistemological deference" are simply shorthand for less wieldy terms such as "deference justified by courts, at least in part, by reference to the superior legitimacy of the decision-maker to whom deference is given" or "deference justified by courts, at least in part, by reference to the likelihood that the decision-maker to whom deference is given will reach the right answer." Any given act of deference within a particular doctrinal category, or even the whole category itself, may well involve multiple reasons, and may thus combine multiple "forms" of deference as we have classified them into a single act. The single act is one of deference. The reasons reflected in our categories are simply an analytical deconstruction of features of that act. They are not themselves doctrinal categories of deference—at least not until and unless courts start applying them that way.

Because we see deference as a single concept, which can be analyzed at least in part in terms of the reasons that prompt it, Professor Daly's metaphysically more potent categories of epistemic and doctrinal deference cross all of our analytical lines. Doctrinal deference, as far as we can tell, can be either mandatory or discretionary for Professor Daly. It describes an allocation of authority, but it says nothing about whether the allocation originates with the judge's choice or is commanded by positive law, such as a constitution or statute. It seems to involve some distinction from epistemic deference regarding the *weight* given to the prior decision; "simply" giving respect under epistemic deference is distinguished from the presumably stronger activity of allocating decisional authority. According to our account, one cannot make a priori judgments about the weight or significance of deference just by looking at the reason-based categories of deference. Epistemological deference could be stronger, weaker, or the same as any other kind of deference, including any kind of mandatory deference, in any given case. As a descriptive matter, one has to look at the particular doctrine under discussion in order to make that judgment, and if one wants to conduct a normative analysis, one will need to look at the particular decision (or category of decisions) on the merits to see what kinds of reasons apply and with what force. One cannot work backward from the reasons to the answers.

In sum, we do not think that we need to modify our account of deference in light of Professor Daly's analysis—not because there is anything wrong with Professor Daly's analysis but just because it does not fit our inductively oriented project.

Since Professor Daly used Brian Foley as his jumping-off point, we might as well explore Mr. Foley's account of deference as well. Since Mr. Foley's book on deference is quite difficult to find in the United States, we refer instead to his Trinity College Dublin doctoral dissertation, which (with many thanks to his home institution for its Trinity's Access to Research Archive) is readily available online.

Mr. Foley's definition of deference presented above, as we saw, has much in common with our own at first glance. His fuller definition provided in his dissertation is similar: "Deference, in the broadest sense, describes a situation where a decision-making body, which we will refer to as 'A', decides a case, 'C', not on the basis of its own independent assessment, but by treating the decision of some other decision-making body, 'B', in respect of C as, in some degree, authoritative for its own (i.e. A's) decision."[12] This definition is general enough to sweep in activity that gives any degree of weight or consideration ("in some degree, authoritative") to another's decision; "there are degrees to which one can defer."[13] The weight might even turn out to be infinite and thus can include complete submission as a kind of deference. Indeed, Mr. Foley labels non-reviewability as a "'justiciability model' of deference,"[14] which thus includes forms of non-reviewability within the compass of deference as a general idea, as do US courts and therefore we as well. His definition—correctly, we think—does not limit who the other to whom one is deferring might be. Nor does his definition try to limit the grounds that would qualify action as deference. In his more detailed discussions, Mr. Foley further identifies and explores phenomena that we would call legitimation deference[15] and epistemological deference[16] that are all subsumed under the broader conceptual category of deference. This is all familiar and friendly territory for us to navigate.

We see only two relevant limits on what kinds of practices Mr. Foley would consider deference that raise eyebrows for us. First, under his definition, the degree of weight given to the other decision must be larger than zero: "The decision maker substitutes, in one degree or another, someone else's will for his own will."[17] If there is literally zero substitution of judgment, there is no deference. As we alluded in an earlier chapter, we agree with this, *provided*— and it is a very important proviso—that one acknowledges that the mere act of consideration of another decision, even if the ultimate judgment is to reject entirely the other decision as worthless, is to some extent a weight larger than zero. At the very least, as we will explain shortly, this kind of consideration treats as to some degree authoritative the other decision-maker's judgment about what decisions and arguments are worth including in the relevant evidence set for decision. The other limitation in Mr. Foley's definition that raises questions for us is that deference must involve giving weight to another's view for some reason other than one's own independent substantive agreement with the decision: "the concept of deference as understood in this thesis refers to the situation where a decision-making body accepts or treats the decision of another body or institution as to how it should decide the case before it as more important than its own independent assessment and on the basis of reasons which are (save in the case of rejecting deference) independent of substantive agreement with the content of the decision to-be-deferred to."[18] According to this account, "a judge acting deferentially is never concerned with whether the legislature [or other decision-maker] has 'got it right' according to his own independent view of what is 'right.'"[19] This notion that a decision to defer must be in some sense content-independent of the other's decision has a very impressive body of support behind it,[20] which we will examine in more detail shortly, and it seems right if understood in a limited fashion. If one only takes into consideration views with which one substantively agrees, then there is no deference involved. But if one considers another view simply because of its pedigree, we regard that as deference even if one ultimately makes one's own independent judgment of the under-lying matter, provided that the other view is part of the relevant evidence set for one's own ultimate judgment. We will say more about this matter in the Section 2 of this chapter.

With those possible qualifications, we thus do not see anything in Mr. Foley's account of deference that is inconsistent with our own. As a result, we do not see anything in it to make us reconsider or recharacterize our own account. Upon approaching Mr. Foley's work, we would not necessarily ex-pect to find anything that would call for reconsideration of our definition. After all, we are principally trying to describe and explain the practice of def-erence in US courts while Mr. Foley is trying to both describe and critique the practice of deference in Irish courts in the limited context of constitu-tional review. There is no a prior reason to expect to see exactly the same framework employed in both settings; the different purposes of the projects might even lead one to expect substantial differences. It is therefore perhaps surprising, and we think encouraging, that the frameworks across those dif-ferent contexts are so similar. If the ultimate goal is to find an account of def-erence that can both describe and explain the practices of US courts *and* have wide application beyond that context, agreement of this magnitude across an ocean and across projects is a good thing.

## 2. Paul Horwitz (et al.)

One of the fullest discussions of deference that we have encountered in US legal scholarship is Professor Paul Horwitz's treatment of the subject.[21] This is an important work of scholarship, and it deserves very careful scrutiny.

Drawing on some earlier thoughts by Professor Robert Schapiro,[22] Professor Horwitz initially defines deference as "a decisionmaker following a determination made by some other individual or institution that it might not otherwise have reached had it decided the same question independently."[23]

Alternatively formulated, deference "involves a decisionmaker (D1) setting aside its own judgment and following the judgment of another decisionmaker (D2) in circumstances in which the deferring decisionmaker, D1, might have reached a different conclusion."[24] From our standpoint, there is much to like in this definition. It puts aside—correctly in our view—questions about what kinds of other determinations or decisions are involved and who made them: "When they defer, courts suspend their own judgment in favor of the judgment of some other party—another branch of government, an adminis-trative agency, a private institutional actor, or a quasi-public actor."[25] It also puts aside—correctly in our view—questions about the degree or scope of deference involved: "In adopting this definition, I set aside for now questions involving the scope of deference. . . . D1 might defer to the judgment of D2 altogether; it might defer only on questions of fact, while reaching its own conclusions on questions of law without any deference to the legal judgment of D2; or it might adopt some other approach. Nevertheless, deference exists as long as D1 follows D2's determinations along at least some dimension."[26] Thus, according to Professor Horwitz, the notion of "deference as a thumb on the scales but not a complete surrender of judgment may qualify as a form of deference."[27] Whether an action is an instance of deference does not depend on the identity of the actor to whom one defers or how much one defers. We agree with all of that. Nor does Professor Horwitz include in his basic defi-nition of deference anything about the potential reasons for deferring. We agree with that as well. Those agreements cover most of the relevant territory.

Indeed, we part from Professor Horwitz definition in only one respect, but it is an important respect. Professor Horwitz, as did Brian Foley, insists that for deference to exist, there must be at least some non-zero substitution of the judgment of the other actor for that of the deferring actor: "if the court ultimately resists substituting D2's position for its own, it may be difficult to call this deference under my definition."[28] Even more specifically: "Nor could we call it deference if D1 only purported to give consideration to D2, while rejecting any conclusions by D2 that it thought wrong."[29] This notion that deference necessarily requires some measure of displacement of judgment, and not mere consideration of another's position, has a storied pedigree; its advocates include Larry Alexander and Fred Schauer,[30] Philip Soper,[31] Henry Monaghan,[32] and Antonin Scalia.[33] It finds strong support in common sense and ordinary language. Recall that an ordinary-language account of defer-ence might well apply the term *only* to instances in which the displacement of judgment is *total*. One might think that it is more than enough of a stretch to let the term apply to graded weights that are less than total displacement of judgment; to stretch it to include instances in which there is *no* displacement of judgment seems like a road too far.

Despite all of these considerations, we respectfully disagree and maintain that deference can exist even when, at the end of the day, the decision-maker gives no weight to the decision of another and the final decision comes out on the merits exactly as the decision-maker would have decided without the other's decision in the mix. We thus stand by our definition of deference as encompassing giving *either* consideration *or* weight to the views of another. We stand our ground for two reasons, one descriptive and one theoretical.

First, as a purely descriptive matter, *Skidmore* deference involves precisely the kind of deference that might, in the end, make no difference to the decision. As we discussed in a previous chapter, *Skidmore* deference requires reviewing courts to *consider* an agency's legal interpretation when making their own decision, but it does not require *any particular degree of weight* to be given to that decision independently of an assessment of various aspects of the decision that bear on its reliability. It is quite possible for a court under *Skidmore* to examine an agency decision and conclude that the decision is entitled to no weight at all because it is poorly reasoned, did not emerge from reliable procedures, seems to be politically driven, and so on. In that circumstance, the court will reach precisely the same result that it would have reached had the agency decision never existed, but the decision process will still be described as deferential. This may be part of the reason why Justice Scalia disliked *Skidmore* so much. In addition to being wide open and very un-rule-like,[34] perhaps he did not regard it as a deference doctrine at all.[35] Nonetheless, as we noted in Chapter 2, references to "*Skidmore* deference" number in the thousands. In light of this usage, an inductively grounded approach to deference cannot possibly exclude from its definition all practices that do not ultimately result in giving positive decisional weight to another decision. An account of deference that does not include *Skidmore* is deeply problematic in the context of US law.

To be sure, there is a linguistic way to (re)characterize *Skidmore* to avoid labeling as deference the mere consideration of views without ultimately giving them decision-relevant weight. One could distinguish *Skidmore deference* from the *Skidmore doctrine*. The *doctrine*, one could say, calls for consideration of an agency opinion followed by an assessment of whether *deference* is appropriate. If one concludes that the agency decision is entitled to no weight, then the *doctrine* will not prescribe any *deference*. According to this account, *Skidmore* only involves *deference* when one makes the second-step decision to yield some measure of one's judgment to the agency. This is perhaps an awkward formulation of *Skidmore,* but it is not an impossible one. If there truly was something conceptually absurd or offensive about using the term "deference" to describe a decision process in which the deferred-to decision seemingly made no difference in the outcome, there might be some grounds for thinking of *Skidmore* in this two-step fashion, to which the term deference could only be applied, contingently, in those cases in which the agency's decision made a difference in the court's ultimate all-things-considered judgment. But on careful reflection, the idea of deference-without-a-difference[36] is not absurd, offensive, or oxymoronic, at least in a context such as *Skidmore.* Quite to the contrary, it makes a great deal of sense. That is because....

Second, as a theoretical matter, there is an important sense in which mere consideration of another's decision as part of one's own decision-making process counts as a meaningful form of deference even if that consideration results in assigning zero significance to the other's decision. This becomes (we think) clear once one unpacks what is involved in a process of decision-making.

We have thus far treated the decision-making process—in any context in which we have addressed it—as a unitary enterprise. One finds facts, or interprets statutes or constitutional provisions, or assesses a policy choice, or reaches an ultimate judgment in a dispute. Deference seems like something that applies or does not apply to this unitary decision-making process. But that is an incomplete, and even deceptive, account of decision-making. And once the decision-making process is properly understood, the importance of "mere" consideration of another's decision stands out.

Every decision process that involves proof of propositions—*every* such decision process in any context and in any discipline—can be broken down into analytical components that must, as a matter of epistemological necessity, be part of that process whether or not they are explicitly identified or recognized. A full discussion and defense of such a claim, and a full treatment of those analytical components, would obviously require a book. One of us has written such a book—and immodestly thinks that he has written it in a way that establishes the claims about the universal features of proof that are necessary for the present argument.[37] The short version of that lengthy argument, which is all that is needed for our present discussion of deference, runs as follows: Any process of decision or proof must run through at least four, and possibly five, steps in order to reach a conclusion. Those steps need not be consciously or expressly identified; indeed, much of the time they are implicit and unrecognized. But those steps—or at least four of them—must all be present in some form in every process of decision-making.

First, one must have some method for identifying what features of the world count for or against a particular conclusion. The world contains an infinite amount of information. No decision process can literally take everything into account. Accordingly, one needs a model of relevance, or admissibility, which tells one which parts of the world deserve attention or focus in any given context. This model of relevance or admissibility determines the content of the evidence set that will ultimately be the basis for the decision. All decisions are based on something, and the operative principles of relevance or admissibility determine of what that something consists. For analytical purposes, it makes no difference at all *what* those principles of relevance or admissibility are; they could be highly restrictive, as in the Anglo-American court system, or as wide open as the limits of cognition permit, as in systems of free proof. The point is only that some such principles, whether explicit or implicit, must exist in every context of decision-making, whether one realizes it or not.

Second, one must have some method for assessing *how much* the relevant, or admissible, evidence that one identifies counts for or against a conclusion. To say that evidence is relevant is not to say *how* relevant, or how significant, it is. The measure of significance need not be, and assuredly cannot be, cardinal, but there must be some operative process for ascertaining, even if only ordinally, the extent to which items of evidence, individually or collectively, point toward a particular conclusion. You need to know what to do with the evidence set once you have it. Again, these principles of significance must exist and be operative whether or not they are expressly recognized. And again, it makes no difference to this abstract analysis what those principles turn out to be.

Third, one must have a standard of proof that indicates *how much* evidence one must have in order to warrant a particular conclusion. Evidence sufficient to warrant a decision by a preponderance of the evidence may not be sufficient to warrant a decision beyond a reasonable doubt. To decide is necessarily to decide in accordance with some standard of proof, again whether or not one chooses to recognize or acknowledge it and regardless of what that standard of proof turns out to be in any given setting.

Fourth, one will sometimes, though not always, need a way to allocate the burden of proof in a decision process. One always starts a decision process from a specific baseline or default position, and it requires considerations of some kind to move one away from that anchor. The specification of the baseline is an allocation of a burden of proof. That allocation will be important in circumstances where not enough evidence comes forth to satisfy the applicable standard of proof for a conclusion contrary to the baseline. That might be often or it might be almost never, depending on the nature of the evidence and the standard of proof. If, for example, the standard of proof is "better than the available alternatives," the range of cases in which a default rule is necessary for a decision might be vanishingly small. If the standard of proof is "beyond a reasonable doubt," the default rule may hold and be decisive in a very large number of cases.

Finally, fifth, one needs some mechanism for determining when the evidence set for a decision is closed. At what point do you stop looking for more relevant and admissible evidence and start deciding? That point must come or there is no decision to analyze.

In a "normal" case of deference, such as deferring to a civil jury's factual findings, the prior decision functions for the reviewing body as relevant, or admissible, evidence of specified (and in this case very substantial) significance. The assignment of a default or baseline for judgment is not itself deference, except as an act of deference toward the authoritative judgment of whoever sets the default; it sets the baseline against which deference, along with other considerations of relevance and weight, operate. The standard of proof and the closing of the evidence set are also factors that set a baseline against which deference operates, though one can certainly imagine courts deferring to others on what the default, the standard of proof, or the principles of closure are in any given case. But as a general matter, when a doctrine of deference calls for giving a certain degree of weight or significance to another's decision, as when courts defer to jury verdicts, it obviously affects what we have described as the second step of the decision-making process, in which one assigns significance to matters within the evidence set. That is surely the step of the decision process that most clearly leaps to mind when one thinks about deference. It is the step most obviously affected by almost all of the doctrines identified by US courts as deference.

There is at least one large exception. *Skidmore* deference, in its mildest form in which a court must at least take into account an agency's interpretation of a statute but need not necessarily do more than that, is instead a doctrine about the content of the relevant evidence set. In the context of *Skidmore*, "[a] court applying deference must at least consider whether to give weight to the agency's point of view, even if it is not required to give such weight. Deference to an administrative interpretation is triggered by the interpretation's 'pedigree'— i.e., the fact that an agency holds the view."[38] In other words, *Skidmore* dictates that the agency's view is among the relevant pieces of evidence that a court must consider when interpreting a statute. By issuing an interpretation of a statute, the agency effectively compels the court to adjust what might otherwise be the court's own independent judgment about what materials bear on the decision before it. Without the agency decision, the evidence set for the court would be X; with the agency decision thrown into the mix by *Skidmore,* the evidence set becomes $X + N$—or perhaps $(X-Y) + N$ if inclusion of the agency decision substitutes for something that would otherwise be part of the evidence set, or even $(X + Y) + N$ if including the agency decision induces the court to add even more considerations to the evidence set. Because that threshold determination of the content of the relevant evidence set is an indispensable part of any decision process, it is meaningful to speak of "mere" consideration as a species of deference—and indeed of mandatory deference from the standpoint of lower courts if they must take the Supreme Court's pronouncement of the significance of *Skidmore* as authoritative— even if that consideration does not ultimately lead to some measure of significance for the other's decision at the significance-assigning phase of the decision-making process. This is why (and how) Professor Daly is right to observe that "[t]o some extent, by virtue of the reviewing court's obligation to take relevant matters into account, weight must be accorded to the decision."[39] The "weight" does not necessarily take place at the stage of determining how much each piece of evidence counts toward a conclusion, as one normally thinks of deference operating, but there is definitely "weight" given to the prior decision in helping fix the relevant evidence set. That is just as vital a part of the decision process as is the consideration of how much the available evidence should count. Indeed, it might be even more important; if evidence never reaches the decision-maker as part of the evidence set, no question ever arises about how to value it.

One can see the cash value of this consequence of *Skidmore* deference by contrasting it with judicial treatment of other expressions of views that do not have the same legal effect on the evidence set as do agency interpretations of statutes. Agencies that do not administer statutes, or that for some other reason are not entitled to *Chevron* deference and thus must rely on *Skidmore* to get their views considered, are not the only entities that offer interpretations of statutes for courts to consider. The parties to the case offer their views in briefs and arguments. In an adversarial system, those views are entitled to a kind of deference equivalent to *Skidmore*: a court does not have to give those views any particular significance if the court does not find those views persuasive, but the court does at least have to consider them. Indeed, it is possible to argue (as one of us has argued) that in an adversarial system, courts should properly limit themselves *only* to the arguments advanced by the parties, though practice in the United States is not wholly consistent with this position.[40] We have no trouble saying that courts in an adversarial system must, in that sense, defer to some extent to the parties, as the parties play a crucial (even if not wholly decisive) role in shaping the process of decision by dictating, in part, what goes into the evidence set considered by the court. Consider by contrast a non-adversarial system; in that setting, there may be no legal obligation even to consider what parties affected by a judgment might think about the law. Indeed, in a theoretically pure non-adversarial system, affected parties may not even be aware of the existence of a legal proceeding affecting them until it is completed, so no occasion for discovering, much less considering, their views ever arises. Adversarial systems are designed, in other words, to require some measure of deference to affected parties through construction of the evidence set for decision.

Other participants in adversarial systems are treated quite differently. Non-parties, for example, sometimes file amicus briefs. Legal scholars sometimes write articles or books designed, in part, to provide material that will influence courts. Government agencies without a claim even to *Skidmore* deference may nonetheless opine on a matter. Courts have no legal obligation to consider these materials. One of us can testify, from experience as a law clerk, that many amicus briefs go unread by at least some of the relevant judicial actors, and the vast majority of scholarship suffers the same fate.[41] Courts *choose* which amicus briefs, books, and articles to consider, and therefore the existence of those sources does not, in and of itself, generate any deference. Courts may elect to defer to some of those sources once they are considered, but the court decides for itself whether and how to consider them. If *Skidmore* truly requires courts to consider agency views, *Skidmore* changes the legal landscape in an important way and thus deserves to be considered a doctrine of deference.

Accordingly, a doctrine that involves giving consideration to a particular kind of decision, simply because of the kind of decision that it is, is properly called a doctrine of deference, even if the significance ultimately afforded any particular decision so considered is zero. In order to conclude that deference is not at work, one must conclude that nothing describable as deference operates at any stage of the decision process, including the process of establishing the evidence set for decision. As Professors Tom Merrill and Kristin Hickman have written, "*Skidmore* is properly regarded as a deference doctrine because the court cannot ignore the agency interpretation—the court must assess that interpretation against multiple factors and determine what weight they should be given."[42] That is why we include, and continue to include, "consideration" of another decision along with "weight" (or significance) given to another decision in our basic definition of deference.

Professor Horwitz offers some further refinements of his definition of deference that provide a useful comparison with our own framework. Professor Horwitz distinguishes deference from *obedience*, which involves following "binding authority." "Deference," says Professor Horwitz, "implies some freedom to act,"[43] while "obedience implies that D1 follows D2's judgment because it has no choice but to do so."[44] As we have noted earlier, we share his intuition that there is something different about giving way to another because one is ordered to do so and giving way because one chooses to do so. But rather than exclude the former action from the definition of deference, we prefer to call it *mandatory deference*, as a subcategory of the wider idea of deference. As we have already argued, we think our account is more descriptive of the way that deference is employed by the US legal system, which describes at least some of what Professor Horwitz considers obedience as a form of deference. Professor Horwitz recognizes this, suggesting that the courts at times "are mislabeling as acts of deference what are actually acts of obedience"[45] as when the Supreme Court says, in the context of deferring to congressional judgments about the exclusion of women from the selective service system: "We of course do not abdicate our ultimate responsibility to decide the constitutional question, but simply recognize that the Constitution itself requires such deference to congressional choice."[46] Under our inductive methodology, we at least initially consider the practices of courts to be data points for our definition of deference rather than potential casualties of it, and we thus resist the idea that we, and the courts, "err in describing the courts as engaging in deference on occasions when they are actually engaging in acts of obedience."[47] We doubt whether much turns on whether one prefers our (and the courts') labeling or Professor Horwitz's on this point; nothing of great consequence that we can see follows if one takes our category of mandatory deference and calls it obedience instead.

Drawing on terminology employed by one of us at an earlier time,[48] Professor Horwitz classifies rationales for deference as either *legal* or *epistemic*. Legal deference corresponds to what we call in this book a form of legitimation deference: One defers because certain actors, such as juries, merit deference simply because of who they are and what role they play in the legal order.[49] Epistemic deference, which is just another term (and quite probably a better one grammatically, given the part of speech involved) for epistemological deference, is deference based on the likely contribution of the other actor to getting the right answer.[50] Since one of us originated this terminology of legal versus epistemic/epistemological deference, he is understandably reluctant to criticize it with much vigor. But, on reflection, the categories of legal (or legitimation) deference and epistemic (or epistemological) deference, while useful analytical tools, are incomplete. We have already added economic deference and signaling deference to the mix. There is nothing wrong with talking about legal and epistemic deference, provided that one does not treat them as the only subcategories of deference worth discussing. With that said, Professor Horwitz provides many illuminating illustrations of what we call legitimation deference and epistemological deference, and we commend his extended discussion of these rationales for deference to any interested readers. But we stand by the terminology that we have employed thus far.

Perhaps Professor Horwitz's most intriguing contribution to the study of deference is something that we did not fully appreciate until reading his work. There are two sides to every act of deference. There is the actor who is deferring and there is the actor to whom deference is given. Legal doctrines focus to near-total exclusion on the deferring actor and its responsibilities, and scholarship has tended to follow the same path. But that is an impoverished view of deference. Professor Fred Schauer raised this point in passing when considering, from a game-theoretic kind of perspective, how one should respond when one knows that one's decisions might be the object of deference:

> Consider, for example, the standpoint of one whose decision might be thought to be mistaken by someone else—call her Alice—and whose decision might nevertheless be the object of deference by someone else. Under such circumstances should Alice not reach the decision she thinks best

because she would not want to put another person—call him Zeke—in the position of having to defer to a decision that he, Zeke, thinks wrong? Should Alice therefore engage in anticipatory deference, deferring to a decision by Zeke that she thinks wrong and thus making what she thinks is the wrong decision in the first instance because she, Alice, wants to defer to Zeke's decision and thus not impose upon Zeke, the deferrer, the burden of reaching a decision he thinks mistaken? Or should Alice instead respect (defer to) Zeke's expected decision to defer by simply reaching what she believes to be the best decision?[51]

These are good questions, and they draw attention to the role of the deferee—the one to whom deference is given—in the legal order. Professor Horwitz develops this insight in considerable theoretical and doctrinal detail.[52] Someone who knows that their decision will be the object of deference has obligations, Professor Horwitz insists, to reach their decision with some measure of care, thoughtfulness, and procedural regularity in order to make the decision worthy of deference:

> Under an epistemically based rule of deference, a party that invokes deference should display a number of qualities. First and most obviously, to the extent that judicial deference to such an institution is based on its epistemic superiority, we should oblige such an institution to actually bring the weight of its expertise to bear on the problem before the court. Conversely, a party invoking its epistemic authority as a basis for judicial deference ought not invoke that authority on questions that are beyond the scope of its expertise.
>
> Second, we might expect a party that invokes deference to reason in good faith on those questions that will be the subject of the judicial act of deference. As [Fred] Schauer observes, to the extent that the obligations of the deferee partake of a moral character, the deferee "would not want to put another person . . . in the position of having to defer to a decision that he . . . thinks [is] wrong" by invoking deference without engaging in good-faith deliberation on the question at hand.
>
> Third, we might expect a deferee to reason thoughtfully toward its conclusions. A conclusion that is reached in haste, or carelessly, or without serious consideration of the complexity of the question, is hardly one that partakes of the quality of epistemic authority that is the basis for judicial deference.

Finally, we might expect a deferee to meet not just a set of substantive obligations when it invokes deference, but also to observe a minimum level of appropriate process in its deliberations. To the extent that it demands deference for its deliberations, those deliberations should be sufficiently structured and transparent to earn the trust of the deferring institution, and the deferee should take some pains to explain its reasons and its process in a way that provides a similar assurance that its conclusions are the result of a meaningful, full, and fair exercise of its expertise.[53]

These duties of deferees are especially important, one might even think, when one is dealing with legitimation deference rather than epistemological deference. With epistemological deference, the deferring institution can always take into account the strengths and weaknesses, and even the pathologies, of the decision under consideration. With legitimation deference, however, that is not part of the picture. One defers because of who the other decider is, not because of how they have decided. Juries get deference even if they do a bad job. Congress gets deference on its legislative fact-finding even if it is a lousy legislative fact-finding body. Would it be appropriate for those bodies receiving deference to revel in their status and take advantage of their opportunity to shape outcomes by foisting decisions on the deferring body that reflect something other than the best judgment of the deferee about the right answer after employing the deferee's best efforts to reach that right answer?

This is an especially poignant question in administrative law, where the deferees—the administrative agencies—are repeat players with a measure of legal sophistication. They know how the game is played, and they are ongoing participants in the game. An administrative agency charged with fact-finding knows that its findings will receive a substantial measure of deference from a reviewing court. Does that mean that the agency fulfills its duty by coming up with findings that have the minimum level of support necessary to survive review? Or does the agency have an obligation to find what it honestly thinks are the objectively correct facts, even if the agency has policy reasons for preferring different findings? Similarly, in a *Chevron* world, does an agency satisfy its obligations by coming up with an interpretation that will survive judicial review as reasonable, or does the agency have an obligation to do its best to interpret the statute correctly?

One of us has tried to answer those questions elsewhere:

Suppose, hypothetically, that an agency knows that its factual findings will be affirmed on review as long as they are supported by substantial evidence. Imagine that the agency then says, "We believe that the facts as presented to us support, by a preponderance of the evidence, a ruling in favor of A. But there is enough evidence in support of B to allow a ruling in favor of B to survive judicial review under the substantial evidence test. We have policy reasons for wanting B to win the case, so we will rule in favor of B, notwithstanding the weight of the evidence." This would constitute the height of arbitrary or capricious decision making. The agency's job is to make correct findings of fact, not to concoct rulings contrary to the evidence that would survive deferential judicial review. Indeed, if the agency does not make a good-faith effort to get the facts right, there is no justification for giving the agency's views deference on appeal (beyond the fact that the legislature may have commanded such sweeping deference without regard to whether any underlying rationale for deference is satisfied in a particular case). Deferential standards of review do not ask reviewing bodies to reach the right conclusion, but someone should be looking for the right answer somewhere in the chain of decision making. It would be outrageous for an agency to use the substantial evidence standard as a tool for initial fact-finding.

The same reasoning holds for questions of law. *Chevron* requires that reviewing courts give deference to an agency's construction of statutes administered by the agency (subject, of course, to the various "step zero" considerations that determine the applicability of *Chevron* under modern law). That means that reviewing courts are not looking to see whether agencies got the right answer but only whether they got a permissible answer. Could an agency take advantage of this deference and say, "In construing this statute, we are going to pick the interpretation that we like on policy grounds, even though we think that a different interpretation represents the best reading of the statute, because we can get away with it on judicial review"? Such reasoning would be a clear abuse of the deferential standard of review. Deferential review is premised on the initial decision maker's good-faith effort to get the right answer. If the decision maker does not try to get the right answer, there is no justification for judicial deference. It would be just as outrageous for an agency to use *Chevron* deference as a tool to protect its initial law findings as it would be for an agency to use the substantial evidence standard as a tool to protect its initial fact findings.[54]

At least one scholar agrees with this assessment in the context of statutory interpretation:

> A responsible agency . . . must reject interpretations that it concludes are interpretively suboptimal, notwithstanding that an ethical, law-abiding reviewing court would acquiesce in those interpretations. This follows directly from the concept of judicial deference itself. A deferential court, by abstaining from finally deciding what a statute means, assigns its law-declaration function to the agency. . . .
>
> When a court defers, therefore, the agency's duties parallel those of the judge in a case where no deference is offered. An agency obliged to say what the law is must do so to the best of its ability. Such an agency takes on what would have been the judicial duty to use available interpretive tools to reach the best account it can of what a statute means. An agency, like a judge, has no business assigning a second-best interpretation to a statute in order to achieve a preferred policy in the knowledge that, as a matter of institutional structure, it has the last word. That institutional structure, the assignment of interpretive finality to a particular decisionmaker, is justifiable only in light of the expectation that the final interpreter will interpret faithfully.[55]

Of course, it is one thing to say that something would be "outrageous." It is quite another thing to say that it would be illegal. In the case of a federal agency's failure to give its best efforts to find a right answer, however, there is a doctrinal basis for merging the two inquiries. Any federal agency action that is subject to the Administrative Procedure Act cannot be "arbitrary, capricious, an abuse of discretion, or otherwise not in accordance with law."[56] An agency that fails to perform as a deferee in accordance with the substantive and procedural standards set forth so well by Professor Horwitz would at least arguably (and one of us thinks clearly) be acting in an arbitrary or capricious fashion. A reviewing court would be entirely within its rights, and quite possibly entirely bound by duty, to reject such a decision even if the agency's decision appeared to satisfy the substance of the relevant deferential standard of substantive review. That is, a finding of fact that matches the record evidence sufficiently, even if only barely, to survive review under a "substantial evidence" test might nonetheless be unlawful if it was reached for reasons other than a best effort to find the facts as they really are. More dramatically, as a federal court put it in 2017, "[a]n agency interpretation [of a statute] would surely be 'arbitrary' or 'capricious' if it were picked out of a hat, or arrived at with no explanation, even if it might otherwise be deemed reasonable on some unstated ground."[57] A court rejecting an agency decision on these grounds *would not* be failing to defer. The court would still defer to the agency's substantive judgment, on the grounds of mandatory deference; courts defer to agency fact-finding because they are ordered to do so by the Administrative Procedure Act or organic statutes, and courts defer to agency legal interpretations when they are ordered to do so by the Supreme Court's adoption of the *Chevron* doctrine. That deference does not go away or have no force simply because the agency committed some other kind of error, such as failing to hold a necessary hearing or behaving in an arbitrary or capricious fashion, that results in rejection of the agency decision. Agency action can be overturned on any number of grounds: procedural, substantive, or decision-process oriented.[58] A failure to fulfill the proper obligations of a deferee falls into the latter category, and the authorization for courts to set aside that action as arbitrary or capricious is independent of the deference due the agency as a substantive fact-finder, law determiner, or policymaker. If one believes that a proper decision-making process must take into account the role of the agency as a potential deferee, then federal administrative law both permits and requires courts to enforce the proper duties of deferees as those duties are aptly described by Professor Horwitz.

Matters are more complicated when one deals with actors who are not subject to provisions for review, such as the arbitrary or capricious standard of the APA, which expressly authorize consideration of defects in the process by which decisions are reached as an independent ground for judicial review. Juries are at the other pole from agencies. Courts faced with jury verdicts do not examine how those verdicts were reached. Indeed, the rules of evidence are designed to prevent courts, or anyone else, from considering the process by which juries reach decisions in all but the most extreme cases. Federal Rule of Evidence 606(b) provides:

(1) *Prohibited Testimony or Other Evidence.* During an inquiry into the validity of a verdict or indictment, a juror may not testify about any statement made or incident that occurred during the jury's deliberations; the effect of anything on that juror's or another juror's vote; or any juror's mental processes concerning the verdict or indictment. The court may not receive a juror's affidavit or evidence of a juror's statement on these matters.

   (2) *Exceptions.* A juror may testify about whether:
      (A) extraneous prejudicial information was improperly brought to the
          jury's attention;
      (B) an outside influence was improperly brought to bear on any juror; or
      (C) a mistake was made in entering the verdict on the verdict form.

The law does not want to know how laws, sausages, or jury verdicts are made. That does not mean that jurors have no obligation to try to reach the right answer. They absolutely have such an obligation. It does mean that courts instructed to defer to jury verdicts cannot attempt an end run around that mandatory deference, as they can with federal agency decisions, by rejecting the process by which the jury decision was reached, unless that process involved a very specific kind of corruption of the jury process. Juries can decide cases using bad, and even irresponsible decision processes, but as far as deference doctrine is concerned, it is damnum absque injuria.

When the deferees are federal legislative or executive agents, the responsibilities of those bodies vis-à-vis courts, and vice versa, gets very complex. The Constitution does not contain an express "arbitrary or capricious" review clause for legislative or executive decisions, as the Administrative Procedure Act does for federal agency action. But it might well contain an implicit one. As we have explored at length in other work, the US Constitution is best seen as a kind of fiduciary instrument.[59] Government officials in such a system function as fiduciary agents for the principal, "We the People," and accordingly owe fiduciary duties to that principal. Those duties include a duty of care in the exercise of their functions.[60] It is not a stretch to think that part of that duty is the obligation to reach decisions with care, thoughtfulness, and procedural regularity when those decisions will be subject to deference by others. Indeed, this same set of constitutional norms might apply to administrative agencies as well; perhaps the Administrative Procedure Act merely makes clear in one context what the Constitution requires in all federal governmental contexts.[61]

Close attention to the obligations of deferees is far beyond the scope of this book, but it is a fruitful avenue for future inquiry, and we should all be grateful to Professor Horwitz for highlighting its importance. Certainly, a legal designer constructing a system of deference would be well advised to think very carefully about the obligations of deferees and how those obligations might be enforced. And US scholars who find persuasive the idea that the Constitution is a fiduciary instrument and government officials are fiduciary agents would be well advised to think carefully about what these fiduciary obligations might mean for deferees.

In sum, we learned a great deal from Professor Horwitz. But in the end, we do not think that we need to make any adjustments to our definition of and vocabulary for deference in light of his analysis. Instead, his profound insights about the role of deferees can be (and should be) added on to our, or anyone else's, account of deference.

We are not alone in finding Professor Horwitz's account enlightening. Israeli scholar Professor Yoav Dotan adopts Professor Horwitz's definition of deference,[62] but with some important modifications. As does Professor Horwitz, Professor Dotan distinguishes deference from obedience: "if D1 has no choice at all but to follow the decision of D2, one cannot talk about deference as defining the relationship between the parties."[63] Deference for Professor Dotan can never be absolute; deference "inherently assumes that the weight given to D2's judgment is not absolute, in the sense that it never denies at least some discretion, or some possibility, that D1 would decide, at the end of the day, not to defer."[64] As we have noted, we agree with the sentiment but think it best to distinguish mandatory deference from discretionary deference, at least in the context of US federal courts. Professor Dotan also signs onto the proposition that deference must make a difference, actually or potentially, in decisional outcomes in order to be deference.[65] Professor Dotan does not consider it an act of deference if the weight given to a prior decision is zero.[66] Again, we agree with the sentiment up to a point: We think that an activity counts as an act of deference if it changes the evidence set that would otherwise be used by a decision-maker, even if the ultimate decision does not change, and even if the weight given to the prior decision at the significance-assigning stage of the decision-making process ends up as zero. Subject to those small but important qualifications, we have little quarrel with Professor Dotan's definition of deference.

Professor Dotan contributes to the process of definition a distinction between two "modes" of deference: disagreement deference and avoidance deference. Disagreement deference involves giving weight to the views of others in some fashion when one would or might have reached a different conclusion on one's own by considering the same factors that drove the deferee's decision.[67] Avoidance deference involves a step in the decision-making process that avoids altogether the need to weigh factors by relying on the deferee's decision in lieu of consideration of those factors.[68] For disagreement deference to function, the deferring decision-maker must have some view about the correct answer to a problem but chooses to look past that view because of another's decision. For avoidance deference to function, the deferring decision-maker need not have a view about the underlying decision; it is enough that the deferee has made a decision.[69]

We have no objection to this distinction, but we do not think that it serves the descriptive function of our enterprise. We are not sure that Professor Dotan will be at all bothered by this conclusion; promoting our descriptive enterprise was not his objective.[70] With one possible exception, US federal courts do not describe what they do in this two-part fashion, and we are doubtful whether one can impose that structure on them analytically. For example, Professor Dotan's chief exemplar of disagreement deference is *Skidmore*, because, he claims, the "content-independent" reasons for deference—the fact that an agency decision is involved—operate on the same level as the "content-dependent" reasons—the substantive persuasiveness of the agency's decision.[71] We are not sure about that. As we have explained, courts must give agencies *Skidmore* deference *with respect to at least one aspect of the construction of the evidence set for decision*, without weighing that content-independent consideration against anything else. Nor is it clear that a distinction between disagreement and avoidance deference explains *Chevron*. If *Chevron* involves two steps, the first step is non-deferential: The court must ascertain whether there is a "clear" meaning to the statute, and that task is performed without giving weight to the agency's views. If there is a second step, it clearly involves what Professor Dotan calls avoidance deference, because the fact that an agency decision is involved by itself establishes a "threshold"[72] of deference; the court is asking only whether the agency decision is reasonable. We have no objection to this form of analysis, but we are not sure how much it explains. If *Chevron* is considered a one-step approach, in which the court determines whether the agency interpretation is reasonable all things considered, taking into account that an interpretation inconsistent with a clear statutory meaning is per se unreasonable, that would also seem to be an instance of avoidance deference, because it sets a threshold for affirmance based on the identity of the deferee. Perhaps there is a way in which this framework explains why *Chevron* must be viewed as a two-step rather than a one-step inquiry, but we are not seeing it.

To be clear, we are not claiming that Professor Dotan's framework has no analytical value. To the contrary, it focuses attention on some salient features of deference by making one examine precisely what kind of work is being done by content-dependent and content-independent aspects of the deferring decision-maker's reasoning process. That is a potentially valuable analytical tool. We simply doubt whether the framework maps well onto a descriptive account of US federal court practice.

## 3. Jonathan Masur and Lisa Ouellette

Many cases are decided under deferential standards of review. Appellate courts often affirm jury verdicts, lower court decisions, or agency decisions even when the appellate courts believe, all things considered, that the prior decision was most likely wrong. When deference operates, as it normally does, at the significance-assigning stage of the decision-making process, this is precisely the result that one would expect.

If an appellate decision finds that another decision is not "clearly erroneous" or "unreasonable," or that a constitutional right was not "clearly established" in a case involving claims of qualified immunity in tort suits against government officials, that is very different from the appellate court concluding that the other decision was "correct" or that a claimed constitutional right does not exist. Sometimes deference leads to an ultimate judgment of correctness, as when one gives epistemological deference to the view of another as part of the determination of the right answer to a problem. But at other times deference is not designed to yield a "correct" answer from the standpoint of the deferring body. On many occasions, the whole point of deference is to stop the deferring body from making its own determination of correctness and to resolve a case with a conclusion far weaker than that one side is "right" and the other is "wrong." Sometimes, all it takes to resolve a case is to find that one side's position is not unreasonable.

All of this is very basic. But what happens if a subsequent court takes a prior decision finding, let us say, no "clearly established" constitutional right and treats that prior decision as a precedent for the absence of a constitutional right altogether. That would clearly be a mistake; it would treat a decision decided under a specific deference regime as though it was decided de novo (or perhaps under a different deference regime).

In an important study, Professors Jonathan Masur and Lisa Ouellette examine and document this phenomenon of what they aptly term "deference mistakes."[73] A deference mistake involves reliance "on precedent without fully accounting for the legal and factual deference regime under which that precedent was decided, thereby stripping the holding from its legal context."[74] We do not here take on the task of analyzing deference mistakes; we broadly agree with Professors Masur and Ouellette that the problem is serious and worth careful attention, and we commend them for raising and studying it. We address their work here only because they include as part of their analysis a definition of deference, which we add to our database of alternative accounts.

Our discussion can be brief, because we agree entirely with their definition (and, we suspect if we may be so presumptuous, they likely with ours). They define deference "broadly to refer to anything that causes a decisionmaker to consider an issue differently from how it would in the first instance, including different standards of review, standards of evidence, or legal presumptions."[75] Alternatively, they see it "to include any situation in which a second decisionmaker is influenced by the judgment of some initial decisionmaker rather than examining an issue entirely de novo."[76] They specifically note that their definition is broader than Professor Horwitz's definition because they include, as Professor Horwitz does not, a complete surrender of judgment within the conceptual scope of deference. The only possible difference that we can see between our definition and theirs comes at the opposite pole: what does it take to "cause[] a decisionmaker to consider an issue differently"? As long as they recognize that consideration of a decision is itself a form of difference or influence, because it changes the evidence set employed by the decision-maker, we are wholly in agreement with this definition because of its descriptive breadth. Indeed, we are encouraged that we are not alone in thinking that a baseline definition of deference can sweep this broadly, without qualifying to whom deference is owed, why it is given, or how strong it is.

## 4. Daniel Solove

It is an interesting commentary on the law's treatment of deference that the first attempt at a comprehensive account of the concept in modern legal scholarship of which we are aware dates from as recently as 1999—and was written by someone who was not at that time a legal academic. Now-professor, then-mere-law-clerk, Daniel J. Solove noted and lamented the fact (and we agree with him that it was a fact) that "while deference has been examined in various contexts, it has never been analyzed in depth as a fundamental issue for constitutional jurisprudence."[77] He worried that a too-broad and too-uncritical use of judicial deference, especially with regard to factual determinations in constitutional cases, could undermine some of the key foundations of judicial review; deference is practiced, he claimed, "with an alarming frequency in cases involving fundamental constitutional rights"[78] and "[t]he practice of deference presents severe problems for maintaining judicial review as an institution that furthers the values of liberalism."[79] His detailed account of deference in US constitutional law remains one of the cornerstone works in the field. His recommended solution "is not to repudiate the deference principle, but to abandon the practice of deference currently associated with the principle and to transform judicial review so that it more adequately deals with facts."[80]

Because Professor Solove was concerned exclusively with deference as it is applied by courts in cases involving fundamental constitutional rights,[81] our project is so different in scope and orientation that comparisons may be unwise. But since Professor Solove's discussion is among the few sustained discussions of deference as a concept in US legal scholarship, we will, with some modest hesitation, give it a go.

Professor Solove defines deference as "the practice of accepting, without much questioning or skepticism, the factual and empirical judgments made by the decisionmaker under review."[82] Alternatively, he sets forth " 'the deference principle'—that judges should not second-guess the decisionmaker under review or impose their own judgments about the wisdom of a policy."[83] He sharply distinguishes deference from non-justiciability or the complete absence of scrutiny: "The deference principle is not carried out by withdrawing certain cases from the scope of judicial review. Deference is not nonjusticiability; unlike political questions, when courts invoke the deference principle, they purport to engage in judicial review."[84] Deference, so defined, has its sharpest bite in "the way courts evaluate the factual and empirical evidence underlying the law or policy at issue. Courts accept uncritically the factual and empirical evidence of the government supporting its laws and policies in a profound number of cases where the deference principle is invoked."[85]

This is actually a pretty fair description of the class of cases discussed by Professor Solove. Those cases are constitutional challenges to legislation or executive action, often in highly charged settings involving the military or prison life. Many of those cases involve findings of legislative facts, to which Congress gets enormous deference when they are found by the legislature and to which executive officials often—not always, but often—get enormous deference as well based on some combination of legitimation, epistemological, and economic deference. But precisely because the context is so limited, it does not make sense to extend Professor Solove's definition to a general definition of deference. That was not his project, and we have no reason to think that he would consider that kind of extension even plausible. We believe, however, that our own framework and vocabulary would have provided useful analytical tools to Professor Solove had they been available to him.

One important question concerning the kind of deference discussed by Professor Solove is whether it was mandatory deference or discretionary deference. For a reform project as ambitious as the one put forward by Professor Solove, which suggests "that the judiciary reform itself—beginning at the level of individual judges—to improve its ability to evaluate empirical evidence,"[86] it might be helpful to know how much of the deference to which he objects is prescribed by positive law and how much is discretionary with the judiciary. That distinction obviously affects which institutions might be capable of altering the existing scheme if that scheme is inadequate. The various rationales that Professor Solove identified as grounding deference in different cases might also helpfully be sorted into categories of legitimation, epistemological, and economic deference. If one is trying to critique deference doctrines, it helps to be able to identify with some precision the kinds of reasons that are and can be advanced in support of it. Those reasons might have different force in different contexts. For example, to what extent is deference to prison administrators on decisions that affect constitutional rights (for example, prison rules that infringe on religious practices or free speech rights of prisoners[87]) based on concerns about who is the most legitimate decision-maker, who is in the best position accurately to assess the consequences of different regulatory regimes, and how costly it will be for the courts to involve themselves in those decisions across a potentially vast range of cases? (It seems unlikely that signaling deference plays much of a role in this context, but we could be mistaken about that.) The strength of the different reasons might vary with the context. Epistemological arguments might be very weak in some cases and strong in others, and in the cases where the epistemological arguments are weak, arguments from legitimation or cost might be strong. We have no judgment at all about how this framework applies in any specific case. But as we read Professor Solove's analysis, we think that our framework is a useful way to organize his arguments. And organizing arguments is a good first step toward evaluating them.

## 5. Aileen Kavanagh

Although our project revolves around practices in US courts, we began this chapter by discussing a Canadian legal theorist (Paul Daley), who in turn was discussing an Irish legal scholar (Brian Foley). This is unsurprising for two reasons. First, while the particular formulations and applications of deference doctrines will surely differ, perhaps dramatically, across jurisdictions, the phenomena that give rise to the concept of deference are universal. Questions about deference arise whenever there is a layered decision-making process and each person in the process must decide whether and how to take into account other decisions (either after those other decisions are made or prospectively in anticipation of those other decisions). Since every legal system is layered, and often very intricately layered, it is not too much to say that anyone thinking about anything in a legal system must at least consider the role of deference in that system. Indeed, that is why we have found it so surprising that deference has not generally been a subject of systematic study. Second, in our anecdotal experience, scholars (and judges) in common law countries other than the United States have been more attentive to the need for conceptual study of deference than have their American counterparts. In searching for discussions of deference as a concept, we consistently come across work from Australia, Canada, Ireland, New Zealand, and the United Kingdom that is, on the whole, more voluminous and, if we may be so bold, more sophisticated than what we see in US scholarship. While we have had to abandon in this book our original project of examining the role of deference across varied legal systems worldwide, we think that exploring the insights of, at the very least, common law scholars and judges outside the United States is a potentially fruitful source of knowledge about the theory and practice of deference.

We focus that exploration on Professor Aileen Kavanagh, who by the time this book reaches print will likely hold the Chair in Constitutional Governance at Trinity College Dublin, Ireland. (As these words are written in November 2018, she is a professor at Oxford.) Professor Kavanagh has written extensively about deference, principally in the context of constitutional adjudication. In a book chapter published in 2008, entitled *Deference or Defiance?: The Limits of the Judicial Role in Constitutional Adjudication*,[88] she set forth a detailed alternative account of deference. She revised and extended that analysis in a subsequent book on *Constitutional Review Under the UK Human Rights Act*.[89] We accordingly engage with her account at some length.

Although Professor Kavanagh is focused on "judicial deference to the elected branches of government in the course of constitutional adjudication" rather than other contexts in which "judges defer to precedent or the factual findings of lower courts or the decisions of specialist tribunals, etc.,"[90] in her 2008 book chapter, she provides a definition of deference that is quite general and that potentially applies in both legal and non-legal settings: "deference is a matter of assigning weight to the judgment of another, either where it is at variance with one's own assessment, or where one is uncertain of what the correct assessment should be. . . . So, if A defers to B's judgment, he assigns more weight to it than he would otherwise judge it to possess on his own determination of what the balance of reasons requires."[91]

If this was the end of the matter, we would have only a modest quibble with this definition. Because we think that consideration of another's view, whether or not it changes the outcome of the decision process, is a form of deference, we would not limit deference only to circumstances where the deferring actor disagrees with the other decision or is not confident of the deferrer's own answer. Professor Kavanagh adds that "if A's assessment of the issue leads to the same conclusion as B, A does not defer to the latter's judgment by agreeing with it."[92] For reasons that we have already given at length, we do not agree with that limitation on the reach of deference. As a descriptive matter, it would not include the full scope of *Skidmore* deference within the concept, and as an analytical matter, mere consideration of another's views has a cognizable effect on the decision process even if it does not alter the outcome. Deference as consideration allows the deferee to determine, to some extent, the evidence set for the ultimate judgment. Indeed, as we shall shortly see, we are not absolutely certain that Professor Kavanagh will stick to her own limitation in all settings. Otherwise, Professor Kavanagh's definition seems largely in accord with our own. It does not purport to limit deference to any specific amount or magnitude of weight. "It could range from treating B's judgment as a persuasive reason (of various strengths) to treating it as a conclusive reason for supporting the outcome favoured by B."[93] Thus, "absolute or complete deference"[94] is still deference. We agree. The definition as presented does not limit deference to any particular reasons or rationales for giving weight. We agree with that as well.

That is not, however, the end of the matter. In her 2009 book, Professor Kavanagh provides a somewhat different definition of deference: "*judicial deference occurs when judges assign varying degrees of weight to the judgment of the elected branches, out of respect for their superior competence, expertise and/or democratic legitimacy.*"[95] This definition adds a finite list of rationales for deference. While the list is expansive, including all aspects of what we would call legitimation deference and epistemological deference, it is too limited as a general definition because it does not contemplate economic deference or signaling deference. As we have said repeatedly, we do not think it is wise to build these kinds of limitations into a basic definition of deference. Even as a description solely of the case law in the United Kingdom applying human rights provisions, we do not think that this limited definition is accurate. Indeed, as we shall see, Professor Kavanagh later finds rationales for deference that do not fit her own definition. Accordingly, we think that the list of reasons should be excised from the definition and made the subject of separate analysis.

Professor Kavanagh's book repeats and elaborates upon her earlier claim that deference conceptually requires either disagreement or uncertainty:

> When we agree with someone on a particular issue, we do not "defer" to them. Rather, we simply assess the pros and cons of the issue ourselves, and come to an independent conclusion which matches the other person's conclusion. We only *defer* to the judgment of another when we are uncertain about what the right conclusion should be, or alternatively where we disagree with them, but nonetheless consider it appropriate to attach weight to their judgment.[96]

Again, we disagree that the concept of deference necessarily requires either uncertainty or disagreement. Deference requires consideration. To be sure, the consideration must be genuine; the other's decision must actually be part of the evidence set for the deferring decision-maker. In that sense, perhaps some small measure of uncertainty is necessary (if one is absolutely and unshakably certain about an answer, there is no point in wasting cognitive energy looking at more evidence, including someone else's view). But we think that Professor Kavanagh has a stronger notion of uncertainty in mind, and we do not think that such a notion should be built into a basic definition of deference.

In her book, Professor Kavanagh also suggests that what we have called mandatory deference is not really deference at all; the only activity that can be called deference is discretionary deference:

> Deference is a doctrine of judicial self-restraint based on concerns about the appropriate roles of the different branches of government. The question

whether judges should defer to the legislature or Executive is not about the legal powers which judges possess. Rather, it concerns the appropriateness of judges *not* exercising those powers, or at least being restrained in exercising them. . . . There is, after all, no *legal* bar on judges making decisions on national security or in cases which have resource implications for government.[97]

We do not want to make too much of this passage. We do not see it as setting out a general definition of deference that categorically rules out mandatory deference as a proper use of language. Instead, we see this as a description of the narrow class of cases on which Professor Kavanagh is focused: courts in the United Kingdom reviewing legislative or executive action that affects fundamental human rights. In that context, her account is entirely correct; there is no authoritative command in positive law dictating that courts defer in those circumstances. That is why she, unlike Brian Foley, distinguishes deference from non-justiciability: "Whilst the doctrines of deference and non-justiciability are both motivated by concerns about the limited institutional expertise and legitimacy of the courts, deference differs from non-justiciability in that it does not remove an issue or subject-matter from the court's supervision altogether."[98] And again: "deference is not a matter of the legal limits on jurisdiction, but rather a matter of judicial restraint."[99] In the contexts in which she is writing, we assume that those observations are accurate descriptions of legal practice. But we do not see them as generalizable to a wider context, and we therefore continue to describe mandatory deference as a kind of deference.

Returning to the rationales for deference, we are not sure that Professor Kavanagh would disagree with us that those rationales do not necessarily limit the conceptual reach of deference and therefore do not belong in a basic definition of the term, but instead should be reflected in subcategories that flesh out the ways in which deference might be employed. Indeed, the bulk of Professor Kavanagh's analysis develops a detailed framework for exploring subcategories of deference, which could easily be built out from the basic definition that she set down in 2008 (or from her 2009 definition without the final qualifying phrase involving reasons for deference). There is much to be learned from that framework, to which we now turn.

Our own framework, recall, distinguishes mandatory from discretionary deference and then identifies subcategories of reasons for deference, including (but not limited to) legitimating reasons, epistemological reasons, economic reasons, and signaling reasons. Professor Kavanagh covers much of the same ground—which we find heartening, as it makes it more likely that we have generated a framework that someone else will find useful—but with some important twists.

As do we, Professor Kavanagh catalogues some of the reasons why courts might engage in deference. She suggests "that the primary reason for deferring to the judgment of another is when that person's judgment is worthy of respect."[100] Read broadly, this could refer to what we have termed legitimation deference (the other's decision is worthy of respect because of the other's institutional role or status), epistemological deference (the other's decision is worthy of respect because it is likely to be good evidence of the right answer), or signaling deference (the other's decision is worthy of respect because it is important to communicate that respect to them). Professor Kavanagh means to include all three of these rationales. The main source of respect, she maintains, is epistemological: "A's judgment will be worthy of respect from B if A possesses some qualities superior to those possessed by B, that is, if A has some skill, expertise, or knowledge that B does not possess, or at least not to the same degree."[101] But while epistemological deference may be the primary motivating force behind much deference, "it is not the only rationale."[102] As we described in the previous chapter, she identifies what we term "signaling deference" as a possible and prominent rationale for deference. Deference "can be a way of showing respect to another whose relationship one values."[103] Respect thus encompasses both respect of the other's decision-making qualities (epistemological deference) and respect in terms of the relationship between the deferring actor and the deferee (signaling deference).

In the context of relationships between courts and other governmental actors such as legislatures or executives, deference as respect counsels in favor of "interinstitutional comity—the requirement of mutual respect between the branches of government."[104] This kind of deference starts to sound very much like legitimation deference: courts sometimes defer to legislatures and executives because those other bodies are the more appropriate decision-makers in certain cases. And, indeed, Professor Kavanagh expressly identifies "competence, expertise, and constitutional legitimacy"[105] as reasons for courts to defer at times to legislatures. That trilogy of reasons shows up, with only minor changes in wording, in her 2009 definition of deference as giving weight to other bodies "*out of respect for their superior competence, expertise and/or democratic legitimacy.*" Legislatures and executives will sometimes merit deference because they have "more legitimacy to assess the particular issue."[106]

This idea of legitimation deference lies behind Professor Kavanagh's account of the relationship between deference and interpretation. She sees legal interpretation as involving two distinct enterprises. First there is the *substantive evaluation*, which "refers to an evaluation of the merits of interpreting a particular constitutional (or legislative) provision in one way or another."[107] Second comes the *institutional evaluation*, which "engages judges' views about the extent and limits of their own role (including the limits of interpretation) and the implications they have for the correct judicial decision in the circumstances of the particular case."[108] Deference, for Professor Kavanagh, "is part of the institutional evaluation since it concerns the desirability of the judiciary interfering with a legislative or executive decision based on concerns about the limits of their institutional role in the constitutional framework."[109] This is a very important set of observations, but only some of them, in our judgment, are right.

By drawing a distinction between substantive and institutional concerns, we think that Professor Kavanagh is really describing the difference between *interpretation* and *adjudication* as legal activities. One of us has spent much of his professional life trying to articulate this distinction.[110] Interpretation is a positive or descriptive enterprise. It involves the ascertainment of the meaning of a text (or of any other potential source of meaning, but in law we are ordinarily dealing with texts as objects of interpretation). It is theoretically possible that a text's meaning could depend on some underlying normative theory, if the terms of the text can best be understood in that fashion, but even then it is a positive question whether any particular text maps onto the moral theory that gives it meaning. Adjudication, on the other hand, is necessarily normative. It involves disposition of real-life disputes, in which the outcome calls into play coercive enforcement mechanisms. Adjudication is all about what certain people ought to do. It is possible that adjudicative outcomes will turn on interpretative conclusions, but that is a decidedly contingent matter. It depends on whether the normative activity of adjudication in any particular instance chooses to make the positive communicative meaning of a text relevant to the normative activity. That might happen, and it might not happen. As one of us has said while discussing original meaning as a method for interpreting the US Constitution:

Originalism can be a theory of interpretation, a theory of adjudication, or both. That is, originalism can be either a theory of ascertaining the meaning of a document—for example, the United States Constitution—or a theory of decision making in cases that at least nominally invoke that document. The relationship between the two kinds of originalism is contingent. One could perfectly well believe that originalism is the interpretatively correct way to understand the United States Constitution, but doubt whether decision makers (such as courts) should make real-world decisions based on that understanding. Similarly, one might believe that originalism is inferior to some other methodology as a tool for ascertaining constitutional meaning, but believe, for institutional and normative reasons, that it is the best tool for resolving real-world disputes in which the Constitution is invoked. And, of course, one might believe that originalism is both a sound interpretative methodology and an appropriate decision making tool-albeit for very different reasons.[111]

In sum, "[i]t is one thing to say that X is the right way to *interpret* the Constitution and another thing altogether to say that X is the right way to *apply* the Constitution. The former statement is a proposition in the domain of interpretative theory, while the latter is a proposition in the domain of moral or political theory, as it prescribes a normative course of action for real-world actors threatening the real-world exercise of the government's coercive power."[112] This is a difference that makes a difference. The kinds of considerations and evidence that go into the ascertainment of communicative meaning might or might not be the kinds of considerations and evidence that determine proper adjudicative outcomes. That depends on the content of the normative theory that drives adjudication. For many people, textual meaning and adjudicative outcomes are closely, and even necessarily, linked, but for others that is not so. As a theoretical matter, there is a clear line between interpreting a text and treating the interpretation of a text as an authoritative guide to action. In principle, the ascertainment of a text whose meaning has real-world implications for at least some people should be no different from the ascertainment of a text (for example, the Rhode Island Charter of 1663) that has no discernible contemporary normative significance.

We say nothing here about whether there is any objectively correct view of the relationship between interpretation and adjudication. It is enough for our purposes that there is a distinction between those activities, and that distinction tracks nicely the similar distinction drawn by Professor Kavanagh. Her notion of substantive evaluation corresponds to our conception of interpretation as the ascertainment of meaning: one determines which interpretation of the relevant text is correct by the lights of whatever interpretative theory one brings to bear. Her notion of institutional evaluation is an accounting of the judicial role, which pertains to the activity of adjudication. Because judges are deciding real-world cases, and doing so within a structure of other real-world institutions exercising life-and-death power over people, it is an open question how, if at all, the conclusions of substantive evaluation (interpretative theory, in our lingo) ought to bear on that adjudicative activity. Professor Kavanagh's distinction is not precisely congruent with ours, because ours is more general and not tied to a specific context of constitutional litigation, but it gets at the same idea.

The distinction, whether framed as interpretation versus adjudication or as substantive evaluation versus institutional evaluation, potentially matters a great deal for a study of deference. According to Professor Kavanagh, "the doctrine of deference is, indeed, a doctrine of constitutional interpretation, but it is not part of the (central) substantive evaluation. Rather, it features in the institutional evaluation that typically accompanies it."[113] Put otherwise, she maintains that deference is not relevant to the positive task of ascertainment of meaning but instead is relevant only (and only potentially) to the normative task of adjudication. We do not agree. Certain kinds of deference, such as legitimation deference and signaling deference, certainly play no role that we can see in the correct ascertainment of textual meaning. But epistemological deference and economic deference might play a fairly major role, especially if the two forms of deference work together. If some other actor is well situated to get the right answer, it might be the optimum interpretative strategy, as a positive matter, to yield to their judgment. That is especially true because interpretation in all real-world settings, whether involving adjudication or ivory-tower speculation, takes place in real time under a scarcity of resources. No one has an infinite amount of time and an infinite amount of resources to devote to any specific problem of interpretation. It is quite possible that the best answer that one is likely to reach, given those constraints, is an answer reached by someone else. That will not always be so, of course, but it might well be so in a non-trivial number of instances. Certainly that is enough to foreclose any categorical judgments about the irrelevance of deference to the interpretative, or substantive, enterprise. (Its relevance to a normative, or institutional, enterprise, is obviously a normative question and is therefore contingent upon whatever the underlying normative theory prescribes.)

Accordingly, we think Professor Kavanagh is on solid ground in trying to identify the quite different activities of interpretation and adjudication and to explore how deference might differently apply in those settings. But the relevance *vel non* of deference to those activities is not as simple as she makes it sound. Deference can be as relevant to interpretation as it to adjudication. Indeed, one can even imagine, without too much effort, an adjudicative theory in which deference would be highly relevant to interpretation and barely relevant, if relevant at all, to adjudication.

While Professor Kavanagh orients her definition of deference, or at least the 2009 version of the definition, around competence, expertise, and legitimacy, she actually introduces an important possible rationale for deference that falls into none of these categories, and which also does not fall directly within any of our four categories of legitimation deference, epistemological deference, economic deference, and signaling deference. She lumps these reasons together under the label "prudential reasons."[114] Prudential reasons for deference involve such considerations as "whether a particular judicial decision would produce a backlash in society, whether society is ready for the legal change, whether it might be counterproductive to introduce it at this particular time or whether the legislature or government would then move to curtail the powers of the courts as a result."[115] Some of these reasons, to be sure, can be slotted in categories such as legitimation deference or signaling deference, and in principle everything and anything can be slotted into a sufficiently broad notion of economic deference, but at least some concerns of this kind have a very different feel. Deferring because one is afraid of the consequences of an independent decision does not fit neatly into any of our categories, but it would be foolish to imagine that no such rationale for deference is ever operative. Indeed, whole theories of constitutional jurisprudence have been constructed around such a notion.[116]

On reflection, we think there is room in the catalogue for a category of "prudential deference," though, as we will explain in more detail in the next chapter, we might prefer to call it "strategic" deference. The term "prudential" potentially covers a great deal of ground, and Professor Kavanaugh has in mind a quite specific exercise of prudence. We thus used the terms "prudential deference," "strategic deference," and "prudential/strategic deference" interchangeably to mean deference based on the perceived institutional consequences to the decision-maker of a failure to defer. Often these reasons will be combined with signaling reasons; in order to obtain or avoid certain consequences, the deferring decision-maker must often make known to other parties the fact of deference. Still, there seems something distinctive about the strategic use of deference. We make no claim that such deference is justified in any particular circumstance. As Professor Kavanagh observes, "many will find the prospect of judicial reliance on prudential reasons deeply objectionable,"[117] though she herself is not among the many.[118] But if our project is truly inductive, we must acknowledge that prudential, or strategic, concerns form a family of reasons that need to be recognized, and we therefore add the category to our list of observable rationales for deference.

One final terminological distinction introduced by Professor Kavanagh bears mention. After noting—correctly—that deference is often a sliding scale with varying degrees of weight assigned to the deferee's decision,[119] she distinguishes between "minimal and substantial deference."[120] "Minimal deference is the judicial attribution of some presumptive weight to the decision taken by the elected body, but it is not a very strong presumption."[121] Substantial deference, which presumably involves a much greater weight being assigned to the other decision, "is only warranted when the courts judge themselves to suffer from particular institutional shortcomings with regard to the issue at hand."[122]

Although this distinction is designed for the specific context of judicial review of legislation for constitutionality, it has potentially broader applications. It certainly reminds US readers of the tiers of scrutiny employed in American constitutional law: rational basis review sounds much like substantial deference, while intermediate and strict scrutiny seem like variations on minimal deference. It also reminds us that there is a very large gap in our treatment of deference in this book. We have said little or nothing about how one goes about ascertaining the weight of deference in any given case (at least cases that are not clearly on the poles of no deference or complete abstention) and how one would distinguish among degrees of deference if it was important to do so. We continue to resist the invitation to say very much about this topic, but we will offer two observations.

First, while a distinction between minimal and substantial deference might well be an adequate framework for describing and explaining constitutional review in the United Kingdom, we doubt whether it provides much of a framework for describing or explaining a broad range of cases in which deference is employed. For our project, then, anything that tried to specify deferential weight would have to be something far more calibrated than a distinction between minimal and substantial deference. We don't see the tiers of scrutiny in US constitutional law faring much better. The simple fact is that US law, at least, presents such a wide range of deference doctrines that it is very unlikely that a simple scale will offer much guidance. From de novo review to strict scrutiny to *Skidmore* deference to hard-look review to clearly erroneous review to *Chevron* deference to intermediate scrutiny to substantial evidence review to review of jury verdicts to rational basis review to preclusion of review, the continuum of deference does not sort itself neatly into fixed points on a curve.[123]

Second, we doubt whether deference, except at extreme poles, is best described as fixed points on a curve or as "degrees" in any fashion that suggests measurability. To the contrary, deference is not a point on a graph; it is an *attitude* toward a prior decision. Degrees of deference represent, for lack of a better phrase, a certain generosity of spirit toward another's decision. That is not something easily analyzed. We suspect that the best that anyone will ever be able to do in trying to pin down degrees of deference is to retreat to Justice Frankfurter's reference to deference as a "mood."[124] That is how we do it when teaching administrative law to students, and we are not prepared to propose anything more rigorous here.

Thus, we think that Professor Kavanagh has usefully reminded us of the need to distinguish interpretation from adjudication and to consider the possibly quite different applications of deference to those two activities. She has correctly pointed out that prudential/strategic deference is a category that must be acknowledged, so that our account of reasons for deference must be broadened to include it. But apart from that, we do not think that we need to alter our definition of deference or our analytical framework in any other fashion at this point.

\* \* \*

After considering all of these alternative accounts of deference, we maintain our definition and our framework mostly intact. We think it is important to focus (as Professor Horwitz urges) on the roles and responsibilities of deferees, it is important to consider (as Professor Kavanagh urges) the distinction between interpretation and adjudication when evaluating claims for deference, we need to add the category of prudential/strategic deference to our list of other rationale-based forms of deference, and we need to remind ourselves that speaking of deference as a sliding scale of weights opens up questions for which we have no good answers. But we continue to believe that our definition of deference as "the action by a legal actor of giving some measure of consideration or weight to the decision of another actor in exercising the deferring actor's function" is the most descriptive definition of US legal practice.

Furthermore, this comparison with other attempts to define deference gives us some confidence that our account of deference has utility as more than just a description of practices. That is, perhaps the framework that we think is implicit in US legal practice actually functions as a useful tool for wider contexts.

The best way to test that hypothesis is to try it. Accordingly, in the next chapter, we explore how our inductively derived definition of deference, and the inductively derived framework for thinking about deference that accompanies it, applies to contexts other than US federal court practices that those courts expressly identify as instances of deference.

## Notes

1. PAUL DALY, A THEORY OF DEFERENCE IN ADMINISTRATIVE LAW: BASIS, APPLICATION AND SCOPE 7 (2012) ("my focus in this book will be on deference being paid by courts to other actors. I will not be addressing, for example, interesting questions about individuals' obligations to obey the law, which might be characterized as deference being paid by citizens to officials.").
2. *See id.* at 25.
3. BRIAN FOLEY, DEFERENCE AND THE PRESUMPTION OF CONSTITUTIONALITY 256 (2008).
4. DALY, *supra* note 1, at 7.
5. *Id.* at 8.
6. *Id.*
7. *Id.* at 9.
8. *Id.* at 9–10 (footnotes omitted). The block quotation within the quotation is from Murray Hunt, *Sovereignty's Blight, in* PUBLIC LAW IN A MULTI-LAYERED CONSTITUTION 337, 346–47 (Nicholas Bamforth & Peter Leyland eds., 2003). The quoted distinction between "submissive deference" and "deference as respect" comes from David Dyzenhaus, *The Politics of Deference: Judicial Review and Democracy," in* THE PROVINCE OF ADMINISTRATIVE LAW 279, 286 (Michael Taggart ed., 1997).
9. R (on the Application of ProLife Alliance v. BBC, [2004] 1 A.C. 185 (HL), ¶ 75.
10. Joseph Vining, *Authority and Responsibility: The Jurisprudence of Deference*, 43 ADMIN. L. REV. 135, 135 (1991).
11. Aileen Kavanagh, *Deference or Defiance?: The Limits of the Judicial Role in Constitutional Adjudication, in* EXPOUNDING THE CONSTITUTION: ESSAYS IN

CONSTITUTIONAL THEORY 184, 189 (Grant Huscroft ed., 2008). *See also* ANDREW LEGG, THE MARGIN OF APPRECIATION IN INTERNATIONAL HUMAN RIGHTS LAW: DEFERENCE AND PROPORTIONALITY 23 (2012) ("Although 'being deferential' in common parlance sometimes refers to a characteristic of bowing to another's preferences, perhaps out of politeness or station, the same sense need not apply to the action of giving deference. In a judicial context, which requires a rational assessment of all of the reasons in a case, there is no room for servility in the practice of deference.").

DALY, *supra* note 1, at 7 ("my focus in this book will be on deference being paid by courts to other actors. I will not be addressing, for example, interesting questions about individuals' obligations to obey the law, which might be characterized as deference being paid by citizens to officials.").

12. BRIAN FOLEY, DEFERENCE TO THE LEGISLATURE: A STUDY OF JUDICIAL DEFERENCE TO LEGISLATIVE CONSTITUTIONAL DECISION-MAKING 5 (2007), http://www.tara.tcd.ie/handle/2262/77983.

13. *Id.* at 23.

14. *Id.*

15. *See, e.g., id.* at 28, 98.

16. *See, e.g., id.* at 279.

17. *Id.* at 25.

18. *Id.* at 29.

19. *Id.* at 25–26.

20. *See* Larry Alexander & Frederick Schauer, *On Extrajudicial Constitutional Interpretation*, 110 HARV. L. REV. 1359, 1363 (1997).

21. Paul Horwitz, *Three Faces of Deference*, 83 NOTRE DAME L. REV. 1061 (2008).

22. *See* Robert A. Schapiro, *Judicial Deference and Interpretive Coordinacy in State and Federal Constitutional Law*, 85 CORNELL L. REV. 656 (2000).

23. Horwitz, *supra* note 21, at 1072.

24. *Id.* at 1073.

25. *Id.* at 1065–66 (footnotes omitted). *See also id.* at 1072 ("Although Schapiro is speaking directly in terms of judicial deference to other branches of government, the point can be generalized to a variety of decisionmakers.").

26. *Id.* at 1073.

27. *Id.*

28. *Id. See also id.* at 1075 ("I have not deferred to my neighbor unless, to some extent, I substitute his judgment for mine, and follow his conclusion even if I would have reached a different decision on my own.").

29. *Id.*, n.72.

30. *See* Alexander & Schauer, *supra* note 20, at 1363.

31. *See* PHILIP SOPER, THE ETHICS OF DEFERENCE 22 (2002).

32. *See* Henry P. Monaghan, *Marbury and the Administrative State*, 83 COLUM. L. REV. 1, 5 (1983).

33. *See* Antonin Scalia, *Judicial Deference to Administrative Interpretations of Law*, 1989 DUKE L.J. 511, 514.

34. *See* United States v. Mead Corp., 533 U.S. 218, 250 (2001) (Scalia, J., dissenting).

35. *See id.* ("the rule of *Skidmore* deference is an empty truism and a trifling statement of the obvious: A judge should take into account the well-considered views of expert observers.").

36. *Cf.* Schapiro, *supra* note 22, at 665 ("deference implies difference").

37. *See* GARY LAWSON, EVIDENCE OF THE LAW: PROVING LEGAL CLAIMS (2017).

38. Kristin E. Hickman & Matthew D. Krueger, *In Search of the Modern* Skidmore *Standard*, 107 COLUM. L. REV. 1235, 1251 (2007).

39. DALY, *supra* note 1, at 138.

40. *See* Gary Lawson, *Stipulating the Law*, 109 MICH. L. REV. 1191 (2011).

41. This includes the numerous articles and books that scholars routinely send to United States courts in order to "aid" the courts in deciding cases. Professor Lawson, as a law clerk, made it a point *never* to look at those materials, on the theory that they were trying to function as amicus briefs without following the procedures required by court rules for filing amicus briefs.

42. Thomas W. Merrill & Kristin E. Hickman, Chevron's *Domain*, 89 GEO. L.J. 833, 855 (2001).

43. Horwitz, *supra* note 21, at 1075.

44. *Id.*

45. *Id.* at 1076.

46. Rostker v. Goldberg, 453 U.S. 57, 67 (1981).

47. Horwitz, *supra* note 21, at 1076–77.

48. *See* Gary Lawson & Christopher D. Moore, *The Executive Power of Constitutional Interpretation*, 81 IOWA L. REV. 1267, 1278–79 (1996).

49. *See* Horowitz, *supra* note 21, at 1079–85.

50. *See id.* at 1085–90.

51. Frederick Schauer, *Deferring*, 103 MICH. L. REV. 1567, 1574 (2005). The point was also noted by Professor Philip Soper, in the book that Professor Schauer was reviewing in the article just cited. *See* SOPER, *supra* note 31, at 182.

52. *See* Horwitz, *supra* note 21, at 1101–5.

53. *Id.* at 1101–2 (footnotes omitted).

54. Gary Lawson, *Dirty Dancing—The FDA Stumbles with the* Chevron *Two-Step: A Response to Professor Noah*, 93 CORNELL L. REV. 927, 932–33 (2008).

55. Aaron Saiger, *Agencies' Obligation to Interpret the Statute*, 69 VAND. L. REV. 1231, 1233–34 (2016).

56. 5 U.S.C. § 706(2)(A) (2012).

57. Catskill Mountains Chapter of Trout Unlimited, Inc. v. EPA, 846 F.3d 492, 521 (2d Cir. 2017).

58. *See* Gary Lawson, *Outcome, Procedure, and Process: Agency Duties of Explanation for Legal Conclusions*, 48 RUTGERS L. REV. 313 (1996).

59. *See* GARY LAWSON & GUY SEIDMAN, "A GREAT POWER OF ATTORNEY": UNDERSTANDING THE FIDUCIARY CONSTITUTION (2017).

60. *See* Gary Lawson & Guy Seidman, *By Any Other Name: Rational Basis Inquiry and the Federal Government's Fiduciary Duty of Care*, 69 FLA. L. REV. 1385 (2017).

61. On how administrative agencies can be viewed as fiduciary actors, *see* Evan J. Criddle, *Fiduciary Foundations of Administrative Law*, 54 U.C.L.A L. REV. 117 (2006).

62. *See* Yoav Dotan, *Deference and Disagreement in Administrative Law*, at 7 (manuscript on file with authors).

63. *Id.* at 10.

64. *Id.*

65. *See id.* at 11–12.

66. *See id.* at 13 n.33.

67. *See id.* at 13–14.

68. *See id.* at 14–15.

69. *See id.* at 14–15, 22–23.

70. *See id.* at 22.

71. *See id.* at 26–27.

72. *Id.* at 29.

73. Jonathan A. Masur & Lisa Larrimore Ouellette, *Deference Mistakes*, 82 U. CHI. L. REV. 643 (2015).

74. *Id.* at 645.

75. *Id.* at 645–46.

76. *Id.* at 652.

77. Daniel J. Solove, *The Darkest Domain: Deference, Judicial Review, and the Bill of Rights*, 84 IOWA L. REV. 941, 945 (1999).

78. *Id.* at 946.

79. *Id.* at 966.

80. *Id.* at 1020.

81. *See id.* at 946 n.19 ("I have limited my inquiry to opinions explicitly implicating fundamental constitutional rights, for this is where deference is at its most problematic.").

82. *Id.* at 946.

83. *Id.* at 948.

84. *Id.* at 953.

85. *Id.*

86. *Id.* at 1023.

87. *See id.* at 965–66.

88. Kavanagh, *supra* note 11.

89. AILEEN KAVANAGH, CONSTITUTIONAL REVIEW UNDER THE UK HUMAN RIGHTS ACT (2009).

90. Kavanagh, *supra* note 11, at 185.

91. *Id.* at 185–86.

92. *Id.* at 186.

93. *Id*

94. *Id. See also* KAVANAGH, *supra* note 89, at 169 n.7, 172.

95. *Id.* at 169 (emphasis in original).

96. *Id.* at 169–70 (emphasis in original).

97. *Id.* at 177.

98. *Id.* at 173.

99. *Id.* at 177.

100. Kavanagh, *supra* note 11, at 187.

101. *Id.*

102. *Id.* at 188.

103. *Id.*

104. *Id.*

105. *Id.* at 192.

106. *Id.*

107. *Id.* at 190.

108. *Id.*

109. *Id.* at 190.

110. *See, e.g.*, Gary Lawson, *Did Justice Scalia Have a Theory of Interpretation?*, 92 NOTRE DAME L. REV. 2143, 2155–56 (2017); Gary Lawson, *Reflections of an Empirical Reader (Or: Could Fleming Be Right this Time?)*, 96 B.U. L. REV. 1456, 1472–73 (2016); Gary Lawson, *Originalism without Obligation*, B.U. L. REV. 1309, 1313–14 (2013); Gary Lawson, *On Reading Recipes . . . and Constitutions*, 85 GEO. L. REV. 1823 (1997).

111. Gary Lawson, *No History, No Certainty, No Legitimacy . . . No Problem: Originalism and the Limits of Legal Theory*, 64 FLA. L. REV. 1551, 1555–56 (2012).

112. *Id.* at 1562.

113. Kavanagh, *supra* note 11, at 190.

114. KAVANAGH, *supra* note 89, at 197.

115. *Id.* at 199.

116. *See, e.g.*, ALEXANDER BICKEL, THE LEAST DANGEROUS BRANCH (1962).

117. KAVANAGH, *supra* note 89, at 198.

118. *See id.* at 198–99.

119. *See id.* at 172 ("deference functions in judicial reasoning by allocating various degrees of presumptive weight in favor of the legislative decision").

120. Kavanagh, *supra* note 11, at 191.

121. *Id.*

122. *Id.* at 192.

123. The same complexity no doubt plagues other legal systems as well. *See* Michael Taggart, *Proportionality, Deference,* Wednesbury, 2008 N.Z. L. REV. 423, 451–53 (describing a "rainbow of review" in New Zealand administrative law).

124. Universal Camera Corp. v. NLRB, 340 U.S. 474, 486–87 (1951). For Professor Lawson's tuneful account of how to describe the various "moods" of deference, *see* GARY LAWSON, TEACHER'S MANUAL TO FEDERAL ADMINISTRATIVE LAW 152–53 (8th ed. 2019).

# 5

# Extensions

Students of jurisprudence will notice a conspicuous absence from the previous chapter, in which we surveyed some alternative accounts of deference
in order to compare them to our own. One of the most complete accounts of
deference in recent times comes from legal philosopher Philip Soper, whose
book[1] contains perhaps the most thorough and extended discussion of deference in modern legal scholarship.

Deference, for Professor Soper, involves "giving weight to the normative
judgments of others even against one's own judgment about the correct action
to take."[2] His discussion of the concept contains virtually all the elements that
we look for in an account of deference. He maintains that deference requires
more than mere consideration of another's views: "Deference suggests that
I am acting in some sense contrary to the way I would normally act if I simply
considered the balance of reasons (including any new information supplied
by your request) that bear on the action."[3] Deference for Professor Soper can
be either absolute (submissive) or partial (weighted); one can either delegate
a decision entirely to another or consider the other's decision as a factor to be
weighed in the balance.[4] Normally, deference is partial; "[o]ne's own judgment is not preempted, but only balanced against the reasons for deferring to
the views of another."[5] While Professor Soper identifies reasons for deference
that correspond roughly to our categories of legitimation deference[6] and signaling deference,[7] his principal categorization of reasons instead contrasts
instrumental and intrinsic reasons for deference,[8] with instrumental reasons
roughly describing utilitarian consequences of deference and intrinsic
reasons having something to do with consistency with values, either objective values or one's own subjective values.[9] He compares and contrasts deference with other ideas, such as authority[10] and obedience.[11] And Professor
Soper pays attention to the obligations of deferees in contexts involving deference.[12] This framework sets up what seems like a natural—and perhaps
even the most natural available—comparison with our own definition and
discussion of deference.

*Deference.* Gary Lawson and Guy I. Seidman, Oxford University Press (2020). © Oxford University Press.
DOI: 10.1093/oso/9780190273408.001.0001

We have left out Professor Soper up to this point, however, for a very simple reason. We have thus far focused entirely on deriving an account of deference in the law inductively by looking specifically to the practices of US federal courts. We derive both our definition and our analytical framework from those practices. Professor Soper has a radically different focus. His book tries to use deference to explain legal obligation: To what extent do citizens (or subjects) have a moral obligation to obey the law, and what kind of moral obligation would that be if they had it? As he explains it:

> It is not uncommon and would not be odd to ask whether one has "reason to defer" to legal authorities in much the same way that one asks whether one has an "obligation to obey" the law. Indeed, as we shall see, the language of deference is often quite naturally in play when one explores the nature of authority and the various reasons for acting in compliance with the advice or requests of those who claim authority. Since political authority is one kind of authority, it should not then surprise that the language of deference could as easily be used in this context as the language of obedience.[13]

There is no good reason to suppose that the relevant "language of deference" that could work to explain legal obligation would be derived inductively from the practice of US federal courts. Given these radically different projects, one would expect that the terminology and frameworks accompanying those projects would be quite a bit different—more different even than descriptions of deferential practice across legal systems. It would be, for example, surprising (though not inconceivable) if economic deference ended up playing a large role in a theoretical justification for legal obligation, while it would be surprising (and perhaps even inconceivable) if it did not play a central role in a descriptive account of deference within a complex legal system.

Nonetheless, there are important lessons for our project in Professor Soper's seemingly unrelated enterprise. While our primary purpose in this book is simply to identify and provide a means for describing and analyzing the practice of deference by federal courts as the courts themselves identify those practices, it would certainly be a bonus if our account had broader utility as a description of other practices as well. Accordingly, in this chapter, we use Professor Soper's discussion as the occasion to ask a broader question than we have posed thus far: Does the definition and account of deference that has emerged in this book, which we are convinced is a good account of deference as the term is expressly employed by federal courts, shed any light on other practices that either are or can be described in terms of deference? To be sure, we have no ambitions of trying to provide a normative account of legal obligation or engaging in any other kind of prescriptive enterprise. Our project was and is descriptive. But there are many other practices that are not always, or even often, described by the courts (or other legal decision-making institutions) as deference which might usefully be analyzed in terms of deference. That was precisely Professor Soper's point: Theorists of legal obligation, he says, normally talk in terms of authority and obedience when perhaps the best answers to their problems are found in the language and practices of deference. We are not taking sides on whether Professor Soper is right in this specific claim about normative jurisprudence; that is far beyond our pay grade. We are simply following his example by taking a vocabulary that has analytical value in one context and seeing whether it might have value in other contexts as well. Accordingly, we aim to look for legal practices that can usefully be analyzed through a framework of deference, as we have thus far defined and described it.

Perhaps the most obvious potential extension of our framework would be to examine court systems other than US federal courts. In particular, it seems apt to ask how well the US federal court framework for deference corresponds to how judicial systems in American states or in other countries employ deference. As we explained in Chapter 1 we initially hoped to make such a comparative project a central part of this book, but we had to abandon that ambition, at least on the international side, for lack of English-language materials. We hope to pursue this comparative project in a subsequent work that brings together scholars from other countries who can speak with knowledge and authority about their own countries' practices. For now, we need to confine ourselves to practices within the United States or other English-speaking countries for which we can find sufficient materials to make useful judgments. Our tentative hypothesis is that deference is a useful way to think about many practices that do not always employ the term. We shall see whether that hypothesis holds up under scrutiny.

## 1. Precedent

We saw in Chapter 2 that US federal courts use deference to describe their relationships with a wide range of institutions, including legislatures, executive agencies, juries, and state courts. Deference is also used to describe the relationship between appellate courts and lower courts, in which appellate courts sometimes defer to the views of prior decision-makers. But what about the inverse relationship between lower and higher courts? When lower courts follow the precedents of higher courts, is that an act of deference? And what about coordinate courts, for which there is no formal hierarchical relationship? If a court follows the prior decision of a coordinate court—such as a district judge following the formally non-binding ruling of another district judge, a circuit court of appeals following the non-binding ruling of another circuit, a state court following the non-binding decision of another state court, or the US Supreme Court following one of its previous decisions—is that activity usefully analyzed in the vocabulary of deference?

We think so. Professor Soper agrees, as he treats precedent within a common law system as a form of deference equivalent to deference to juries or administrative agencies.[14] Analytically, we think this is clearly right. There is no obvious conceptual difference between, for example, an appellate court deferring to the factual findings of a trial court and a trial court deferring to the legal findings of an appellate court. The strength of the deference might (or might not) vary, and the reasons for deference might (or might not) be different in those cases, but both seem like instances of deference. If there is a general framework that is useful for understanding and describing deference in the law, that framework should apply in both instances.

It is not our task here to set out a theory, either a descriptive or a prescriptive theory, of precedent. That is a task for another life. Our limited goal is to show that the framework for deference inductively derived from the practices of federal courts sheds light on the practice of precedent even though the federal courts do not typically describe precedent as an act of deference. To be sure, there are plenty of times when courts and scholars do explicitly describe precedent in terms of deference.[15] We are saying only that precedent is not always, or even typically, discussed in those terms. For example, a recent volume assembled by the remarkable Bryan Garner and a passel of distinguished federal judges comprehensively surveys the practice of precedent in US courts.[16] While there are occasional references in the work to "deference to precedent,"[17] on the whole there is relatively little discussion of precedent as a species of deference. The sparse references to deference seem incidental. Accordingly, we think that applying the language and framework of deference to precedent is best viewed as an extension of our analysis rather than part of the database from which that analysis was induced.

Our basic definition of deference, recall, is "the giving by a legal actor of some measure of consideration or weight to the decision of another actor in exercising the deferring actor's function." This obviously fits the practice of precedent, in all of that practice's many manifestations. Indeed, we could have included—and considered including—precedent in the database from which we drew our definition of deference. But as we just noted, we thought it warranted separate treatment because the description, by courts and other actors, of the practice as deference is not as consistent as the description of the other practices from which we draw our account.

The language of deference easily and naturally applies to precedent. Some forms of precedent count as mandatory deference while others are discretionary. Lower courts are normally considered legally obliged to follow the precedents of higher authorities within their own system: "Federal and state courts are absolutely bound by . . . precedents . . . delivered by higher courts within the same jurisdiction."[18] This system of so-called vertical precedent[19] is "a virtually undiscussed axiom of adjudication,"[20] contested by almost no one.[21] While the mandatory character of deference to vertical precedent may seem grounded more in custom than in authoritative legal command, one of us has argued that the labeling of certain courts as "inferior" in the US Constitution entails that those inferior courts must, as a matter of positive law, follow the precedents of superior courts.[22] Even if that is not right as a matter of US constitutional law, the uniform expectation of judicial actors in the United States is that precedents of higher courts will be followed by lower courts as a matter of legal design, even if the precise contours and textual sources of that design are not clear. As a matter of ordinary legal practice, it is not up to the lower courts to choose whether to be bound by vertical precedent.

Other forms of precedent, however, are decidedly discretionary. Horizontal precedent—the following of precedents at coordinate levels of the judicial hierarchy—is a practice long established but not commanded by authoritative text or legal design. The US Supreme Court, for example, presumptively follows its own prior precedents unless there are compelling reasons to overrule prior decisions,[23] but there is nothing in the nature of the US legal system that requires this result. The Supreme Court could choose tomorrow to abandon its practice of horizontal precedent.[24] Courts of one state sometimes look to the courts of other states for guidance, but there is no principle of law that commands this practice. So what kinds of considerations drive those discretionary decisions?

A study of precedent, even in this limited fashion, is a book in itself.[25] But even a cursory look at the practice shows how the categories of reasons for deference induced from federal court practice apply to precedent. The ensuing discussion is *not* meant to be an endorsement of any particular practice of precedent or a suggestion that any of the rationales advanced for precedent are persuasive to any degree in any setting. We are simply describing commonly advanced reasons for deference to precedent and showing how they map onto the structure of deference derived from the book thus far.

Reasons from legitimation might be thought to justify precedent if one thinks, for example, that the US Constitution contains structural inferences that suggest, even if they do not inexorably command, deference to judicial precedent. Professor Randy Kozel has advanced exactly such an argument with considerable sophistication,[26] maintaining that the practice of precedent is implicit in the judicial function of courts in the federal structure. In that sense, one might think that prior courts have a claim to legitimacy, justifying at least a presumptive weight for their decisions in subsequent cases, which is exactly what the doctrine of presumptive precedent prescribes. The deliberate construction by constitutional drafters of at least some forms of mandatory deference can be justified, as a matter of legal design, by the same kinds of considerations. More generally, one might think that "the past can teach valuable lessons inherently worthy of our respect,"[27] meaning that there is some legitimation value in the act of referring to, and seeking authority from, prior practices. But can this kind of deference really play a role in discretionary rather than mandatory applications of precedent? When would a coordinate body—in the past or in the present—ever really have more legitimacy than the body actually making the decision? As it happens, this could occur quite often without any reference to contingent issues of constitutional structure. Indeed, later in this chapter, we will consider one context in which that is quite likely to occur. We accordingly postpone the discussion for the moment, other than to note, with more to follow later, that legitimation deference is a useful analytical category for examining at least some forms of precedent.

Epistemological deference as a rationale for deference surfaces most often in connection with vertical precedent. Just as trial judges have more experience, and presumably more expertise, at fact-finding and trial management than do appellate courts, and therefore merit deference in their fact-finding and trial management, so one might think that appellate courts have more experience, and presumably more expertise, in pure law finding than do trial courts, which warrants constructing a regime of vertical precedent as a matter of legal design. Decision-making by multimember bodies, which is the typical form for appellate review in the United States, may further the epistemological advantages of appellate tribunals.[28] But one can easily see epistemological deference functioning at the horizontal level as well. One example, well known to scholars of administrative law, is the deference given by other federal courts of appeals to the decisions of the D.C. Circuit on matters of administrative law.[29] The D.C. Circuit hears a steady diet of federal administrative law cases and thus acquires at least the potential for an expertise in the subject that no other court will ever reach. As a result, D.C. Circuit decisions tend to carry special weight, on purely epistemological grounds, on administrative law questions. Decisions of the Second Circuit have long carried similar epistemological weight on matters of securities law.[30] More mundane examples involve deference to the views of particular judges who are seen as having expertise in specific fields or general legal wisdom. How many times has one heard a phrase such as "in an opinion authored by Judge/Justice XXX . . ."? Why does it matter who authored the opinion if there are not differences in expertise or wisdom that are relevant for epistemological deference? Examples of this kind of judge-specific deference abound.[31]

A legal designer will surely want to consider epistemological deference when constructing models of precedent. All else being equal, surely one would want decisions that are more likely to be right to be given more weight. That consideration, of course, could be outweighed by other concerns (a decision-maker can, for example, have more legitimacy than another even if the "legitimate" decision-maker is less competent), but all else equal, it is hard to see why a legal designer would not at least try to take epistemological concerns into account. When the application of precedent is discretionary rather than mandatory, as when coordinate bodies consider each other's decisions (and each Supreme Court panel is coordinate with every other Supreme Court panel), epistemological deference may call for some careful judgments about what kinds of decisions might or might not merit deference. Not all judges, and not all courts, are created equal. If a court is looking to precedent "not because precedent, right or wrong, binds, but because precedent can teach and help find the right answer,"[32] one will want to be attentive to whether and when precedent is actually good evidence of the right answer. At a minimum, one will want to know whether the prior decision-maker was applying a methodology calculated to produce right answers. Someone who thinks, for example, that right answers to questions of constitutional interpretation come from attempting to ascertain the original communicative intentions of the relevant text will not learn much from most prior Supreme Court decisions,[33] as one could probably count on one hand the number of such decisions driven by an informed application of original meaning. By the same token, someone who thinks that constitutional meaning comes from deep engagement with first principles of moral philosophy will also likely be disappointed by the work product of the US Supreme Court. That is not a body noted for the depth and sophistication of its moral philosophizing. On the other hand, someone who thinks that constitutional meaning emerges from a common law process of judicial decisions may well find a large bulk of prior decisions persuasive, partly because the courts may actually be pretty good at reading and applying prior opinions and partly because the interpretative methodology might make those opinions themselves the data points from which meaning is derived. The extent to which epistemological deference makes sense in any context cannot be determined without knowing the correct interpretative theory and the likelihood that the deferee in any given case will provide useful material in light of that theory. As there is no consensus view of the correct interpretative methodology, there is unlikely to be a consensus view of the correct application of epistemological deference in the context of precedent. But we think we can plausibly postulate a consensus that epistemological deference, in the abstract, is a category relevant for understanding and assessing the practice of precedent.

Economic deference obviously plays a major role in judicial precedent. One huge advantage of a system with precedent is that it economizes on decision costs. If every issue had to be rethought on each occasion, the systematic costs could be enormous. "[C]ourts, litigants, and the public at large gain something from a system that doesn't require each case to be litigated anew and instead allows resort to rules already at hand."[34] As with deference to administrative agencies, deference to precedent changes the decision process from one in which the decision-maker must look for the right answer to one in which the decision-maker must look for special circumstances that justify looking for the right answer (and then expends resources looking for the right answer only when those special circumstances are satisfied). That not only allows for an easier decision process in many circumstances, but it also makes many other disputes so clear in their outcomes that it does not make sense to bring them before a court, and there is accordingly no need for any official decision process regarding them. As Professor Michael

Gerhardt puts it: "judicial precedent, at its most basic, settles disputes be-tween parties . . . and clarifies the rules of the game for what litigants need to do in order to prevail."[35] Again, we are not saying that these cost consider-ations objectively justify the practice of precedent in any particular context. (Indeed, one of us affirmatively thinks that they do not justify the practice of horizontal precedent in federal constitutional cases.) We are saying only that the category of economic deference is a useful tool for analyzing the practice of precedent.

It may seem at first glance as though there is little room for signaling defer-ence in the practice of precedent. To whom, after all, is the signal being sent? As it happens, there is considerable power to the idea of signaling deference in some very important contexts involving precedent. We will see later in this chapter how signaling deference can play a crucial role in at least some prece-dent practices, so we again postpone that discussion for the moment.

Finally, the category of prudential, or strategic, deference, which we added to our catalogue of rationales for deference at the inspiration of Professor Aileen Kavanagh, encompasses some of the most important and common rationales for precedent. That is perhaps a warning sign for use of our anal-ysis. If prudential/strategic deference is simply a dumping ground for every rationale that does not fit within a more precise analytical framework, the framework may not provide much utility. A framework with that kind of built-in safety net will of course be able to explain and accommodate everything—by fiat. We think, however, that Professor Kavanagh's notion of prudential/strategic deference is more cabined than that. She clearly had in mind deference as a means for preserving the status and role of the court within a larger governmental structure. Courts prudentially defer when they perceive that deciding by their own lights without deference will generate adverse reactions from other governmental institutions or the public that could endanger the court's ability to decide cases accurately (by the court's own non-deferential lights) in the future. That is why we suggest the label "strategic deference" as perhaps more descriptive and less prone to undue expansion, as it emphasizes that the focus is on preserving the court's lim-ited decisional capital. We will, however, continue to use the label prudential deference on occasion, but with the understanding that we see it as a rela-tively specific rationale rather than a catch-all category. With that in mind, we think that the standard rationales offered for judicial precedent fit neatly within some combination of the categories that we have identified, as we will now demonstrate.

Precedent can be sought to be justified as a form of constraint on judges, so that decisions do not come entirely from the mind of a single judge.[36] There is an obvious epistemological element to this rationale; if one believes that prior decision-makers possessed a degree of skill or wisdom, drawing on that temporally diverse group mind might lead to better decisions. But there is much more to this constraint-based rationale than just drawing on sources of wisdom. The clear worry is that decisions that are seen to come from individual judges rather than from an impersonal "law" lack legitimacy, or at least lack a perception of legitimacy. "[B]y seeking to ensure some consistency in outcomes among decision-makers, the doctrine of precedent may simultaneously promote respect for the judiciary as a neutral source."[37] While this smacks of both legitimation and signaling deference as rationales for precedent, it also seems different from both of those rationales in important ways. Legitimation deference focuses on the superior legitimacy of the prior decision-maker. In this case, the focus is on securing the legitimacy of the present deferring decision-maker, which perhaps can be enhanced by invoking precedent as a ground for decision. That sounds very much like a counsel of prudence, as we have construed Professor Kavanagh's category of prudential deference, though concerns both of legitimation and signaling play an important role in this rationale. After all, the reason why it might matter whether a decision is seen as representing the rule of men rather than the rule of law probably has something to do with public acceptance of the judicial role, which is precisely what the category of prudential deference is meant to include.

Other oft-advanced rationales for precedent are stability in the law and the equal treatment of litigants.[38] One of the Supreme Court's most oft-cited litanies of justifications for precedent claims that following precedent "promotes the evenhanded, predictable, and consistent development of legal principles, fosters reliance on judicial decisions, and contributes to the actual and perceived integrity of the judicial process."[39] Again, these rationales do not fit squarely into the non-prudential categories of deference, though they partake of them to some degree. Even-handedness and equality are presumably values because they enhance the legitimacy of the decision-making process—not necessarily because the prior decision-makers are more legitimate than the present one but because the legitimacy of the present decision-maker depends on acceptance by other legal actors, which in turn depends on perceptions of even-handedness. As with impersonality, these seem like precisely the kinds of consideration that Professor Kavanagh's category of prudential deference was trying to capture. They are practical concerns about the operation of a legal system and the role and status of judges, whose authority depends on political and public acceptance rather than the control of armies, within that system.

Consistent development of legal principles and reliance upon those principles, by contrast, sounds more in economic deference. Precedent, recall, is largely a cost-saving device. Precedent insures that "scarce judicial resources are not squandered over endless relitigation of every conceivable question."[40] But precedent can only serve that function if parties actually rely upon it and if the norms embodied in precedent are knowable and usable. Assuming that those conditions hold, precedent can dramatically reduce decision costs system-wide.

Do we gain anything by deconstructing precedent into the language and categories of deference? That is not something for which we want to make strong claims, but we suspect that the answer can be yes. Breaking down the multifaceted rationales for deference into a compact set of categories can help one think about whether and how those rationales apply in different settings and how the practice of precedent can be shaped to promote those rationales. For example, if it is important in some settings to maintain the public acceptability of judicial institutions, and if precedent as a form of prudential deference can be a mechanism for securing that acceptability, one surely wants to think about whether any of the other kinds of deference also play a role in justifying the practice. If they do, the case for precedent is obviously strengthened. If they do not, one will have to decide whether prudential deference alone is sufficient to justify the practice. By the same token, if the principal justification for precedent in a context is thought to be drawing upon the wisdom of the past, thinking in terms of epistemological deference may sharpen attention to the need to consider carefully whether the processes of decision-making that led to prior decisions are well calculated to produce wisdom. And if one focuses on the economic features of deference as devices to reduce decision costs, that focus may prescribe how a system of precedent should function in order to generate those cost savings. In other words, the language of deference provides a means for organizing and structuring thought about precedent. It does not, and is not designed to, answer questions, but it provides a way in which those questions can perhaps be better understood and more productively formulated. That is, at the end of the day, the goal of this book.

At the risk of tedium, it is not our goal here to prescribe any particular outcomes. We are not even saying, for example, that prudential deference is (or is not) ever appropriate as a normative matter. We are merely trying to provide a framework and vocabulary that can be used, in a modular fashion, as part of more jurisprudentially deep analyses than we aim to provide here. Our only bottom line is that legal designers may want to consider these deference rationales when designing systems of precedent, and it is a certainty that at least some judges actively consider them when making discretionary decisions to adhere to precedent. Focusing on the precise categories can lead all of these actors to clearer thinking. Or so we hope and maintain.

## 2. Deference to Courts by Other Actors

Our focus thus far has been on deference as practiced by federal courts. But other governmental institutions also practice deference. Any layered decision-making process will have some role for deference. Courts are simply the institution of government for which the practice is easiest to identify and study.

Legislative and executive institutions have their own practices and traditions of deference within themselves. Units of the executive may defer to other executive units, either by legal command or by institutional choice. For example, US federal agencies with litigating authority must, by regulation, defer to the Office of the Solicitor General, within the Department of Justice, on matters involving appellate litigation.[41] The Office of Legal Counsel, also within the Department of Justice, sometimes speaks with the delegated authority of the Attorney General,[42] in which case its views in theory could be thought to command mandatory deference within the executive department, though whether such formal mandatory deference to Attorney General opinions actually exists within the executive department is a thorny, and probably contingent, question.[43] In practice, the question of the formal bindingness of Attorney General opinions may be moot, as enforcing such conformity across the executive department is likely impossible.[44] The one exception is an executive order promulgated in 1979 which requires federal agencies that disagree on legal matters to refer the dispute to the Office of Legal Counsel before they take the matter to court.[45] If they are not taking the matter to court, the disagreeing agencies are "encouraged to submit the dispute to the Attorney General."[46] Even apart from this dispute-resolving function, there is room, of course, for discretionary deference to the Office of Legal Counsel by other executive actors, and the possible institutional reasons for such deference have been canvassed by others.[47]

An accounting of how deference functions within an institution as vast and complex as the federal executive in the United States is best left to political scientists (our brief description above, for example, concerns only the role of the Department of Justice with respect to legal interpretation, which is a tiny fraction of the activity that can plausibly involve deference of some kind). Legislatures, for their part, may defer to committees, and any given committee may defer to specific members with expertise, clout, or both.[48] Legislative bodies may also have traditions of decorum or procedural practices to which current bodies defer to some degree. As with internal executive deference, a study of these legislative practices is beyond the scope of this book; it would require political scientists far better trained in empirical methods than are we even to begin to describe the inner workings of such bodies.

There is, however, one practice of the US President and Congress that we can, as purely legal scholars, identify and discuss here as an instance of deference: Those bodies routinely defer to the federal courts, especially on matters of constitutional interpretation. On the rare occasions when the modern Congress engages in serious constitutional analysis before it acts,[49] that analysis is likely to focus on the consistency of proposed action with Supreme Court decisions when such decisions are available. (For "political questions" that will never result in decisions by the courts, there is obviously nothing from the courts to which to defer, though even in those instances analogous court decisions are the universal starting point.) The executive department devotes considerable resources to constitutional analysis to guide agencies and to advise the President on everything from whether to sign or veto legislation to the legality of proposed unilateral executive action. One of us can testify from experience in the legal arm of the executive that virtually all of that legal analysis focuses on consistency with court decisions. Even when the President is exercising the presentment power, for which no judicial review is available, executive legal analysis is oriented around court decisions. As one of us wrote, with Christopher D. Moore, back in 1996:

> It is well understood that presidents can, and even should, consider the constitutionality of legislation before signing it, but we suspect that the ordinary expectation in much of our legal community is that such

constitutional review will consist of a careful study of court decisions on the relevant question—much the same way that courts themselves typically address such questions. In other words, while no one really doubts that Congress and the President, in their legislative capacities, have the power and duty to consider the constitutionality of their actions, "constitutionality" is often taken to mean "consistency with Supreme Court (and perhaps lower federal court) decisions about the Constitution." In particular, we doubt whether the legal community is prepared to swallow whole the idea that, in presidential deliberations about the proper exercise of the presentment power, Supreme Court decisions need not play any larger role than do law review articles or memoranda from staff attorneys in the Justice Department's Office of Legal Counsel.[50]

This legislative and executive deference to courts is so much a routine matter that it is easy to take it for granted. But it is neither legally nor politically inevitable.

Indeed, not only is such a practice not inevitable, it is actually puzzling, and even a bit baffling, once one thinks about it carefully. The power of legal interpretation is an enormous governmental power. Texts frequently are not self-interpreting or self-executing. That is especially true in an era in which statutes are often so vague as to be literally meaningless and in which constitutional provisions are seen as open-ended invitations to interpretative updating. In those circumstances especially, and in all circumstances to some degree, the power of legal interpretation is among the most formidable of all governmental powers. The power to shape (or just flat-out declare) the meaning of legal texts is comparable in scope to the power to enact them in the first instance. Why would governmental institutions ever relinquish that power to other actors?

And by "governmental institutions," we mean the real-world people who staff those institutions. Those people are people—and people do not suddenly become a different species of creature simply by assuming government office. The founders of the US Constitution knew this well.[51] They understood that, given human nature and "the encroaching spirit of power,"[52] one should expect governmental actors to seek to aggrandize their own influence. As James Madison memorably put it, "[t]he legislative department is everywhere extending the sphere of its activity, and drawing all power into its impetuous vortex."[53] The more general words of Madison from 1787 still resonate today:

Ambition must be made to counteract ambition. The interest of the man must be connected with the constitutional rights of the place. It may be a reflection on human nature, that such devices should be necessary to control the abuses of government. But what is government itself, but the greatest of all reflections on human nature? If men were angels, no government would be necessary. If angels were to govern men, neither external nor internal controls on government would be necessary. In framing a government which is to be administered by men over men, the great difficulty lies in this: you must first enable the government to control the governed; and in the next place oblige it to control itself.

A dependence on the people is, no doubt, the primary control on the government; but experience has taught mankind the necessity of auxiliary precautions. This policy of supplying, by opposite and rival interests, the defect of better motives, might be traced through the whole system of human affairs, private as well as public. We see it particularly displayed in all the subordinate distributions of power, where the constant aim is to divide and arrange the several offices in such a manner as that each may be a check on the other that the private interest of every individual may be a sentinel over the public rights. These inventions of prudence cannot be less requisite in the distribution of the supreme powers of the State.[54]

Was Madison right about how a great many—not all, but a great many—people within governmental institutions are likely to behave? We think that history—thousands of years of it—amply confirms Madison's suspicions that enough people will behave as he (and pretty much all members of the founding generation) predicted they would behave to make it prudent to expect some measure of aggrandizement from governmental institutions. To be sure, aggrandizement is not the only motive driving government action, and one will not even necessarily be able to generate reliable predictions from a model that assumes aggrandizement to be the principal force in government action.[55] But it is surely at least a force with which to be reckoned. So why would government officials give way to others on one of the most important powers to be found in government?

One possible answer is that they are ordered to do so by a source which they consider authoritative. If the Constitution of the United States commands legislative and executive deference to courts, that would be a reason, both descriptively and prescriptively, for legislative and executive actors to defer.

As with other instances of mandatory deference, the only choice facing those actors would be the choice to obey or disobey the law.

It is possible that some contemporary legislative and executive actors believe that the US Constitution commands mandatory deference to the legal views of courts. That is an empirical question on which we do not have conclusive data. If that belief was universal or near-universal, it would solve the descriptive puzzle. But however widespread that belief might be, it is clearly not universal.

American executives, from Thomas Jefferson to Andrew Jackson to Abraham Lincoln to Franklin Roosevelt to Ronald Reagan to Donald Trump, have a long history of challenging the exclusivity of courts as interpreters of the US Constitution.[56] In 1987, Attorney General Edwin Meese III made the point simply and powerfully when he said that a judicial decision "binds the parties in a case and also the executive branch for whatever enforcement is necessary. But such a decision does not establish a supreme law of the land that is binding on all persons and parts of government henceforth and forevermore. This point should seem so obvious as not to need elaboration."[57]

As a matter of original constitutional meaning, Attorney General Meese was clearly right. The US Constitution mandates only a very limited form of executive deference to judicial decisions—far more limited than the current practice reflects. One of us has discussed this point at great length elsewhere[58]; we present here only the barest outline of the argument.

The US Constitution nowhere confers on any federal department or official an express, much less an exclusive, power of legal interpretation. Indeed, all actors must swear an oath to uphold the Constitution,[59] which suggests that it is the responsibility of all actors to interpret the Constitution that they are sworn to uphold. The federal courts assuredly have the power to interpret the law. They are vested with the "judicial Power of the United States,"[60] which is the power to decide cases in accordance with governing law. In order to apply that power, one must ascertain the governing law, so a power of legal interpretation is incidental to the exercise of the judicial power. As Chief Justice John Marshall aptly said in 1803: "Those who apply the rule to particular cases, must of necessity expound and interpret that rule."[61] This much is clear.

But legislative and executive actors equally apply constitutional rules to cases whenever they act. A legislator deciding how to vote on a bill applies (if the legislator is conscientious and follows his or her oath of office) constitutional rules to the particular case at hand. Presidents deciding whether to sign or veto legislation, or how to allocate enforcement resources, make similar applications of constitutional rules to particular cases. For exactly the same reasons that the power of interpretation is incidental to the judicial power, it is also incidental to the legislative and executive powers. All interpretative powers under the Constitution are incidents to other granted powers. The Constitution contains no express "legal interpretation clause."

But doesn't this contravene the famous declaration in *Marbury v. Madison* that "[i]t is emphatically the province and duty of the judicial department to say what the law is"?[62] Only if one fundamentally misunderstands what was at issue in *Marbury* and what Chief Justice Marshall was claiming.[63] *Marbury* involved, inter alia, the constitutionality of a statute purportedly conferring original jurisdiction on the Supreme Court over mandamus cases.[64] For the statute to have reached the Supreme Court, Congress must have enacted it and the President must have signed it (or vetoed it and then have the veto overridden by supermajorities in both houses of Congress). Thus, governmental actors in coordinate departments had already determined, through their actions, that the statute was constitutional. Was the Supreme Court bound, by mandatory deference, to accept those prior legislative and executive determinations of constitutionality? Chief Justice Marshall said no, the Court was not conclusively bound by the views of Congress or the President. The Court has the power and duty to make its own judgment about the meaning of the Constitution; that is part of what it means for the federal courts to be a coordinate department of government. Thus, the declaration that it is the "province and duty of the judicial department to say what the law is" means that courts have a responsibility to interpret the law that is not canceled or eliminated by some kind of mandatory deference to the views of the other federal departments. That is why interpretation is both a province and a *duty*. To be sure, there may be reasons in the exercise of that duty for *discretionary* deference to legislative or executive precedents. Chief Justice Marshall himself invoked such precedents as the principal reason for upholding the constitutionality of the second Bank of the United States in *McCulloch v. Maryland*:

> The first question made in the cause is—has congress power to incorporate a bank? It has been truly said, that this can scarcely be considered as an open question, entirely unprejudiced by the former proceedings of the nation respecting it. The principle now contested was introduced at a very early period of our history, has been recognised by many successive legislatures,

and has been acted upon by the judicial department, in cases of peculiar delicacy, as a law of undoubted obligation.

It will not be denied, that a bold and daring usurpation might be resisted, after an acquiescence still longer and more complete than this. But it is conceived, that a doubtful question, one on which human reason may pause, and the human judgment be suspended, in the decision of which the great principles of liberty are not concerned, but the respective powers of those who are equally the representatives of the people, are to be adjusted; if not put at rest by the practice of the government, ought to receive a considerable impression from that practice. An exposition of the constitution, deliberately established by legislative acts, on the faith of which an immense property has been advanced, ought not to be lightly disregarded.[65]

But invoking that discretionary deference is quite different from saying that the courts are *disabled* from exercising independent judgment once the legislature and/or the executive have spoken. *Marbury* rejects that latter view.

*Marbury* is not about judicial supremacy. It is about judicial *equality*.[66] The courts are not bound by legislative and executive precedents, because courts are instead bound by the Constitution itself, whose meaning the courts have the power and duty to ascertain as much as do the President and the Congress. But exactly the same arguments marshalled (no pun intended) by *Marbury* for this conclusion equally support the proposition that legislators and executives are not conclusively and mandatorily bound by judicial precedents, because those bodies are bound by the Constitution itself, whose meaning the Congress and the President have the power and duty to ascertain as much as do the federal courts. All constitutional powers of interpretation are equally incidental to the three great vested powers. The Constitution creates an interdepartmental interpretative coordinacy, not an interpretative hierarchy. *Marbury* recognized this coordinate regime and the place—the co-equal place—of the federal courts within it. That regime allows, and requires, courts to exercise their own independent judgment about the constitutionality of legislation.[67] It does not deny the same power and duty to other actors.

The Supreme Court did not assert a claim to judicial supremacy or exclusivity in interpretation until 1958, when it was provoked by official state resistance to federal court desegregation orders stemming from the decision in *Brown v. Board of Education* mandating desegregation of public schools.

In *Cooper v. Aaron*[68] in the face of that resistance, the Court claimed that *Marbury* had "declared the basic principle that the federal judiciary is supreme in the exposition of the law of the Constitution, and that principle has ever since been respected by this Court and the Country as a permanent and indispensable feature of our constitutional system."[69] That was obviously (if understandably, given the context and the times) flatly wrong both as a description of *Marbury* and as a proposition about the Constitution's allocation of interpretative authority.[70] Apart from the fact that it would be circular reasoning in any event to use a Supreme Court decision (*Marbury*) to establish the supremacy of Supreme Court decisions, *Marbury* did not contemplate the kind of supremacy for which it was represented in 1958.

To be sure, the Court in *Cooper* was right about one very important point (other than its substantive interpretation of the Fourteenth Amendment). The Constitution does mandate a very strong, near-but-not-quite-absolute obligation of executive deference to court decisions in one specific context: The enforcement of judgments in specific cases. When courts enter judgments, those judgments have legally binding force, which other actors are obligated to obey unless those judgments are so unreasonable that they exceed the bounds of the "judicial power." The argument for that claim is made at length elsewhere,[71] but almost no one contests that judgments are, at the very least, presumptively binding.[72] Indeed, the most likely objection will be to our qualification that, at least in extreme cases, judgments might not be absolutely binding.[73] We can take as given that there is, at least in ordinary cases, some form of mandatory deference for court judgments in specific cases.

The opinions that accompany those judgments and explain the reasoning behind them, however, have no such mandatorily binding force. Indeed, nothing in the Constitution or in the nature of judicial power even requires the issuance of opinions with judgments. It might be a very good practice, but it is not legally required.[74] From a strict constitutional standpoint, opinions are akin to press releases; the true exercise of judicial power comes in the form of a judgment. The principles of coordinacy that were (correctly) laid out in *Marbury v. Madison* preclude any kind of mandatory deference to judicial pronouncements that extend beyond the bare judgment in the case.

Of course, even if the US Constitution does not in fact prescribe mandatory legislative and executive deference to courts, one would still be able to explain the fact of such deference if legislative and executive actors uniformly believed in such a prescription. Possibly enough legislative and executive actors hold that belief to explain away the practice, though, as we have noted, we doubt whether that is true at least of executive actors. Especially in administrations that purport to take seriously the idea of original constitutional meaning, one is likely to see strong representation at the highest levels of the executive legal arm of the "departmentalist" view that each coordinate institution has its own power and duty of legal interpretation. Accordingly, we still face the key question: If legislative and executive deference to courts, outside of the enforceability of specific judgments, is discretionary rather than mandatory, why do we see so much of it? Why would powerful political actors choose to give way on such an important matter as constitutional interpretation?

Ultimately, that is a question that others far better versed than we in political science have sought to answer,[75] and in the final analysis we leave the field to them. We think, however, that one can profitably think about the subject through the lens of deference. Are there legitimation, epistemological, economic, signaling, or prudential/strategic reasons for such deference?

There are no legitimation arguments for such deference. There is nothing in the text or design of the Constitution that suggests that courts are more—or less—legitimate as interpreters than any other legal actor. The courts must interpret in their own spheres, but that says nothing about what legislative and executive actors should be doing in their respective spheres. Each of the three departments is vested with a particular kind of governmental power, and the power and duty of interpretation is equally incidental to each of those powers. There is nothing unique or special about the judicial power in this regard.

Of course, as a descriptive matter, it is possible that some actors believe, however mistakenly, that courts are somehow more legitimate as interpreters than are legislators and executives. Certainly there are a good many judges who take that view. Consider this statement from the joint opinion of the US Supreme Court in *Planned Parenthood of Southeastern Pennsylvania v. Casey*:

> Like the character of an individual, the legitimacy of the Court must be earned over time. So, indeed, must be the character of a Nation of people who aspire to live according to the rule of law. Their belief in themselves as such a people is not readily separable from their understanding of the Court invested with the authority to decide their constitutional cases and speak *before all others* for their constitutional ideals.[76]

We have no hard data on how many judges, of the Supreme Court or lower federal courts, share this somewhat exalted view of the judicial role in the constitutional design, though Professor Lawson, for his part, suspects (with nothing but anecdotal evidence to support him) that the number is fewer today, after several decades of discussion of departmentalism, than it was in the 1980s and 1990s, when federal courts threw temper tantrums whenever executive actors tried to think for themselves.[77] But as that past judicial (over)reaction to executive action that does not meekly follow the courts illustrates, departmentalist thinking had penetrated into the executive department even by that time, especially in Republican administrations where arguments from original meaning were likely to carry more sway with Department of Justice officials. Accordingly, we doubt whether one can explain the vast amount of executive deference to judicial decisions simply by reference to legitimation concerns.

Arguments from epistemological deference to courts are of dubious merit as a matter of first principles, unless one is wedded (as are some very smart people) to an interpretative methodology in which court decisions are considered good evidence of right answers simply because they are court decisions.[78] That is, it is possible to have a theory of interpretation in which the "right answer" is ascertained by determining the "right answerer." On this model, court decisions are entitled to epistemological deference simply because they are court decisions and the meaning of legal texts comes from—is defined by—court decisions.[79] We are not fans of this approach, but because this book is not about legal interpretation, we do not want to engage it on the substance.[80] We assume that most people, including most government officials, have some idea about how to interpret legal texts that does not reduce entirely to "whatever interpreter X says" (though perhaps that view is better represented in the real world than we credit). For anyone who has a view of interpretative meaning that is external to court decisions, those decisions will only be good evidence of right answers if factual conditions for epistemological deference are satisfied. Are the courts actually looking for right answers, as defined by whatever one's theory of right answers might be, or are they instead (to paraphrase the song) "looking for law in all the wrong places"? If they are looking in the right places, are they doing it well? Are they even doing it at all, or is most of the work being done by law clerks barely a year out of law school? And are they doing it comparatively better than any other competing sources of interpretation? It is very hard to argue that the legal staff of Congress or the executive is utterly lacking in interpretative expertise. It is possible that some courts at some times have some kind of comparative advantage over these other actors, but it is not at all hard to imagine—or witness—instances in which it is the other way around. There are, after all, people in the Department of Justice who have devoted their entire lives to studying a relatively narrow band of questions and have thus acquired an expertise in those questions that no court will ever approach.

This is not a categorical argument against epistemological deference to court decisions. As we just said, we do not believe that categorical arguments, of any kind, can be made in this context. It is only to say that one cannot justify wide-ranging legislative and executive deference to court decisions, of the kind that characterizes actual legislative and executive legal interpretation in the face of court decisions, based on epistemological concerns.

Whether one can descriptively explain such deference in epistemological terms is also doubtful. Legislative and executive interpreters are, in our experience, keenly aware of their own talents and expertise, and they are keenly aware of the limitations of judges (and the judges' barely-out-of-law-school law clerks). The idea that judges know best simply does not ring true as a position held so dominantly by governmental actors that it fully explains modern legal practice.

Economic deference may be more plausible, both as a justification and an explanation, for widespread legislative and executive deference to courts. The volume of decisions that must be made in a modern government the size of the US government is beyond massive. To assess each of those decisions from scratch in light of whatever happens to be the governing interpretative theory of the institution (which is likely to change somewhat as the institutional personnel change) would be a mammoth undertaking. It is not clear that either the legislature or the executive has the resources to undertake it. Instead, the assumption is that on most matters, the legislative and executive interpreters will "free ride" on the efforts of the courts, unless the stakes are high enough to warrant investment of resources in an independent assessment of the matter. As a descriptive matter, this explanation has an element of plausibility. Whether it serves as a justification depends on how one understands the "duty" to say what the law is. If that duty is not delegable, because it is a function vested personally in various governmental agents who thus have obligations personally to exercise their discretion, even very substantial cost savings may not justify the practice of deference, though if resources are scarce enough to foreclose independent assessment in all cases, there might be a sufficient necessity to allow delegation of the interpretative function to carry the day.[81]

Another kind of economic argument for deference focuses on the benefits of uniformity. If the legislature, executive, and judiciary (and the various state governmental actors as well) all have an independent power of interpretation, the costs of ascertaining "the law" go up. Especially if the various actors do not agree, that creates compliance costs and legal risks for those seeking to conform to "the law." The whole point of law, one might argue, is to provide a mechanism for the settlement of disputes. A regime of multiple interpreters reduces the effectiveness of that settlement function. These concerns have led some very notable (and very, very smart) jurisprudential thinkers, such as Larry Alexander and Fred Schauer, to conclude that judicial supremacy is a *normative* imperative even if it is not interpretatively prescribed by the US Constitution.[82] The settlement function of law, they say, requires a supreme interpreter, and even if the Supreme Court is not ideal, it is the best available choice for that role. While the authors of this argument do not frame their case in the language of economic deference, it slots into that category very nicely. The costs that are minimized in this model are not necessarily the decision costs of judges (though that might play a role as well) but the decision costs of those who must comply with the commands of the legal system. Those costs are very real, so they are entirely sensible subjects for an analysis based on economic deference.

One of us has previously responded to this argument at a length brief enough (if only barely) to reproduce here:

> Consider the more general case for a regime that divides governmental power through separation of powers and bicameralism. Separation of powers, as its critics are quick to point out, is very messy. The American system of separation of powers and bicameralism, which provides for the possibility, and even likelihood, of divided government, is especially messy. The lawmaking process is slow, cumbersome, and difficult. The laws that emerge from such a divided regime are likely to lack coherence, and thus likely to lack some of the characteristics that make law valuable. The separation of execution from lawmaking increases the cumbersomeness, unpredictability, and incoherence of the system: the actual effect of laws will vary enormously across space and time with variations in enforcement regimes. Throw in a separate judicial body and the problems of predictability and coherence multiply. Separation of powers and bicameralism significantly

threaten the settlement function of law. The same arguments can be made about federalism. The dispersion of authority among distinct governmental actors creates the possibility of conflicts among jurisdictions and reduces the clarity of signals sent by any one jurisdiction to its subjects. Federalism significantly threatens the settlement function of law.

Separation of powers, bicameralism, and federalism are all mechanisms for dispersing power that make it more difficult for wise lawmakers to produce and enforce a stable, coherent body of law and make it more difficult for subjects to conform to the commands of their masters. If one was confident that the governmental masters were likely to be wise and benevolent rulers who would do the right thing a substantial percentage of the time, it is hard to imagine why one would ever adopt a regime containing these structural features. That may be why many countries have not in fact adopted such a regime and why modern America has effectively abandoned it through adoption of administrative mechanisms that mostly dispense with the structural niceties of the Constitution.

But there is nonetheless a powerful normative case for an eighteenth-century-American style system of separated powers, bicameralism, and federalism. Quite simply, separation of powers works better than more concentrated systems, whether parliamentary or dictatorial, if governments are likely to reach a lot of wrong results—whether through corruption, stupidity, disinterest, or lack of knowledge. Put bluntly, separation of powers reduces the amount of damage that any particular bad people can do. . . . Separation of powers, federalism, and bicameralism are destabilizing, or un-settling, to the point that they seriously threaten some of the core reasons for having law in the first place. Maybe they are in fact a bad idea. But maybe they aren't. It doesn't take very much risk aversion to think that dividing power is, all things considered, likely to work better across a broad range of real-world scenarios than concentrating it in one authority.[83]

In other words, the calculation of costs from concentrating (or dispersing) interpretative authority is much more complex than is conveyed by a simple observation that settlement matters to the law. That does not mean that arguments for judicial supremacy based on economic deference are wrong. It just means that they are difficult and complicated. As always, our goal is to provide a framework for discussion rather than to prescribe right answers.

There might also be signaling and prudential reasons for deferring to legal interpretations by courts, though it is not entirely obvious to whom the signal is being sent or who the legislature or executive fears will take action against them if they do not obey. Nonetheless, it is quite possibly in the category of prudential, or strategic, deference that the best explanation for the modern practice of deference to courts lies.

In the end, the best descriptive explanation for the near-universal practice of legislative and executive deference to courts may be, as Professor Keith Whittington has eloquently argued, that legislators and executives often find it politically expedient to pawn their responsibility off on another actor, who can take the blame for unpopular decisions and provide additional political support for positions that the legislature or executive favor. As Professor Whittington puts it:

> Relative judicial independence and authority can help elected political officials overcome a variety of political dilemmas that they routinely encounter. In particular, the authority of the federal judiciary is rooted in concerns for electoral success and coalitional maintenance and the complications for political action create by the American constitutional system of fragmented power.[84]

To be sure, it is unlikely that legislative and executive actors will openly announce their strategic goals in deferring in this fashion, so such motives must be inferred from their actions. We leave the task of defending such an inference to political scientists, though we find the analysis of one very, very good political scientist—Professor Whittington—plausible, and even compelling, on this point. Whether this strategic deference rationale has justificatory power we leave to the judgment of the reader. Our contribution (we hope) is simply to provide a framework and vocabulary through which these arguments can be assessed.

## 3. Intra-Agency Deference

Governments are normally defined by their institutions. In the case of the US government, the main institutions are the three great departments: the legislative department, the executive department, and the judicial department. There are subunits within each department: The Congress has the House, the Senate, and various committees; the executive has the presidency, the vice presidency, and numerous agencies and subagencies; and the federal courts have the Supreme Court, the courts of appeals, and the district courts, as well as subordinate bodies such as bankruptcy courts, magistrates, and the like. (The territorial governments form their own distinct category.)

All these institutions are merely forms. They are shells that need to be filled in by people in order to function. Whenever one speaks of the actions of an institution—and this is true outside government as well as within—one speaks metaphorically. It is always and only individual people who act.

Nonetheless, institutions can be designed so that the metaphor of institutional action has significant descriptive and analytical content. People act, but they sometime act in certain, and certain predictable, ways when placed in specific institutional settings. This is why we can meaningfully speak of activities of bodies, such as the Supreme Court, Congress, the President, the Environmental Protection Agency, and so forth, when in fact those bodies consist of shifting assemblages of people who may have very little, culturally or intellectually, in common with their predecessors. The persons who populate the Supreme Court of 2019 are not at all like the persons who populated the Supreme Court of 1819 in many important respects, but the Court continues to speak of itself as an enduring institution; it will use the royal "we" to describe what long-dead people from a two-centuries-gone culture said. There is some positive-law grounding for this metaphor. The US Constitution vests the "judicial Power" in "one Supreme Court, and in such inferior Courts as the Congress may from time to time ordain and establish."[85] The power is vested in the institution, not in the individual people who staff the positions within that institution.

Continuity of this kind also exists within executive institutions. Statutes vest power in, for example, the Administrator of the Environmental Protection Agency (EPA). The person who holds that position, and thus wields the statutory power, changes over time; the Administrator of the EPA in an Obama administration may have as little in common with the Administrator of the EPA in a Trump administration as the modern Supreme Court has in common with its eighteenth- or nineteenth-century predecessors. Nonetheless, the institution of the EPA has an enduring form, both in positive law (statutes) and in practice. Relatively few of the personnel within a federal agency turn over with changes in the presidency. Only a few thousand of the several million federal employees are "political appointees" who can expect to be replaced with changes in control of the presidency. The vast bulk of agency activity, in any federal agency, proceeds on its routine business without much regard for what is happening at the top of the agency's organization chart.

Can this intra-agency continuity be usefully explained or analyzed by viewing it as a form of deference? To a large extent, we think it can.

We have already seen how deference to judicial precedent can be analyzed in terms of deference. We have also seen how courts sometimes give deference to decisions of agencies. Agencies also often give deference to previous action by (different incarnations of) that agency, for many of the same reasons of epistemology, economics, signaling, and prudence/strategy that explain practices of judicial precedent. (It is hard to see how prior incarnations of an agency could be more "legitimate" than a current one, though we suppose that one could concoct scenarios in which that is plausible.) There are a few features of intra-agency deference, however, that differ from what happens with intra-court deference that merit a few words.

Federal agencies do not have any strict legal obligation to obey their own adjudicative precedents. If they promulgate valid rules, they must follow those rules until and unless they are properly repealed, at least when those rules concern substantive rights (or perhaps procedural rights that are closely tied to substantive rights).[86] But adjudicative orders do not have the same binding status. Agencies with adjudicative authority are free to abandon or overrule prior precedents, and those new precedents can sometimes be applied retroactively in the cases in which they are adopted.[87]

That does not mean, however, that agencies do not owe any kind of mandatory deference to their prior adjudicative decisions. To the contrary, they owe those internal precedents a somewhat stronger form of deference than is prescribed by *Skidmore* for federal courts reviewing agency legal interpretations that do not merit *Chevron* deference: Adjudicating agencies must *acknowledge and consider* their prior decisions, and if they choose not to follow them, they must *explain why they made that choice*.[88] (Pure *Skidmore* deference would require consideration of the prior decisions, but would not impose the additional requirement of an explanation for departure from them.) As one court has summarized the doctrine, an agency is "not at liberty to ignore its prior decisions but must instead provide a reasoned justification for departing from precedent."[89] This requirement stems from the more general requirement imposed on federal agencies of reasoned decision-making, principally through the Administrative Procedure Act's provision instructing courts to set aside agency decisions that are "arbitrary, capricious, an abuse of discretion, or otherwise not in accordance with law."[90] Modern courts maintain that it is "arbitrary or capricious" to fail to consider past decisions that are on point, and they further maintain that those decisions create at least a modest anchor that requires some affirmative explanation for any change from the status quo. That explanation need not be especially detailed,[91] and it can involve nothing more than a conclusion that the previous agency had the wrong policy, but the explanation must exist, at the very least to counter any reliance interests created by past decisions.

Agencies can, of course, avoid following precedents without discarding or overruling them by acknowledging those precedents and then distinguishing them. Interestingly, federal agencies in these contexts of distinguishing past agency decisions appear to get no deference from courts in the interpretation of the agencies' own prior decisions.[92] The courts decide for themselves what the agency decisions mean and whether they are consistent. That is in sharp contrast to the deference given to agencies (at least as of 2019, pending an overruling of *Auer v. Robbins*) in the interpretation of the agencies' own regulations.

The foregoing all deals with mandatory deference, in which courts compel agencies to give some measure of deference to their prior adjudicative decisions. Agencies are free to give their prior decisions discretionary deference, based on all of the same reasons that might justify the practice of discretionary deference by courts to their own decisions. One might, at first glance, suspect that there is likely to be less discretionary deference within federal agencies than within federal courts. Agencies, after all, are bodies that change with the political winds, at least at the top decision-making levels, more quickly than do courts. Top agency officials either serve at the pleasure of the President or serve fixed terms that seldom exceed five years, so turnover at that level will be far more rapid than with a life-tenured judiciary. Depending upon the ideological commitments of the outgoing and incoming administrations, there could be very large swings in policy preferences among top decision-makers; surely Donald Trump's and Barack Obama's Secretaries of Education, for example, do not share policy views across a wide range of important matters

Nonetheless, while we have no empirical data on which to base this judgment, our anecdotal sense is that policy changes, and especially policy changes resulting from adjudications, are considerably less dramatic than either political rhetoric or political reality might suggest. For a good chunk of the regulated world and the regulators who oversee it, life goes on more or less without regard to who wins elections and who gets appointed to run the agencies. This is not to say that changes in administrations are unimportant; of course they are important. But there is (without our being able to quantify this assertion) more continuity than change in government over time. We are neither political scientists nor empiricists, so we do not want to make strong claims along these lines. We do think there is room for those who do have the necessary expertise to explore the matter, and we hope that our framework for deference can help explain this phenomenon, if we are right that it is a phenomenon that bears explanation.

The same considerations of epistemology and economics that drive much discretionary judicial deference to precedent surely apply as well to agencies. Agencies have limited times and limited budgets. Even if they were inclined to reconsider everything from scratch, the costs are just too high. The sheer volume of activity governed by federal adjudicative authority makes some kind of intra-agency deference inevitable; in 2017, for example, the Social Security Administration alone processed more than two million claims for disability benefits.[93] Moreover, much agency decision-making takes place at lower rather than higher levels of the agency's structure. For epistemological purposes, those lower-level decisions might sometimes (not always, but sometimes) carry more epistemological weight than decisions made by higher-ups. Much of the low-level structure consists of career, or at least long-term, employees who may have substantial expertise, both from training and experience, and whose views therefore merit some epistemological deference. As with discretionary judicial deference to precedent, of course, much may depend on what the later decision-maker thinks that the prior decision-maker was doing. If the suspicion is that prior decision-makers were not really applying expertise to a problem but were instead concealing a naked political agenda (and an agenda contrary to that of the current administration) in the language of technocracy, one will be disinclined to give those decisions much weight, just as courts might (justifiably) be suspicious of prior judicial decisions based on what the later court regards as faulty methodology. In these respects, internal agency decision-making can be analyzed using the same terms and considerations that one uses to analyze judicial precedent.

There is, however, perhaps a prudential, or strategic, element to discretionary agency deference that might not be present for courts. Agencies, unlike courts, have an ongoing responsibility to monitor and shape behavior. They adjudicate in pursuit of specific missions and not simply as dispute-resolving mechanisms. They resolve disputes created by their own policies (or by those of the legislature, which then commits implementation of those policies to the agencies). However broadly one thinks that courts actually are policymaking bodies, the courts do not have the same direct oversight responsibilities over primary behavior. Agencies accordingly may want, or need, to employ some notion of deference to their prior decisions as a means of securing compliance and cooperation from regulated parties. As Professor Aaron Nielson has pointed out,[94] agencies often pursue regulatory strategies that will only succeed if regulated parties behave a certain way over an extended period of time. But regulated parties will be understandably reluctant to make investments in certain behaviors if the agencies' requirements are likely to change. In order to induce desired long-term investments in behavior, agencies need credible commitment mechanisms that can provide at least some measure of assurance that change will not happen too rapidly. Judicial doctrines that place constraints on the agencies' ability to shift positions quickly and easily may serve that function, and agencies can perhaps contribute by adopting— and credibly sticking to—discretionary practices of deference to their own decisions. We make no empirical claims about how often this rationale drives agency practice, but it does seem like something that is more applicable to agency than to court decision-making. Courts are less likely to act with specific repeat players in the regulated world in mind.

In sum, agencies have multiple reasons for engaging in intra-agency deference. Sometimes that deference is mandatory; the agency's only choice is whether to obey the law, either statutory or judge-made, that orders the agency to defer to its prior decisions. Sometimes that deference is discretionary; agencies have the same epistemological and economic incentives as do courts to defer, and agencies may have prudential/strategic reasons for internal deference that courts do not. Our sense is that jurisprudential scholars have paid much less attention to intra-agency deference than to intra-court deference. Given the relative importance of agencies and courts in the modern world, we are not sure that this is a desirable allocation of scholarly resources. Looking at internal agency decision-making through the lens of deference is a promising research agenda.

## 4. Judicial Deference to Foreign Law

In 2010, voters in the state of Oklahoma overwhelmingly approved a state constitutional amendment providing:

The [Oklahoma state] Courts . . . , when exercising their judicial authority, shall uphold and adhere to the law as provided in the United States Constitution, the Oklahoma Constitution, the United States Code, federal regulations promulgated pursuant thereto, established common law, the Oklahoma Statutes and rules promulgated pursuant thereto, and if necessary the law of another state of the United States provided the law of the other state does not include Sharia Law, in making judicial decisions. The courts shall not look to the legal precepts of other nations or cultures. Specifically, the courts shall not consider international law or Sharia Law. The provisions of this subsection shall apply to all cases before the respective courts including, but not limited to, cases of first impression.[95]

This provision never took effect because it was held unconstitutional by a federal court[96] and consequently was not certified by the Oklahoma Board of Elections as a validly enacted amendment. That is surely a good thing for Oklahomans. Suppose that an Oklahoma business engages in a transaction with a company in Mexico, and both parties agree that resolving contract disputes according to Mexican law is the most efficient choice-of-law rule even if jurisdiction over the dispute arises in Oklahoma courts. Such choice-of-law provisions are commonplace in commercial transactions, and the law of US jurisdictions will not always be the agreed-upon law of choice. The proposed Oklahoma amendment would, on its face, have forbidden Oklahoma courts from applying these contractual choice-of-law provisions—or any other choice-of-law rules that would normally govern which might point to foreign law as the appropriate substantive rule.

It is a fair guess that preventing application of such commercial choice-of-law agreements was not the motivating force behind this proposed—and, let us not forget, electorally approved—constitutional amendment. Two considerations rather obviously drove it. One is evident on the face of the provision: Voters in Oklahoma did not want their courts to apply Sharia law (or even the law of other American states that are willing to apply Sharia law). The second, and broader, undercurrent that drove this amendment has deeper foundations.

In the decade preceding the vote on this amendment in Oklahoma, there was much discussion, both scholarly and popular, throughout the United States about the appropriateness of using the law of foreign countries in American legal decisions.[97] There was, of course, no real controversy about the appropriateness of enforcing choice-of-law provisions in commercial contracts. There was immense controversy, however, about the appropriateness of invoking foreign law and practices in the interpretation of the US Constitution. Some Justices of the US Supreme Court invoked foreign law and practices when deciding, as a matter of US constitutional law, cases on such hot-button topics as the constitutionality of the death penalty for juvenile offenders[98] or the criminalization of homosexuality.[99]

The 2005 case involving the juvenile death penalty, *Roper v. Simmons*, involved an especially controversial use of foreign law. It was settled (even if, from the standpoint of original meaning, erroneous) law in 2005 that under the Eighth Amendment's prohibition of cruel and unusual punishments,[100] the constitutionality of any criminal sentence, including imposition of the death penalty, was to be evaluated by reference to "the evolving standards of decency that mark the progression of a maturing society."[101] The defendant who was sentenced to death in *Roper* committed his crime—and it was an appallingly gruesome and brutal crime[102]—when he was seventeen years old. The majority found the death sentence unconstitutional because the Eighth Amendment, in its judgment, categorically forbids the death penalty for offenders under the age of eighteen. Most of the majority's opinion in *Roper*, authored by Justice Anthony Kennedy, focused on the practices of American states, in an effort to identify "objective indicia of consensus . . . that today our society views juveniles . . . as 'categorically less culpable than the average criminal.'"[103] While the dissenting opinions by Justices O'Connor and Scalia strongly contested the persuasiveness of the empirical evidence mustered in support of such a national consensus,[104] the real fireworks came from the following discussion in the majority opinion:

> Our determination that the death penalty is disproportionate punishment for offenders under 18 finds confirmation in the stark reality that the United States is the only country in the world that continues to give official sanction to the juvenile death penalty. . . .
>
> . . . Article 37 of the United Nations Convention on the Rights of the Child, which every country in the world has ratified save for the United States and Somalia, contains an express prohibition on capital punishment for crimes committed by juveniles under 18. No ratifying country has entered a reservation to the provision prohibiting the execution of juvenile offenders . . . .
>
> . . . [O]nly seven countries other than the United States have executed juvenile offenders since 1990: Iran, Pakistan, Saudi Arabia, Yemen, Nigeria,

the Democratic Republic of Congo, and China. Since then each of these countries has either abolished capital punishment for juveniles or made public disavowal of the practice. In sum, it is fair to say that the United States now stands alone in a world that has turned its face against the juvenile death penalty.

. . . .

It is proper that we acknowledge the overwhelming weight of international opinion against the juvenile death penalty. . . . The opinion of the world community, while not controlling our outcome, does provide respected and significant confirmation for our own conclusions.

. . . It does not lessen our fidelity to the Constitution or our pride in its origins to acknowledge that the express affirmation of certain fundamental rights by other nations and peoples simply underscores the centrality of those same rights within our own heritage of freedom.[105]

Justice Scalia, joined by Chief Justice William Rehnquist and Justice Clarence Thomas, took grave exception to the majority's use of foreign law and practice to interpret the Eighth Amendment:

. . . [T]he basic premise of the Court's argument—that American law should conform to the laws of the rest of the world—ought to be rejected out of hand. In fact the Court itself does not believe it. In many significant respects the laws of most other countries differ from our law—including not only such explicit provisions of our Constitution as the right to jury trial and grand jury indictment, but even many interpretations of the Constitution prescribed by this Court itself. The Court-pronounced exclusionary rule, for example, is distinctively American. . . .

Most other countries—including those committed to religious neutrality—do not insist on the degree of separation between church and state that this Court requires. . . .

And let us not forget the Court's abortion jurisprudence, which makes us one of only six countries that allow abortion on demand until the point of viability. . . .

. . . .

The Court responds that "[i]t does not lessen our fidelity to the Constitution or our pride in its origins to acknowledge that the express affirmation of certain fundamental rights by other nations and peoples simply underscores the centrality of those same rights within our own heritage of freedom." To begin with, I do not believe that approval by "other nations and peoples" should buttress our commitment to American principles any more than (what should logically follow) disapproval by "other nations and peoples" should weaken that commitment. More importantly, however, the Court's statement flatly misdescribes what is going on here. Foreign sources are cited today, *not* to underscore our "fidelity" to the Constitution, our "pride in its origins," and "our own [American] heritage." To the contrary, they are cited *to set aside* the centuries-old American practice—a practice still engaged in by a large majority of the relevant States—of letting a jury of 12 citizens decide whether, in the particular case, youth should be the basis for withholding the death penalty. What these foreign sources "affirm," rather than repudiate, is the Justices' own notion of how the world ought to be, and their diktat that it shall be so henceforth in America.[106]

Apart from Justice Scalia's objection to the selective use by the majority of foreign law, these passages reveal a deeper disagreement about the implications of the use of foreign law for US *sovereignty*. Does it denigrate the US Constitution, and the US legal tradition, to rely on foreign sources as legal authority in this fashion? The voters of Oklahoma surely had this kind of question in mind (however inarticulately) when they sought to limit Oklahoma courts to the use only of domestic law.

Posed this way, the question about the relationship between sovereignty and the use of foreign law has broader significance. Tribunals frequently make use of, or defer, to foreign law. Sometimes, that is a direct application of mandatory deference; there are many circumstances, as we have noted, in which a domestic choice-of-law rule or an express agreement among parties will point to foreign law as the rule of decision. Domestic law can thus directly, as a formal matter, incorporate foreign law into its content (though the distinction between foreign and domestic law in those circumstances can still be highly relevant for matters such as the methods for proof of the applicable law). *Roper* was not such a case; any deference to foreign law in that setting was entirely discretionary with the Court. The US Constitution does make specific reference to foreign law when it gives Congress power to "define Offenses against the Law of Nations,"[107] but nothing suggests that the law of nations, or the law of any specific nation, helps define the meaning of the rest of the Constitution. The *Roper* Court's reference to foreign law as a source of meaning for the Eighth Amendment was not commanded by any domestic choice-of-law rule.

This kind of discretionary deference to foreign law is a worldwide phenomenon. A book authored in 2006 by Professors Basil Markesinis and Jörg Fedtke chronicles the practices—sometimes open, sometimes covert—of seven national courts with respect to the use of foreign law in domestic disputes: the United States, for which we have already seen evidence of strong dispute regarding the legitimacy of the practice in some contexts[108]; Italy and France, whose courts use foreign law, but do not overtly admit to it[109]; England and Germany, whose courts openly cite foreign materials[110]; and Canada and South Africa, whose courts make wide-ranging use of foreign law.[111] Israeli courts as well make more than occasional use of foreign law. A good example comes from a 2017 case in which Israeli Supreme Court Vice President Justice Elyakim Rubinstein used foreign law much as did the US Supreme Court in *Roper* to buttress the conclusion that prisoner overcrowding in Israeli prisons was unlawful:

> The topic of the proper living space for prisoners and detainees engaged many countries in the world, of all kinds, both those considered well-ordered and those who have not acquired a good reputation in this area. . . .
>
> While we have not overlooked respondents' position, arguing for caution in comparing foreign laws to the balance made by the Israeli legislator, and while clearly every country has its nature, needs and capabilities, I am of the opinion that the sheer scope of comparative law treatment of the issue at hand—together with the fact that, to a large extent, this is a universal issue of human dignity—require that we also cast our look overseas. Clearly, this does not mean the outright adoption of the regime applicable at a certain state into our legal system; the survey is only meant to enlighten us, as we seek a solution to an issue that is at our doorstep. The inmate-man in of himself is one and the same across the universe. History and literature are laden with interpretation and stories on incarceration and incarceration conditions in regimes to which we have neither been nor will we be alike in any form and fashion, not only in past eras but also in generations close to us and in our generations, between calaboose and gulag. Israel wishes to be to be seen as the most orderly of states, and this topic, while physically in the "back yard," is normatively front window.[112]

The precise scope and contours of this practice in specific countries are not important for our project; it is enough for now to observe simply that the practice of referring to foreign law in judicial decisions is widespread.

We thus propose to take a brief look beyond the boundaries of the United States to the phenomenon of deference to foreign law.[113] Specifically, we will look at what Professor Michal Bobek has identified as "non-mandatory references to foreign law by a national judge in interpreting domestic law for the purposes of solving a domestic dispute."[114] Our focus is on the extent to which discretionary deference to foreign law raises concerns about sovereignty and whether our account of deference can help shed light on these concerns. Such worries about the effect on sovereignty of the use of foreign law by domestic courts, one should note, are not limited to Justice Scalia and the voters of Oklahoma. Concerns about loss of sovereignty because of deference to foreign tribunals has been an active topic of conversation throughout the world for some time.[115]

To be sure, the use of foreign law can be controversial even apart from any concerns about sovereignty. Justice Scalia's dissenting opinion in *Roper* raised the problem of inconsistent application of foreign law; it appears to be invoked when it supports the personal views of the judges rather than in accordance with some neutral principle that would specify in advance when and how foreign law might be relevant. Moreover, at least in recent times in the United States, foreign law is discretionarily invoked seemingly uniformly in favor of "liberal" or "progressive" outcomes, such as the unconstitutionality of the juvenile death penalty or criminalization of homosexuality. One can approve of the results in such cases (as the two of us often do, though not always or necessarily in sync) while still worrying about the intellectual consistency that underlies the decision-making process. Moreover, the use of foreign law raises the well-worn problem of the methodological weakness of much of comparative law. As we have written elsewhere:

> In more than a century of research and study in the modern era, comparative law has failed to adopt or evolve a clear methodology stating how comparisons are to be made, and the result is often a free-for-all in which partisans pick their favorite sources without rigorous guiding principles. A judge who has an interest in comparative law can try to persuade his brethren to take into account—or reject—the law of any other jurisdiction—of any size, continent, legal history, or socio-economic makeup—that she sees fit.[116]

For this project, we simply note these concerns without addressing or evaluating them. We concentrate on issues regarding national sovereignty. Why would national courts ever defer to the views of courts of other countries on matters of domestic law, and does the practice threaten the sovereignty of the deferring nation?

Start with the "why" question. Our framework for analyzing deference fits neatly into the practice of deferring to foreign courts on matters of domestic law.

One might initially wonder how or why a foreign tribunal could ever be seen to have more legitimacy than a domestic tribunal on a question of domestic law. But on reflection, legitimation deference is a perfectly reasonable ground for deference in a wide range of circumstances. Consider the situation of an emerging or developing country. This is a common phenomenon in the modern world. At the end of World War II, there were fewer than 100 countries in the world (the exact number depends on what one counts as a country).[117] In 2018, the number was roughly twice that amount (again subject to differing understandings of what counts as a country),[118] with thirty-four of those countries dating from 1990 onward.[119] How should a new country organize its legal system, and what forms of law should it draw upon? The answer obviously depends on how well developed, and acceptable, a legal system existed in the country before nationhood. It may well be that the most legitimate source of law for a new country will be found in another country with a better established legal tradition.

An example is readily at hand. In 1776, thirteen new countries emerged on the North American continent; their status as countries was confirmed by treaty and the international community in 1783, upon conclusion of a war against the colonial empire that previously exercised sovereignty over the territory. Those new nations needed to establish forms of government and legal systems. They could have constructed domestic legal institutions from scratch, but instead they uniformly relied on the law of the former colonial occupier. In constitution after constitution, these new nations, which were eventually going to consolidate into a single United States of America, adopted provisions declaring that the law of England was to be the law of those nation/states. For example, the Declaration of Rights in the Maryland Constitution of November 11, 1776, provided that

the inhabitants of Maryland are entitled to the common law of England, and the trial by Jury, according that law, and to the benefit of such of the English statutes, as existed at the time of their first emigration, and which, by experience, have been found applicable to their local and other circumstances, and of such others as have been since made in England, or Great Britain, and have been introduced, used and practiced by the courts of law or equity; and also to acts of Assembly, in force on the first of June seventeen hundred and seventy-four, except such as may have since expired, or have been or may be altered by facts of Convention, or this Declaration of Rights-subject, nevertheless, to the revision of, and amendment or repeal by, the Legislature of this State.[120]

The New York Constitution of April 20, 1777, similarly provided that "the good people of this State, ordain, determine, and declare that such parts of the common law of England, and of the statute law of England and Great Britain, and of the acts of the legislature of the colony of New York, as together did form the law of the said colony on the 19th day of April, in the year of our Lord one thousand seven hundred and seventy-five, shall be and continue the law of this State, subject to such alterations and provisions as the legislature of this State shall, from time to time, make concerning the same."[121]

It is not difficult to imagine modern conditions in which developing countries might find it helpful to incorporate the law from other jurisdictions that have more fully developed legal systems—conceivably even if those countries are the very colonial empires from which the new countries emerged. The long establishment of those systems might well give them a legitimacy that a ground-up attempt to construct a new legal order might not have. In that sense, deference to foreign law may be more legitimate than a purely domestic order.

Many of the same considerations underlying legitimation deference to foreign law may also support epistemological deference. Justice Stephen Breyer, who has long championed the use of foreign law in cases such as *Roper*, defends this usage by noting:

cases sometimes involve a human being working as a judge concerned with a legal problem, often similar to problems that arise here [in the United States], which problem involves the application of a legal text, often similar to the text of our own Constitution, seeking to protect certain basic human rights, often similar to the rights that our own Constitution seeks to protect.[122]

These epistemological views find support in the economics of information, which suggest that groups can draw on dispersed knowledge to reach better decisions than can individual actors.[123] As legal systems become more transnational in general, the occasions for this kind of learning across systems is sure to increase. As with domestic law, sometimes an independent search for a right answer suggests that the best course of action is to defer to someone better positioned to reach that answer. Obviously, this is not a recipe for deference to others in all circumstances, but it can support deference in limited situations when the conditions for epistemological deference are satisfied.

One suspects that the new American nations/states in the eighteenth century chose to incorporate, at least presumptively, the laws of England not only for legitimation and epistemological reasons but also because crafting a set of common law and statutory norms from scratch would take too long and cost too much. There are evident reasons grounded in economic deference for giving weight, and sometimes dispositive weight, to the views of foreign tribunals whose legal norms are likely to be decent fits with the deferring legal system. Again, this is especially likely to be true with emerging or developing legal systems that do not have their own long traditions, practices, and bodies of norms. Those traditions, practices, and bodies may well develop over the course of time, but in the short term deference to foreign tribunals may be the most attractive option. To be sure, there is always bound to be some mismatch between foreign law and domestic circumstances, but the costs of precisely calibrating the one to the other can be prohibitive:

> Sometimes reliance on someone else who has already dealt with a problem saves time and other resources. Perhaps such reliance will not yield the absolutely best answer by the criteria of the domestic legal system, but it is an interesting jurisprudential question whether courts are or should be aiming at the best answer without regard to costs. Perhaps an adequate answer that comes cheaply is better than a perfect answer that comes at the expense of many other potentially adequate answers in other cases. As we have said in another context, "[a]nyone who says there is no price tag on justice understands neither price tags nor justice."[124]

Thus, there can be reasons for deferring to foreign precedents that are comparable, in terms of legitimation, epistemology, and cost, to the reasons for deferring to domestic precedents or other domestic institutions. Those conditions may be more likely to hold in emerging rather than developed legal systems, but there is ample room within even the most developed legal system for some kind of reference to foreign law. Again, we do not endorse (or criticize) any particular practice, or the practice in general. We are not taking sides in the Kennedy-Scalia squabble or any other particular dispute about the propriety of the use of foreign law to help determine domestic norms. We simply offer the observation that our framework for deference is a helpful way both to describe and to assess those practices.

As a matter of description, however, one of the most important reasons for discretionary judicial deference to foreign law may have nothing to do with establishing the normative legitimacy of domestic law, reaching the right answers from within the internal perspective of domestic law, or reducing decision costs within the legal system. It may be that a non-trivial amount of judicial deference to foreign law can be explained (though not necessarily justified) as a form of signaling deference. The key is to decode the signal and to ascertain its intended audience.

A substantial literature exists on the use of foreign law as a judicial signaling device. One of the most elaborate signaling models comes from Professor Eyal Benvenisti.[125] National courts sometimes gain strength from the parallel practices of other national tribunals. On some occasions, the norms themselves become more effective if they are coordinated across a number of jurisdictions; ready examples include human rights norms and pollution control regulations. On other occasions, courts can band together to combat the threat to their individual national sovereignties from supranational forces. In those circumstances, what might seem at first glance like a denial of sovereignty (deference to foreign tribunals) can be part of a global judicial strategy to promote national sovereignty in the long run. For any of these kinds of global judicial cooperation to function, there must be channels of communication among the judges. In theory, one could accomplish such coordination through conferences, list-serves, or old-fashioned phone calls. In practice, this kind of overt judicial coordination is rare, no doubt partly because of appearances and also partly because talk is cheap. Judicial decisions, however, can serve as strong, because legally significant, signals to other potential coordinating partners, and the language of those signals may well be citation to decisions in other jurisdictions. As Professor Benvenisti argues:

> Courts that wish to signal readiness to cooperate will tend to use the language that other courts understand: comparative law (primarily comparative constitutional law) and international law. The use of comparative analysis indicates that courts are willing to learn from

one another, or are seeking support from other jurisdictions for their judgments, or both. More significantly, they learn from each other's legal systems how to balance the competing common interests and how to manage the conflicting common risks to their societies. . . . By referring to each other's interpretation of a shared text, they not only signal readiness to cooperate, but also to a certain extent impede the future retreat of one of them from the shared interpretation: as courts carefully watch each other, the one that backs away has to offer an explanation to its peers.[126]

A simpler, but perhaps in the end even more powerful, model comes from Professor Shai Dothan, who argues that courts at all levels often seek to enhance their own reputations and hence their own influence over other actors.[127] At any given moment in time, certain courts and institutions will enjoy reputational advantages. Weaker bodies, especially in emerging or newly developing legal systems, can enhance their own reputations, and thus increase the chances of compliance with their judgments, by aligning themselves with stronger institutions through deference. Those stronger institutions might well be foreign tribunals, in which case deference to those tribunals can simultaneously serve legitimating, epistemological, economic, and signaling functions. We are not social scientists, so we are in no position to evaluate the extent to which these or other models actually explain or predict judicial behavior. But again, we think our analysis may provide a useful framework through which those models can be assessed.

Because we are not social scientists, we hesitate—for more than a brief moment—before offering our own possible account of how deference to foreign tribunals can send signals to a very different audience than we have been discussing thus far. But as the old saying (and a moment's reflection will reveal just how old a saying, and therefore just how old the authors) goes, "in for a nickel, in for a dime."

One data point that we observe anecdotally, even if we cannot verify it rigorously, is that the debate in US law over the use of foreign law to help interpret the US Constitution divides largely along "left-right" lines. The "liberal" justices, such as Justice Breyer, tend to be much more enthusiastic about this particular use of foreign law than are "conservative" justices such as Justice Thomas and the late Justice Scalia (with former-Justice Kennedy, perhaps characteristically, straddling the middle). More broadly, the voters in Oklahoma approved a constitutional amendment that would never make it to the ballot in California or Rhode Island. We cannot prove it, but we perceive real differences across populations in attitudes toward the use of foreign law.

We are skeptical that US Supreme Court justices engage in the kind of strategic, cooperative signaling to other tribunals postulated by Professor Benvenisti (though we could be wrong about that). We suspect that they use foreign law as a signal to a different audience.

Our starting point is an observation by Professor Steven Calabresi noting the disjunction between "liberal elite" views on the use of foreign law and the attitudes of the general population in the United States toward the practice:

> This is a tale of two cultures. The first culture is that of the United States Supreme Court and the lawyerly elite. In that culture, it is not only socially acceptable for the Court and law professors to rely on foreign law in deciding American cases, it is obligatory that they do so. . . . The other culture . . . is the popular culture of the vast majority of American citizens, as shaped by those citizens' political leaders and opinion elites. In this second culture, there is a decidedly different view of the relationship between the United States and foreign legal systems. American popular culture overwhelmingly rejects the idea that the United States has a lot to learn from foreign legal systems, including even those of countries to which we are closely related like the United Kingdom and Canada. Most Americans think instead that the United States is an exceptional country that differs sharply from the rest of the world and that must therefore have its own laws and Constitution.[128]

Perhaps, then, the signal being sent by the use of foreign law is a species of what is sometimes called (almost always disparagingly) "virtue signaling," in which one shows one's membership in a particular social group or adherence to a particular set of norms considered virtuous by that group. The signal, in other words, is not necessarily to political actors in an effort to secure institutional support for the judiciary but to a lawyerly, scholarly, and political community to show one's "globalist" and cosmopolitan bona fides (while sticking a thumb in the eyes of those rubes in Oklahoma who keep voting for Republicans). As we have said elsewhere:

> This signaling function, to the extent that it really operates, makes sense with reference to citation of foreign materials as well as with domestic scholarly sources. The United States is almost singular, among rich, Western nations, in not providing universal health care, in keeping and applying the

death penalty, in not participating in the International Criminal Court, and in its limited control over private ownership of firearms. Whether one likes it or not,[129] there is a reason for these differences, and they are deeply rooted in American constitutionalism, tradition, and public policy. It would not be entirely strange for judges, who are people who likely have some regard for their reputations, to use the tools at their disposal to situate themselves along these divides.[130]

It also sets terms of debate that are likely to be favorable to the liberal side. "Consider this: the only nations not party to the Paris climate accord are Syria and Nicaragua; the only European country to hold an execution in 2016 was Belarus; and the only countries to execute persons who were underage when they committed the offense were Iran and Saudi Arabia."[131] If constitutional interpretation comes down to counting western European countries, US conservatives are going to lose on almost everything (except perhaps abortion, but that is a story for another time).

Assuming that this virtue-signaling function explains at least part of the deference to foreign law shown by US courts in constitutional cases, it is an interesting definitional question whether it can properly be called deference. If foreign law plays no role at all in the actual decision process, not even as an addition to the relevant evidence set, but serves purely as a rhetorical add-on, then we are doubtful whether it deserves to be called deference. More plausibly, however, signaling considerations have the effect of at least making foreign law part of the evidence set, and we have already seen at length how and why that counts as a form of deference.

We can now address whether and when deference to foreign law poses a threat to national sovereignty. We have already seen how Professor Eyal Benvenisti postulates circumstances in which such deference enhances national sovereignty, and that is surely going to be true in some instances. In other instances, however, there is surely some loss of sovereignty involved in delegating the lawmaking and law-interpreting processes to foreign tribunals. It may be a very small price to pay for large legitimating, epistemological, and/or economic benefits, but it is a price that should at least be noted. Much turns on how and why tribunals defer to foreign law. We stand by the tentative answer that we reached when first pondering this question:

If the judges are really still deciding for themselves, there is neither delegation nor loss of independence.... If they defer as a result of an independent process of analysis that leads to the conclusion that a foreign source is likely to be very good evidence of the right answer (what we have called "epistemological deference"), then there is no delegation or loss of independence. The judges are deciding a matter of domestic law using the best available materials. If those materials happen to come from a foreign source, there is no obvious reason why use of that source to help get the right answer is not a full execution of the judicial function. But if deference results from either a concern about political legitimacy or a desire to save on costs [or signaling or prudential concerns of some kind], there does seem to be an inescapable element of delegation and at least a modest sacrifice of judicial independence. We are not arguing here that deference of that kind is therefore illegitimate. That would require a complex judgment grounded in a deep theory of jurisprudence that we neither have nor present here. But it does seem to be a feature of the practice that is worth noting.

Whether there is any loss of sovereignty in the process depends on the same considerations. When strict application of national law in pursuit of a right answer points outward, there is no more reason to fear loss of sovereignty from that process than to fear it from mandatory applications of foreign law. The judges are determining domestic law as best they can, and they are merely following where the evidence leads. The domestic courts themselves perform the relevant acts of interpretation. That is no more delegation or loss of independence than is consideration of the briefs and arguments of parties. However, if courts defer to foreign sources in the determination of domestic law out of concerns regarding legitimacy or cost savings, then at least part of the decision has seemingly been "outsourced" to foreign interpreters. Again, we say nothing here about whether that practice is good or bad. We simply observe its consequence for anyone who finds it interesting.

In sum, one needs to know *why* a court defers before one can say much about the merits or consequences of that act of deference. We think this is true universally of all instances of deference, and it is therefore true of the particular case of deference to foreign legal sources.[132]

And that seems like an apt thought on which to conclude. Our goal, as we have repeatedly said, is not to tell courts, officials, or scholars what to do. Our goal has been to provide some tools that can be used by courts, officials, and scholars to understand better what they do and why they do it when they defer to other actors, whether those other actors are foreign tribunals, other units of domestic government, or prior decisions by the deferring actor. There is a common analytical framework that can be applied to all these diverse contexts. That framework will not tell anyone how to decide a case or design a legal system. But it might make those processes more transparent and rigorous. That is all we want, and it is all we offer. We hope that at least someone finds it to be enough to justify reading the book.

# Notes

1. PHILIP SOPER, THE ETHICS OF DEFERENCE: LEARNING FROM LAW'S MORALS (2003).
2. *Id.* at 169. *See also id.* at 45 ("deference requires that extra weight be given to the authoritative decision and thus requires one sometimes to act in ways inconsistent with one's own view of the correct judgment").
3. *Id.* at 22.
4. *Id.* at 175–76.
5. *Id.* at 45.
6. *Id.* at 44–45 ("When courts defer to the judgments of another court or agency, we may plausibly describe the situation as one that involves recognizing the subordinate institution's authority to make an initial determination, not necessarily because of greater expertise but because of a prior decision to allocate the 'right to decide' to particular institutions.").
7. *Id.* at 25 (deference can be "a signal about how I value my friends and the ideal of friendship").
8. *See id.* at 24–25, 136–37.
9. These descriptions of instrumental and intrinsic reasons are our own interpolation. Professor Soper defines these terms more by example than by verbal definition. For the clearest account in his own words, *see id.* at 136–37.
10. *See id.* at 44–45.
11. *See id.* at xiii.
12. *See id.* at 182.
13. *Id.* at xii.
14. *See id.* at 45.
15. *See,* e.g., Director, Office of Workers' Comp. Programs, Dep't of Labor v. Greenwich Collieries, 512 U.S. 267, 277 (1994) ("[a] cursory answer to an ancillary and largely unbriefed question does not warrant the same level of deference we typically give our precedents"); Randy J. Kozel, *Precedent and Constitutional Structure,* 112 Nw. U.L. REV. 789, 791 (2018) (discussing "deference to precedent").
16. BRYAN A. GARNER ET AL., THE LAW OF JUDICIAL PRECEDENT (2017).
17. *Id.* at 5, 12. *See also id.* at 6–7 ("Not infrequently the Supreme Court reaffirms debatable decisions on the ground that they warrant deference as precedent").
18. *Id.* at 27.

19. We ran a WESTLAW search for "vertical precedent" to try to find the first use of the term. To our surprise, the earliest entry in the database is Thomas W. Merrill, *Judicial Opinions as Binding Law and as Explanations for Judgments*, 15 CARDOZO L. REV. 43, 61 n.79 (1993)—which attributes the language to one of us: "I have borrowed the useful nomenclature distinguishing between horizontal and vertical precedent from Gary Lawson, *The Constitutional Case Against Precedent*, 17 Harv. J.L. & Pub. Pol'y (forthcoming 1993)." The final version of the cited article by Professor Lawson, as it happens, does not actually contain the term "vertical precedent," though the concept certainly shows up in the article sans the label. *See* Gary Lawson, *The Constitutional Case Against Precedent*, 17 HARV. J.L. & PUB. POL'Y 23, 24 (1994). Probably the term was in an earlier draft and got dropped in the editing (Professor Merrill and Professor Lawson were colleagues at the time, so Professor Merrill would have had access to the draft). Professor Lawson has no recollection of considering himself an innovator in this respect; he is reasonably confident that, a quarter century ago, he got the terms "horizontal precedent" and "vertical precedent" from somewhere else (the name "Larry Alexander" sticks in his mind for some reason). On the other hand, the leading modern survey of precedent notes only: "Not until the early 1980s did scholarly commentators first use the antonyms *horizontal* and *vertical* in reference to precedents." GARNER ET AL., *supra* note 16, at 27. No citation to any source is given. In any event, the classic treatment of vertical, or "hierarchical," precedent is Evan H. Caminker, *Why Must Inferior Courts Obey Supreme Court Precedents?*, 46 STAN. L. REV. 817 (1994).

20. *Id.* at 820.

21. For the notable scholarly exception to the acceptance of vertical precedent, *see* Michael Stokes Paulsen, *The Intrinsically Corrupting Influence of Precedent*, 22 CONST. COMMENTARY 289 (2005); Michael Stokes Paulsen, *Accusing Justice: Some Variations on the Themes of Robert M. Cover's Justice Accused*, 7 J.L. & RELIGION 33 (1990).

22. *See* Steven G. Calabresi & Gary Lawson, *The Unitary Executive, Jurisdiction Stripping, and the Hamdan Opinions: A Textualist Response to Justice Scalia*, 107 COLUM. L. REV. 1002, 1032 (2007).

23. *See*, e.g., Janus v. American Fed'n of State, County, and Mun. Employees, Council 31, 138 S. Ct. 2448, 2460 (2018) ("we recognize the importance of following precedent unless there are strong reasons for not doing so"); Planned Parenthood of Southeastern Pa. v. Casey, 505 U.S. 833, 864 (1992) ("a decision to overrule should rest on some special reason over and above the belief that a prior case was wrongly decided").

24. Indeed, one of us has urged it to do so on the ground that, at least in constitutional cases, the practice of following precedent is affirmatively unconstitutional. *See* Lawson, *supra* note 19; Gary Lawson, *Mostly Unconstitutional: The Case Against Precedent Revisited*, 5 AVE MARIA L. REV. 1 (2007). This is, to say the least, not a view that is widely shared either in the academy or in government, though Professor Lawson, over the course of three decades, has heard more than one federal judge say, not for attribution, that they agreed with the basic thesis.

25. Or several books. *See, e.g.,* GARNER ET AL., *supra* note 16; MICHAEL J. GERHARDT, THE POWER OF PRECEDENT (2011); RANDY J. KOZEL, SETTLED VERSUS RIGHT: A THEORY OF PRECEDENT (2017).

26. *See* Kozel, *supra* note 25.

27. GARNER ET AL., *supra* note 16, at 9–10.

28. *See, e.g.,* Caminker, *supra* note 19, at 846–47.

29. *See* GARNER ET AL., *supra* note 16, at 245–46.

30. *See id.* at 245.

31. *See id.* at 164–65, 248–52.

32. Akhil Reed Amar, *Foreword: The Document and the Doctrine,* 114 HARV. L. REV. 26, 43 (2000).

33. *See* JOHN O. MCGINNIS & MICHAEL B. RAPPAPORT, ORIGINALISM AND THE GOOD CONSTITUTION 187 (2013) ("Many cases have deserved no weight on epistemic grounds because they have not attempted to derive their results from the Constitution's original meaning.").

34. GARNER ET AL., *supra* note 16, at 10.

35. GERHARDT, *supra* note 25, at 158.

36. *See* Randy J. Kozel, *Original Meaning and the Precedent Fallback,* 68 VAND. L. REV. 105, 112–17 (2015).

37. GARNER ET AL., *supra* note 16, at 10.

38. *See,* e.g., Epic Sys. Corp. v. Lewis, 138 S. Ct. 1612, 1623 (2018) ("The law of precedent teaches that like cases should generally be treated alike").

39. Payne v. Tennessee, 501 U.S. 808, 827–28 (1991).

40. GERHARDT, *supra* note 25, at 4–5.

41. *See* 28 C.F.R. § 0.20 (2018).

42. *See id.,* § 0.25(a).

43. *See* Nelson Lund, *Rational Choice at the Office of Legal Counsel,* 15 CARDOZO L. REV. 437, 489 n.128 (1993).

44. *See id.* at 488 ("The Justice Department, however, has never succeeded in gaining anything close to a monopoly over the provision of legal advice within the government.").

45. Executive Order 12,146, *Management of Federal Legal Resources,* § 1-402, 44 Fed. Reg. 42,657 (1979).

46. *Id.,* § 1-401.

47. *See* Lund, *supra* note 43, at 492–95.

48. It is conceivable that the legislature could also defer to the executive on legal matters, and vice versa, but there is little empirical evidence of either practice of which we are aware.

49. Congresses in the founding era took constitutional analysis much more seriously, perhaps because they did not have a body of judicial doctrine on which to fall back. Consider, for example, the extensive debates over the removal power culminating in the "Decision of 1789." *See* Saikrishna Prakash, *New Light on the Decision of 1789,* 91 CORNELL L. REV. 1021 (2006). To be sure, the early Congress did not always distinguish itself through its efforts, *see* Gary Lawson, *The Constitution's Congress,* 89 B.U.

L. REV. 399 (2009) (describing how the very first statute enacted by the first Congress was flagrantly unconstitutional), but at least it tried.

50. Gary Lawson & Christopher D. Moore, *The Executive Power of Constitutional Interpretation*, 81 IOWA L. REV. 1267, 1291 (1996) (footnote omitted).

51. *See* Steven G. Calabresi & Gary Lawson, *Foreword: Two Visions of the Nature of Man*, 16 HARV. J. L. & PUB. POL'Y 1 (1993).

52. James Madison, THE FEDERALIST NO. 48 (1787).

53. *Id.*

54. *Id.* No. 51.

55. *Compare* WILLIAM A. NISKANEN, BUREAUCRACY AND REPRESENTATIVE GOVERNMENT (1971) (advancing the aggrandizement thesis as an explanation for agency action) *with* James Q. Wilson, *The Politics of Regulation, in* THE POLITICS OF REGULATION 372 (James Q. Wilson ed., 1980) (doubting whether aggrandizement explain most agency action).

56. For a short and readable summary of the history, *see* KEITH E. WHITTINGTON, POLITICAL FOUNDATIONS OF JUDICIAL SUPREMACY: THE PRESIDENCY, THE SUPREME COURT, AND CONSTITUTIONAL LEADERSHIP IN U.S. HISTORY 31–39 (2007).

57. Edwin Meese III, *The Law of the Constitution*, 61 TUL. L. REV. 979, 983 (1987).

58. *See* Lawson & Moore, *supra* note 50.

59. *See* U.S. CONST. art. 2, § 1, cl. 7 & art. VI, cl. 3.

60. *Id.*, art. III, §1.

61. Marbury v. Madison, 5 U.S. (1 Cranch) 137, 177 (1803).

62. *Id.*

63. For a detailed account of the real meaning and significance of *Marbury v. Madison, see* Michael Stokes Paulsen, *The Irrepressible Myth of* Marbury, 101 MICH. L. REV. 2706 (2003).

64. Whether the statute actually did any such thing is an open question as a matter of first principles. *See* AKHIL REED AMAR, AMERICA'S CONSTITUTION: A BIOGRAPHY 232 (2005).

65. *See* McCulloch v. Maryland, 17 U.S. (4 Wheat.) 316, 401 (1819).

66. *See* Paulsen, *supra* note 63, at 2714–16. *See also* Gary Lawson, *Interpretative Equality as a Structural Imperative (or "Pucker Up and Settle THIS!")*, 20 CONST. COMMENTARY 379 (2003).

67. The Court in *Marbury* was probably wrong about the power of Congress to enlarge the Supreme Court's original jurisdiction, but that is a matter for another time. *See* Steven G. Calabresi & Gary Lawson, *The Unitary Executive, Jurisdiction Stripping, and the* Hamdan *Opinions: A Textualist Response to Justice Scalia*, 107 COLUM. L. REV. 1002, 1036–47 (2007).

68. 358 U.S. 1 (1958).

69. *Id.* at 18.

70. *Cooper* involved an assertion of coordinate interpretative authority by a state official, not by a coordinate federal department. But the principle of interpretative coordinacy applies to state actors as well as federal ones, because state actors also swear an oath to uphold the Constitution, and the federal courts are no more given an express

interpretative power superior to those of state officials than they are given a power superior to those of other federal officials.

71. *See* Lawson & Moore, *supra* note 50, at 1319–29.

72. The lone dissenter is Professor Michael Stokes Paulsen. *See id.* at 1322–24.

73. Another possibility is that judgments are binding unless the issuing court had no jurisdiction over the case. *See* William Baude, *The Judgment Power*, 96 GEO. L.J. 1807, 1809 (2008) ("the judicial power vested in Article III courts allows them to render binding judgments that must be enforced by the Executive Branch so long as those courts have jurisdiction over the case").

74. Whether Congress can require federal courts to issue opinions, or findings of fact and conclusions of law, raises interesting questions about the scope of congressional power to "carry into Execution" the judicial power that are best left for another time.

75. *See, e.g.*, WHITTINGTON, *supra* note 56.

76. 505 U.S. 833, 869 (1992) (emphasis added).

77. When an executive agency adopted a constitutional viewpoint different from that of the court, a panel of the Court of Appeals for the Ninth Circuit held that it was bad faith warranting an award of attorney's fees against the government. *See* Lear Siegler, Inc. v. Lehman, 842 F.2d 1102, 1119–26 (9th Cir. 1988), *rev'd and remanded*, 893 F.2d 205 (1989) (en banc). The general reaction to nonacquiescence by federal agencies in the 1980s was not materially different. *See* Joshua I. Schwartz, *Nonacquiescence, Crowell v. Benson, and Administrative Adjudication*, 77 GEO. L.J. 1815, 1821 n.15, 1823 n.23 (1989).

78. *See, e.g.*, DAVID A. STRAUSS, THE LIVING CONSTITUTION (2012).

79. For an illustration of this model of "right answerer-ism," *see* Burt Neuborne, *The Binding Quality of Supreme Court Precedent*, 61 TUL. L. REV. 979 (1987); Burt Neuborne, *Panel: The Role of the Legislative and Executive Branches in Interpreting the Constitution*, 73 CORNELL L. REV. 375 (1988).

80. For an extended answer to this position by one of us, see Lawson & Moore, *supra* note 50, at 1293–98.

81. On the agency-law principle that exercises of discretionary governmental power are presumptively non-delegable, absent specific authorizations or a strict necessity, *see* GARY LAWSON & GUY SEIDMAN, "A GREAT POWER OF ATTORNEY": UNDERSTANDING THE FIDUCIARY CONSTITUTION 107–29 (2017).

82. *See* Larry Alexander & Frederick Schauer, *On Extrajudicial Constitutional Interpretation*, 110 HARV. L. REV. 1359 (1997); Larry Alexander & Frederick Schauer, *Defending Judicial Supremacy: A Reply*, 17 CONST. COMMENT. 455 (2000).

83. Lawson, *supra* note 66, at 381–83 (footnotes omitted). One of the omitted footnotes challenges the assumption of Professors Alexander and Schauer that if one must have a supreme interpreter, the Supreme Court is the most plausible choice among the available options. That is a point on which Professor Lawson declares them "embarrassingly wrong," *id.* at 381, because, in his words: "The best candidate for supreme interpreter is, obviously, me. The second best candidate is probably Mike Paulsen, though I suppose that reasonable people could disagree on the proper sequence once we get past me on the list. In any event, there are going to be quite a few people who

are well ahead of the Supreme Court. Of course, I am not mentioned anywhere in the Constitution as a potential authoritative interpreter, but it is unclear why that is relevant to a preconstitutional argument." *Id.* at 381 n.10. Professor Lawson was and is entirely serious about this. If one uses the Constitution to limit the universe of possible interpreters, then the argument is not really pre-constitutional (and then why not use the Constitution to ascertain the assignment of interpretative responsibility?). Is the claim that the Supreme Court is epistemologically superior to all other interpreters on the planet? That seems so implausible as not to warrant discussion.

84. WHITTINGTON, *supra* note 56, at 27.

85. U.S. CONST. art. III, § 1.

86. *See* Thomas W. Merrill, *The* Accardi *Principle*, 74 GEO. WASH. L. REV. 569 (2006). Rules that regulate agency procedures rather than the rights of third parties can be, and sometimes even must be, waived rather than followed, though the case law on this point is notoriously obscure. *See* Leslie v. Attorney Gen. of the United States, 611 F.3d 171, 175–80 (3d Cir. 2010).

87. Retroactive application of new adjudicative precedents is not always allowed. *See* Verizon Tel. Cos. v. FCC, 269 F.3d 1098, 1109 (D.C. Cir. 2001) ("This is not to say that agency adjudications that modify or repeal rules established in earlier adjudications may always and without limitation be given retroactive effect. To the contrary, there is a robust doctrinal mechanism for alleviating the hardships that may befall regulated parties who rely on 'quasi-judicial' determinations that are altered by subsequent agency action."). The courts have not had an easy time figuring out when new principles of law announced in adjudications can be applied retroactively. *See id.* ("This court has not been entirely consistent in enunciating a standard to determine when to deny retroactive effect in cases involving 'new applications of existing law, clarifications, and additions' resulting from adjudicatory actions.").

88. *See* GARY LAWSON, FEDERAL ADMINISTRATIVE LAW 828–45 (8th ed. 2019).

89. W & M Props. of Conn., Inc. v. NLRB, 514 F.3d 1341, 1346 (D.C. Cir. 2008) (citation omitted).

90. 5 U.S.C. § 706(2)(A) (2012).

91. *See, e.g., W & M Props.*, 514 F.3d at 1347–48 (breezily accepting the agency's rationale that a change in doctrine would simplify the decision-making process).

92. *See*, e.g., United States Dep't of the Treasury, Bureau of Engraving & Printing v. FLRA, 995 F.2d 301 (D.C. Cir. 1993).

93. *See* Washington v. Commissioner of Soc. Sec., 906 F.3d 1353, 1355 (11th Cir. 2018).

94. *See* Aaron L. Nielson, *Sticky Regulations*, 85 U. CHI. L. REV. 85 (2018).

95. H.J. Res. 1056, 52d Leg., 2d Reg. Sess. (Okla. 2010). The full text of the proposed amendment is available at https://www.sos.ok.gov/documents/legislation/52nd/2010/2R/HJ/1056.pdf

96. Awad v. Ziriax, 670 F.3d 1111 (10th Cir. 2012).

97. *See, e.g.,* Steven G. Calabresi & Stephanie Dotson Zimdahl, *The Supreme Court and Foreign Sources of Law: Two Hundred Years of Practice and the Juvenile Death Penalty Decision*, 47 WM. & MARY L. REV. 743 (2005); Steven G. Calabresi, Lawrence, *the Fourteenth Amendment, and the Supreme Court's Reliance on Foreign Constitutional*

*Law: An Originalist Reappraisal*, 65 OHIO ST. L.J. 1097 (2004). For a more recent survey of the field, *see* Steven G. Calabresi & Bradley G. Silverman, *Hayek and the Citation of Foreign Law: A Response to Professor Jeremy Waldron*, 2015 MICH. ST. L.J. 1.

98. *See* Roper v. Simmons, 543 U.S. 551 (2005).

99. *See* Lawrence v. Texas, 539 U.S. 558 (2003).

100. U.S. CONST. amend. VIII ("Excessive bail shall not be required, nor excessive fines imposed, nor cruel and unusual punishments inflicted.").

101. Trop v. Dulles, 356 U.S. 86, 101 (1958).

102. *See* 543 U.S. at 556–57.

103. *Id.* at 567 (quoting *Atkins v. Virginia*, 536 U.S. 304, 316 (2002)).

104. *See id.* at 594–98 (O'Connor, J., dissenting); *id.* at 608–15.

105. *Id.* at 575–78 (citations omitted).

106. *Id.* at 624–28 (citations and footnote omitted).

107. U.S. CONST. art. I, § 8, cl. 10.

108. *See* BASIL S. MARKESINIS & JÖRG FEDTKE, JUDICIAL RECOURSE TO FOREIGN LAW: A NEW SOURCE OF INSPIRATION? 54–62 (2006).

109. *See id.* at 62–66.

110. *See id.* at 66–82.

111. *See id.* at 82–108.

112. Association for Civil Rights in Israel v. Minister of Internal Security, JCJ 1892/14 (2017). For discussion of the case, *see* Hillel Sommer & Guy I. Seidman, *Courts, Prisons, Budgets and Human Dignity: An Israeli Perspective*, 8 AZ. ST. L.J. FOR SOCIAL JUSTICE 135 (2017).

113. We discuss the subject at more length in Gary Lawson & Guy Seidman, *Deference and National Courts in the Age of Globalization: Learning, Applying, and Deferring to Foreign Law*, *in* 2 IUS DICERE IN A GLOBALIZED WORLD 431 (Chiara Antonia d'Allesandro & Claudio Marchese, eds. 2018).

114. MICHAL BOBEK, COMPARATIVE REASONING IN EUROPEAN SUPREME COURTS 19 (2013).

115. *See, e.g.*, Eyal Benvenisti, *Reclaiming Democracy: The Strategic Uses of Foreign and International Law by National Courts*, 102 AM. J. INT'L L. 241 (2008) (noting these concerns without endorsing them).

116. Lawson & Seidman, *supra* note 113, at 445.

117. *See* https://en.wikipedia.org/wiki/List_of_sovereign_states_in1945

118. *See* https://en.wikipedia.org/wiki/List_of_sovereign_states

119. *See* https://www.thoughtco.com/new-countries-of-the-world-1433444

120. http://avalon.law.yale.edu/17th_century/ma02.asp

121. http://avalon.law.yale.edu/18th_century/ny01.asp

122. Norman Dorsen, *The Relevance of Foreign Legal Materials in U.S. Constitutional Cases: A Conversation Between Justice Antonin Scalia and Justice Stephen Breyer*, 3 INT'L J. CONST. L. 519, 523 (2005).

123. *See* Calabresi & Silverman, *supra* note 97, at 17–18.

124. Lawson & Seidman, *supra* note 113, at 448 (quoting LAWSON & SEIDMAN, *supra* note 81, at 170).

125. *See* Benvenisti, *supra* note 115.

126. *See id.* at 251–52 (footnotes omitted).

127. SHAI DOTHAN, REPUTATION AND JUDICIAL TACTICS: A THEORY OF NATIONAL AND INTERNATIONAL COURTS (2014).

128. Steven G. Calabresi, *"A Shining City on a Hill": American Exceptionalism and the Supreme Court's Practice of Relying on Foreign Precedents*, 86 B.U. L. REV. 1335, 1336–37 (2006).

129. "One of us dreads the prospect of socialized medicine, is fine with the death penalty, suspects that the ICC is likely to be a vehicle for politicized anti-Americanism, and is a life member of the National Rifle Association." Lawson & Seidman, *supra* note 113, at 450 n.67. The other one of us tolerates the first with resigned bemusement.

130. *Id.* at 450.

131. *Id.* at 450 n. 62.

132. *Id.* at 455–56.

# Index

For the benefit of digital users, indexed terms that span two pages (e.g., 52–53) may, on occasion, appear on only one of those pages.